House of Horrors

FAMILIAL INTIMACIES IN CONTEMPORARY AMERICAN HORROR FICTION

HORROR STUDIES

Series Editor
Xavier Aldana Reyes, Manchester Metropolitan University

Editorial Board
Stacey Abbott, Roehampton University
Linnie Blake, Manchester Metropolitan University
Harry M. Benshoff, University of North Texas
Fred Botting, Kingston University
Steven Bruhm, Western University
Steffen Hantke, Sogang University
Joan Hawkins, Indiana University
Alexandra Heller-Nicholas, Deakin University
Agnieszka Soltysik Monnet, University of Lausanne
Bernice M. Murphy, Trinity College Dublin
Johnny Walker, Northumbria University
Maisha Wester, Indiana University Bloomington

Preface
Horror Studies is the first book series exclusively dedicated to the study of the genre in its various manifestations – from fiction to cinema and television, magazines to comics, and extending to other forms of narrative texts such as video games and music. Horror Studies aims to raise the profile of Horror and to further its academic institutionalisation by providing a publishing home for cutting-edge research. As an exciting new venture within the established Cultural Studies and Literary Criticism programme, Horror Studies will expand the field in innovative and student-friendly ways.

House of Horrors

FAMILIAL INTIMACIES IN CONTEMPORARY AMERICAN HORROR FICTION

AGNIESZKA KOTWASIŃSKA

UNIVERSITY OF WALES PRESS
2023

© Agnieszka Kotwasińska, 2023

All rights reserved. No part of this book may be reproduced in any material form (including photocopying or storing it in any medium by electronic means and whether or not transiently or incidentally to some other use of this publication) without the written permission of the copyright owner except in accordance with the provisions of the Copyright, Designs and Patents Act. Applications for the copyright owner's written permission to reproduce any part of this publication should be addressed to the University of Wales Press, University Registry, King Edward VII Avenue, Cardiff, CF10 3NS.

www.uwp.co.uk

British Library Cataloguing-in-Publication Data

A catalogue record for this book is available from the British Library.

ISBN   978-1-83772-012-5
eISBN 978-1-83772-013-2

The right of Agnieszka Kotwasińska to be identified as author of this work has been asserted in accordance with sections 77 and 79 of the Copyright, Designs and Patents Act 1988.

Typeset by Chris Bell, cbdesign

Printed by CPI Antony Rowe, Melksham, United Kingdom

Contents

Acknowledgements	ix
Introduction	**1**
1. Uncanny in the House of Fear	**23**
Introduction	23
Uncanny Houses	27
Void Dreams in *Dead in the Water*	31
Unhomely Funhole in *The Cipher*	37
The Queer (Uncanny) Desire in *Drawing Blood*	43
Conclusion	50
2. Grotesque Monsters and Hybrid Subjectivities	**55**
Introduction	55
Grotesque Bodies	58
Hybrid Lesbian Bodies in *The Drowning Girl*	63
Male Grotesque in *Sineater*	74
Monstrous Girlhood in *The Rust Maidens*	82
Conclusion	90
3. Blood(y) Ties in Vampire Fictions	**93**
Introduction	93
Towards Abjection	98
Gilda's Sensual Vampires	102
Escaping the 'Little Wife' in *Black Ambrosia*	109
Prodigal Children (Not) Coming Home	120
Conclusion	129

4.	**Spectral Kinship and Ghostly Selves**	**133**
	Introduction	133
	The Ghostly Other in Horror Fiction	137
	Dangerous Dis/possessions in *Come Closer*	140
	The 'Wandering Subject' in *The Between*	150
	Familial Disintegration in *Within These Walls*	158
	Conclusion	168
	Afterword	**173**
	Notes	177
	Bibliography	209
	Index	227

Acknowledgements

IT IS HARD TO PINPOINT the exact moment that I began this project. The official starting point was, of course, enrolling in the doctoral programme at the University of Warsaw in 2011 to write about family and horror fiction. But my interest in horror by women writers takes me back to my Goth teenage years and specifically to my mother giving me Kathe Koja's *Skin* because she felt that I would like it. Full confession: I loved it with a kind of frenzied intensity only teenagers are capable of. But reading horror was an even earlier development. I have vivid memories of using my mother's library card (with her blessing) to borrow books from the adult section when I was still a kid – I read Stephen King's *It* when I was the same age as its protagonists, which, in hindsight, was perhaps a bit too soon. Three decades later I'm still reading horror, watching horror and thinking horror – and writing about it.

I've looked at writing from both sides now, to paraphrase a classic. I know that writing can be a joyful and creative experience, but it can also be a profoundly lonely and disheartening process, which is why I am grateful to the women in my life who have supported me over the years. Fellow gender studies and American studies researchers in the doctoral support group, Latający Uniwersytet, read an earlier draft and offered kind feedback on how to tease out the intimacies without losing the horror. Thank you, Agata Chełstowska, Ludmiła Janion, Anna Kurowicka and Marta Usiekniewicz. Agata, you have been my rock for more than twenty years. A heartfelt thank you to the peer reviewers at University of Wales Press for their insightful comments and to Sarah

Lewis, the Head of Commissioning, for her understanding and unending patience. Sarah's kindness kept me going when my daughter's arrival forced me to reorganise my life and, soon after, when covid-19 fractured everyone's world. I am also indebted to Professor Marek Paryż, my PhD adviser at the Institute of English Studies, University of Warsaw, for guiding me and keeping me on track – a massive task considering how easily distracted I can be. Lastly, huge thanks to Stefan 'Steve' Rabitsch for proofreading parts of the book.

My eternal gratitude goes to Marcin, my lifeline and best friend, and to Dagna, who is busy learning that monsters can be way more fun than people.

Introduction

IN 2014, *Nightmare Magazine* produced a special issue titled *Women Destroy Horror!*, written and edited entirely by women. Four horror writers, Kate Jonez, Helen Marshall, Rena Mason and Linda Addison, discussed the North American publishing industry and the gender politics of writing horror as a woman. In a roundtable discussion they covered the gendered aspects of the publication process, reactions to horror fiction by women writers, the popularity of torture porn and misogyny in horror fiction, their own approach to horror and genres and, finally, how horror critics, readers and publishing houses read and categorised their work. While some described their work as 'feminine' in that it revolved around women, others challenged the feminine/masculine dichotomy and expressed uneasiness and ambivalence towards current definitions of femininity. Describing the gender binary as problematic, Jonez stated that, as a writer, it was impossible for her to think in such categories.[1] While Addison and Mason were comfortable with being labelled 'female horror' or 'dark fiction' writers, Jonez and Marshall were wary of this terminology. Marshall described the need for such terms as the 'New Weird' or 'dark fantasy' to put some distance between contemporary horror creations and earlier fiction, which customarily, and perhaps unconsciously, reproduced the same tedious plotlines in which women's bodies were abused either for the sake of male protagonist's development or for cheap thrills.[2] Their discussion provides a fascinating glimpse into the contentious politics of

2 • House of Horrors

writing in a genre chiefly associated with male writers and audiences, as well as readerly pleasures that are coded masculine.

For the simple reason that the majority of horror scholarship focuses on male writers, and thus avoids issues relating to representation and female and/or feminised experiences of the body, I am drawn primarily to female experiences and female representations in both my professional and private reading practices. Although cultural representation remains an important way for people to recognise and organise their own identity, corporeality and social position in relation to other social agents, the politics of representation have been challenged in recent years by post-structuralist thought, postcolonial criticism and queer theory.[3] Thus, feminist scholarship focusing on women's output and female experiences must tread lightly to avoid essentialising or reifying loaded and intrinsically destabilised/destabilising concepts such as womanhood, femininity and the female experience. Rather than analyse those popular horror writers who 'happen' to be mostly white, middle-class men, I focus on writers whose horror fictions have been marginalised or assigned to different genre categories due to a perceived divergence from the canon of horror fiction. In doing so, I investigate how different femininities – as well as masculinities – play out in intimate relationships within a diverse set of female and/or feminised experiences, previously identified and homogenised as 'domestic horror' or 'female horror'.

I use 'women writers' rather than simply 'women' to emphasise the way that authorial subjects have been received and shaped by general reading practices and publishing and marketing processes. I envision contemporary women's horror writing as a vibrant assemblage in which femininity acts as a flow or intensity, rising and ebbing over time and subject to external pressures and internal propensities. One of my main goals is to examine the generic borders that inform how women writers' horror fictions are read, publicised and critiqued, how the very category of 'horror' is sustained, co-curated and challenged by women writers, and how the instability of generic definition may be welcome in horror scholarship. Tracing female and feminised experiences in horror fiction does not amount to ascertaining a monolithic definition of femininity or womanhood, neither does it determine what horror fiction by women writers is or does. Rather, I study the ways in which femininity is deployed by various, lesser-known authors from diverse literary backgrounds who bring unique voices to contemporary horror literature. In this sense, horror fictions by women writers function as a minor literature, written in the majoritarian language of mainstream, white, male horror literature to express the concerns and lived experiences of a minority, such as female and feminised subjects, queer subjects and racialised subjects.[4] It is my contention that particular embodiments, lived experiences and material conditions shape cultural texts produced by gendered subjects.

With otherness defining both my subject matter and my own subjectivity, I am strongly drawn to Adrianne Rich's politics of location and Donna Haraway's situated knowledges, two pedagogic tools that compel me to acknowledge my own position as an early career researcher; a white, middle-class cis-woman living in the capital of Poland, supported by her husband and family; an able-bodied person with a largely invisible history of depression; and an Eastern European citizen whose name remains unpronounceable to English-speaking colleagues from the West. All this and more have shaped my choices in terms of subject matter, personal politics and engagement with feminism, my theoretical toolkit and conceptual framework, the authors that I have included and excluded, the research questions that I have formulated and the methods that I have applied. It would be insincere and pointless to insist on a pretence of academic objectivity, especially since my subject matter is horror, a bodily genre that actively disrupts the long-standing Western infatuation with logic, reason and a neat split between body and mind, culture and nature, 'us' and the Other.

Gender matters in horror, a genre that has been constituted as a predominantly male and masculine field in terms of both creators and consumers. Consequently, being identified as a woman *and* a horror writer translates into a corpus of work that, by definition, resides on the margins. Paradoxically, such a marginal position enables the twelve writers whose work I discuss to engage more freely with themes that have been deemed uninteresting or too benign, and which are often associated with other genres of the fantastic, such as urban fantasy or Gothic. Importantly, two authors, Caitlín R. Kiernan and Poppy Z. Brite/Billy Martin, do not identify as women; however, their fiction was first published and received as women's genre fiction, which is why I decided to include their works. In my study I focus on twelve novels published over the course of the past three decades, between 1988 and 2019. The choice of 1988 as my starting point is not accidental: I trace the development of contemporary horror fiction from the moment it began to veer away from realist horror in the vein of Stephen King's massively popular novels; a moment later associated

4 • House of Horrors

with the publication of Clive Barker's *Books of Blood* in the mid-1980s. The novels selected for this monograph showcase a remarkable diversity of themes, types of narration and textual devices, and thus enter a fascinating, if ambivalent, dialogue with mainstream horror fiction. All underscore the increasingly visible instability of the generic categories on which the conventional recognisability of horror rests.

Historically, literary horror scholarship has been devoted to the study of fear and terror, the community and the individual, the social Other(s), and the workings of Freudian repression, as well as various aesthetic and political considerations. Yet, little attention has been given to the intimacies that take shape in familial relations, which often become the true source and context of horror, especially for female and/ or feminised and marginalised subjects. Examining how kinship, intimacy, sexuality, corporeality and reproduction are approached by ten women-identified American authors, one non-binary person and one trans man whose output formed a crucial part of women's horror fiction during the 1990s, enables me to consider contemporary horror beyond the typical theoretical frameworks that emphasise examination of the characteristic tropes and genre formulas historically associated with horror fiction and horror studies.[5]

My reliance on intimacy as an analytical category brings both the materiality and discursive relationality of horror into sharp relief. Thus, I problematise the source of horror by drawing attention to how the most intimate of all social relationships – the family – supports and replicates social hierarchies, violent exclusions and struggles for dominance. Far from being a vehicle for material comfort, the nuclear family and other kinship structures become sources of disquiet and intimate dread. Looking at horror narratives through the lens of kinship, intimacy and corporeality permits me to rethink genre boundaries, question the efficacy of certain genre tropes and consider feminist contributions to the development of American horror fiction in a new light.

Many of the novels analysed in this study are rarely, if ever, read as horror fiction, which raises the issue of what considerations place a particular work of fiction within or outside the horror literary tradition. Here, I not only examine genres structurally, through the specific themes and tropes employed, but also through the historical and material changes that the category of 'horror' has undergone over the past three decades.[6] In contrast to the 1980s, when horror literature enjoyed peak popularity, the turn-of-the-century publishing market appeared far more wary of using 'horror' as a label for work that did not easily fit preconceived notions of the genre and could thus be shifted to potentially more marketable shelves. A great many horror authors had their work described and marketed as dark fantasy, urban fantasy, serial-killer fiction, neo-noir, grimdark, supernatural thriller, young adult, neo-Gothic, supernatural romance and/or erotica, the New Weird or simply literary fiction with supernatural elements. This was especially true of newcomers and authors already pushing genre boundaries established by the bestselling horror formulas of the 1970s and 1980s. While the past couple of years have witnessed a decidedly wider acceptance of horror as a marketing category and genre indicator, the reasons for this are unclear. One explanation is that, just as the 1970s horror fiction boom was tightly linked with the success of cinematic horror, an analogous situation may now be unfolding.

My decision to focus exclusively on American horror fiction stems from the cultural hegemony of mainstream American horror, which not only dwarfs the horror output of other nations in terms of sales and recognition but has also established a blueprint for defining all American horror production, themes, formal features, intended audiences and reception. Combined with the near collapse of the horror publishing market in the 1990s and 2000s, this blueprint has effectively concealed a number of works by women within American horror fiction, long associated with towering white, male writers, such as Stephen King, Peter Straub, Dan Simmons, Richard Matheson, Harlan Ellison and Jack Ketchum, with a few token women writers – most notably Anne Rice, Joyce Carol Oates and Shirley Jackson – thrown into the mix.

Defining Horror

At its core, horror is about plunging the consumer into a state of fear, shock, disgust, dread and unease. While an unsuccessful horror narrative will be met with a shrug or a yawn, an effective one, whether in a video game, short story or TV show, will frighten and excite the receiver. This corporeal preoccupation presents us with two questions: how does horror trigger such affective states; and why do people seek out such experiences? Although these two questions are to an extent inseparable, most horror scholarship is preoccupied with the latter, hence the popularity of critical theories explaining and legitimising the social, cultural and political functions of horror.[7] As Joseph Grixti discussed in *Terrors of Uncertainty*, horror may function as a culture's reservoir for the social and cultural anxieties that need to be debated and worked through in the safe cocoon of fiction.[8] Conversely, horror may be the abode of monstrous sociocultural Others,[9] a place to work through repression[10] or to go through a ritualised encounter with the abject.[11] Some scholars have applied a feminist psychoanalytic framework to horror narratives,[12] while others have opted for Marxist and psychoanalytic approaches to horror as a cultural production.[13] While some have traced horror's affinity with the fantastic,[14] others have concentrated on the weird tale[15] or the Gothic.[16] As Isabel Cristina Pinedo has stated, horror can be read as a perfect embodiment of postmodern cultural production, a latter-day Frankenstein's creature, in which the contemporary infatuation with the monstrous, the fragmented and the meta-textual comes to the fore.[17] Some, like Terry Castle, have diachronically investigated terror as an aftershock and side effect of the Enlightenment,[18] while others, like Noël Carroll, have synchronically discussed excess, norm disturbance and monstrosity.[19]

All these and many more studies of horror are founded on the assumption that the genre is carrying out important, if slightly misunderstood, 'cultural work,' a term borrowed from Jane Tompkins's 1985 classic *Sentimental Designs*.[20] While some critics explicitly cite Tompkins,[21] others, I believe, work in the spirit of her groundbreaking exploration and critical recovery of yet another much maligned genre, nineteenth-century American sentimental fiction. Rather than simply listing the major themes and functions of horror, such analyses move towards a more culturally and socially engaged form of critical thought, one intended to examine how horror fiction not only represents society's repressed fears and anxieties but can 'redefine and reorder the socialscape'.[22] Holland-Toll's approach to horror – based on a sense of cultural dis/ease produced through 'antinomy, however unrecognized and unarticulated'[23] – approximates my own understanding of horror literature as texts that cannot be contained within a single type of critical reading and exceed a conservative/transgressive binary. Holland-Toll's division into affirmative and disaffirmative horror emerges from this binary, with the former confirming the status quo, the latter allowing no such respite. Due to its formulaic inclinations and fleeting transgressions, Stephen King has described horror as an intrinsically reactionary genre, 'as conservative as an Illinois Republican in a three-piece pinstriped suit'.[24] However, Clive Bloom has noted that for writers such as Whitley Strieber, horror is essentially '*the* literature of conspiracy and therefore a *politicized* literature'.[25] Clive Barker has similar faith in the subversive qualities of the genre.[26] In contrast, Mark Jancovich concentrates on how the genre is 'based on the process of narrative closure in which the horrifying or monstrous is destroyed or contained', thus, transgressive elements are expunged and order restored.[27]

Horror exists not only at the margins of the respectable and the proper, in the romanticised 'outside', but at vulnerable borders between cultural categories, 'where our sense of certainty, integrity, unity is suddenly profoundly challenged, destabilized'.[28] Horror narratives reveal – and revel in – the stickiness and slipperiness of the building blocks of identity that mould modern Western societies, the axes of sexualisation (that is, becoming a sexed subject), racialisation (becoming a racialised self) and naturalisation (becoming human).[29] I believe horror makes a double movement, conservatively reinforcing differences, between life and death, masculine and feminine, male and female, human and non-human, proper and abject, white and BIPOC (Black, Indigenous and people of colour), the Global North and Global South, etc., but also challenges these binarisms and exposes their limitations as agents of interpellation, resulting in a deep sense of unease or dis/ease.[30] Such an unsettling, if thrilling, experience is invariably linked to how any disturbance of sociocultural 'norms' moves straight into somatic and affective territory. In other words, horror never happens only 'in our heads', but rather, as its etymology suggests – in Latin *horror*: to stand on end, to bristle; and in old French *orror*: to shudder – it *moves* our bodies, which in the Western scopic regime are forced to carry so many of the categories that horror destabilises.

This study is not intended to provide a systematic history of the horror genre or an overview of the most prominent figures in the field. My main goal is to present a generative definition of horror fiction, one that can be found in the tensions and contradictions between different affects, effects, themes and stylistic choices. This definition returns to the corporeal features of horror: the body of the reader affectively reacting to the narrative and the imagined bodies affected through and by the flows and movements of the narrative. Echoing Linda Williams's theorisation of cinematic horror as a body genre (along with melodrama and pornography), I read horror fiction as a type of literature that can 'produce intimate reading encounters'; a literature that not only describes intimate encounters but can also 'create or enhance the intimacy represented' and engage the reader 'intimately by deliberately prompting emotional responses'.[31]

Horror and the Gothic

The differences between the Gothic and horror are often of degree, not kind, and the two are used interchangeably, with literary horror regularly subsumed under the former's somewhat more spacious label.[32] Although the Gothic eludes easy categorisation – is it a mode, an aesthetic, a historical formation, a sensibility, a particular grouping of themes and tropes, or all of the above? – the definition that speaks most to me is hinted at by Catherine Spooner in her essay on the affinities between crime and Gothic fiction. Although Spooner mentions 'Gothic vestigiality' only in passing, and in reference to Robert Mighall's and Charles Rzepka's writings, it is a concept that perfectly encapsulates the Gothic preoccupation with family secrets, inheritance and patriarchal abuse.[33] Coupled with a penchant for the 'melodramatic imagination' and a thirst for the sensational, the Gothic remains an open-ended literary and cultural formation rather than a fully defined genre.[34] Thus, contemporary Gothic may follow carefully delineated forms and reference eighteenth and nineteenth-century Gothic romances populated by moody male anti-heroes and motherless women fighting for their sanity and autonomy, but it can also engage playfully with campy vampires, haunted houses and evil dolls, without exhibiting much reverence for past Gothic production. Even when lacking the particular themes or protagonists associated with the lineage's earlier output, today's Gothic can emerge in a stifling atmosphere of familial secrecy, a deep sense of dread coupled with eroticised thrill, terror lurking between the lines or a preoccupation with surfaces and artificiality.

Following Anne Williams, I agree that Gothic exceeds the ramifications of a 'genre', 'mode' or 'tradition'; however, for the sake of clarity, I retain the term here to indicate two aspects.[35] First, a particular mode of writing and presenting potentially horrifying and/or sensational material, one that accentuates Gothic vestigiality, an obsessive preoccupation with limits and boundaries, and familial secrecy, as, after all, 'all Gothic stories are family stories'.[36] Secondly, a recognisable set of literary themes and conventions rooted in both European and American traditions of Gothic romances, but also the direct descendants, third cousins and long-lost acquaintances, such as the Victorian and Edwardian ghost story, the Southern Gothic, neo-slave narratives, contemporary horror and the neo-Gothic. Thus, a significant intrusion of the Gothic into horror fiction is often signalled by excess, transgression, play with surfaces, as well as a fascination with repetition compulsion, inversion and monstrosity.

Introduction • 9

It is clear from the briefest glance at Gothic scholarship that there is a greater accommodation of women writers than in horror studies. By the late 1970s, the term 'Female Gothic' had entered critical vocabulary concerning eighteenth and nineteenth-century work centred on women's experiences, terror of patriarchy, absent mothers and tyrannical patriarchs, as well as the dangers lurking at home for female and/or feminised subjects.[37] It is in Gothic studies that we can find the largest concentration of critical work showcasing women's approaches to haunted houses, vampires, ghosts and monsters. Still, reading fiction through the Gothic lens necessitates a different historical perspective and origin story, and only a handful of contemporary authors can successfully be incorporated into the Gothic theoretical frame. While I refer to various Gothic formations, I want to stress that placing these twelve authors in the horror category is no mere rhetorical gesture, but a decision with particular theoretical ramifications.

Women Writers in Horror Fiction and Horror Studies

The critical and financial success enjoyed by horror fiction in the 1970s and early 1980s began to dissipate in the late 1980s. Part of this decline related to changes in marketing categories and a more relaxed approach to horror's generic boundaries among practitioners and fans.[38] As Jeanne Cavelos has suggested, horror has always struggled as a genre and the division into other categories over the course of the 1990s, such as young adult, supernatural romance, dark fiction and urban fantasy, came as no surprise.[39] Other reasons for this decrease in popularity included a consolidation around major bestselling authors and the subsequent disappearance of middle-range or mid-list authors, as well as a general economic slump within the American publishing industry that resulted in the cessation of most horror lines by major publishing houses during the mid-1990s.

One line that went against the grain was Dell's paperback imprint Abyss, which opened with Kathe Koja's *The Cipher* in February 1991 and went on to publish various important works by such newcomers as Nancy Holder, Kristine Kathryn Rusch, Poppy Z. Brite/Billy Martin and Melanie Tem. Over one-third of all Abyss titles were by women writers, an unprecedented move by any horror line before or since. Under Jeanne Cavelos, series editor and its biggest champion, Abyss became synonymous with highly original horror. After Cavelos left and critical acclaim failed to translate into financial success, Abyss closed with Poppy Z. Brite's/Billy Martin's *Lost Souls* in 1998. In his overview of Dell's horror imprint, Steffen Hantke noted the uniqueness of the forty-three Abyss titles, with their edgy covers, 'artsy but sexy, more reminiscent of pop art's boldness that [sic] the gothic's doom and gloom',[40] dedication to novelty and a clear break with the stylistics and themes of the 1970s and 1980s bestsellers, exemplified by Stephen King's hefty, multi-character, realist novels. Cavelos championed novels that were more succinct, more focused in their scope and less concerned with the social and communal than with the intimate and individual. For Hantke, who sees the supernatural as a twentieth-century remnant of the Gothic, this also meant abandoning the 'return of the repressed' rationale for horror and a switch to 'the space of individual psychology'.[41] Yet, as Hantke has lamented, the Abyss line never approached the level of cultural impact enjoyed by 1980s horror fiction, perhaps due to its introverted stance and preference for 'tight, claustrophobic novels in which little of the larger world – the social world or the vast universe of horror itself – would impinge on the mad minds of its protagonists'.[42]

Important anthologies of women's horror fiction at that time include *Women of Darkness* (1988)[43] and *Women of Darkness II* (1990),[44] both edited by Kathryn Ptacek and published by the Tor Horror imprint (closed in 1990), and Lisa Tuttle's edited collection, *Skin of the Soul* (1991).[45] These three anthologies provide a glimpse into horror fiction by established horror and Gothic authors such as Joyce Carol Oates and Chelsea Quinn Yarbro, writers associated primarily with other genres such as science fiction and fantasy such as Cherry Wilder, Suzy McKee Charnas, Tanith Lee and Nina Kiriki Hoffman, and literary fiction, including Karen Jay Fowler, and the late 1980s/early 1990s newcomers, Elizabeth Massie, Nancy Holder, Lucy Taylor, Melanie Tem, Poppy Z. Brite/Billy Martin, Yvonne Navarro and Lisa W. Cantrell. Three anthologies of vampire fiction and vampire erotica – two *Love in Vein* volumes edited by Poppy Z. Brite/Billy Martin in 1994 and 1997,[46] and *Daughters of Darkness: Lesbian Vampire Stories* edited by Pam Keesey in 1993[47] – also showcase a number of women writers associated with 1990s horror, such as Kathe Koja, Elizabeth Engstrom, Christa Faust, Jewelle Gomez and Caitlín R. Kiernan. A 1980s/1990s list of names would not be complete without Charlee Jacob, Nancy A. Collins, Nancy Kilpatrick, Tananarive Due, Elizabeth Hand, Kristine Kathryn Rusch, P. D. Cacek and Lisa Tuttle. The popularity of the short-story format continued well into the 2000s with a number

Introduction • 11

of critically acclaimed standalone anthologies and anthology series, a great many edited or co-edited by Ellen Datlow.[48]

My decision to focus on women's fiction stems from the evident gaps in literary horror scholarship, especially the continuing under-representation of work by women. Although the past two decades have witnessed an increase in the number of articles and book-length studies of the literary output of contemporary women authors, most of these are firmly embedded in the Gothic traditions: Gina Wisker's *Contemporary Women's Gothic Fiction: Carnival, Hauntings and Vampire Kisses*,[49] Paulina Palmer's *Lesbian Gothic: Transgressive Fictions*,[50] Benjamin A. Brabon and Stephanie Genz's (eds) *Postfeminist Gothic: Critical Interventions in Contemporary Culture*,[51] Sarah E. Whitney's *Splattered Ink: Postfeminist Gothic Fiction and Gendered Violence*,[52] Diana Wallace and Andrew Smith's (eds) *The Female Gothic: New Directions*,[53] Andrew Hock Soon Ng's *Women and Domestic Space in Contemporary Gothic Narratives: the House as Subject*,[54] Avril Horner and Sue Zlosnik's (eds) *Women and the Gothic: an Edinburgh Companion*,[55] Helene Meyers's *Femicidal Fears: Narratives of the Female Gothic Experience*,[56] to name only a few. Yet a glimpse at the analysed works reveals that while some horror writers are readily adopted by the Gothicists – most notably Anne Rice, Poppy Z. Brite/Billy Martin, Shirley Jackson, Joyce Carol Oates and Toni Morrison – a great many do not fit within the Gothic brackets. For this reason, I have decided to include a wide spectrum of writers: from the virtually forgotten horror paperback writers of the 1980s and early 1990s, Elizabeth Engstrom and Elizabeth Massie, through contemporary authors of speculative and horror fiction Caitlín R. Kiernan, Jewelle Gomez and Tananarive Due, to literary fiction writers whose works are not often considered via the horror lens, such as Sara Gran.

I cannot say that I am surprised by the relative dearth of women writers in scholarship devoted to horror fiction published before the 1980s boom; to an extent, this is understandable, as women writers were simply more difficult to locate in a maze dominated by easily recognisable male names, although such books as the recent *Monster, She Wrote*[57] by Lisa Kröger and Melanie R. Anderson prove such archival recovery work is possible and much needed. However, what is disappointing is the continued disregard of the not insignificant output of women writers in the past thirty to forty years.[58] One could argue that this is simply a matter of the popularity of certain authors, but it does not explain why, for instance, Thomas Ligotti is accorded such an important place in so many overviews,

12 • House of Horrors

given that most of his work had been out of print until a 'Ligotti revival' was triggered by a popular HBO show in 2014. To put it bluntly, just as Jeanne Cavelos chose to include more women in the Abyss line, critics and scholars must make a conscious effort to cover the work of women writers, even if this means conducting extra work, reading a few more anthologies and actively resisting the lure of the male canon.[59]

Fortunately, the times are changing. The popularity and critical recognition of Caitlín R. Kiernan, Kathe Koja and Poppy Z. Brite/Billy Martin has risen steadily over the past decade, with more articles, chapters and parts of monographs devoted to their work.[60] In the wake of the enormous success of Jordan Peele's *Get Out* and *US*, Black horror fiction has gained more mainstream recognition, although it should be stressed that horror writers such as Tananarive Due, Linda D. Addison – the first African American winner of the Bram Stoker award – and L. A. Banks have been publishing for years, alongside a whole line-up of authors associated with the Gothic and other genres of the fantastic, such as Toni Morrison, N. K. Jemisin, Octavia E. Butler and Nnedi Okorafor. Hopefully, with Jess Nevins' comprehensive overview of horror fiction in the twentieth century, more inclusive work will follow.[61] Plus, thanks to the impact of Grady Hendrix's *Paperbacks from Hell* (co-written with Will Errickson), a number of 1970s and 1980s paperback originals by women writers are now being reissued by Valancourt Press, including Elizabeth Engstrom's *Black Ambrosia*, to which I will return in Chapter 3.[62]

My decision to concentrate on the relationship between body and kinship was inspired by the dearth of scholarship devoted to personal relationships in literary horror. Interestingly, personal and familial relationships are analysed far more frequently in scholarly works on sexual politics, gender and sexuality in cinematic horror.[63] Such examinations, often informed by feminist criticism and queer theory, engage readily with familial concerns. Similar analyses of literary horror remain rare. The few exceptions are academic works focusing on evil or 'creepy' children[64] and haunted houses,[65] and while undeniably valuable and informative, these studies do not begin to exhaust the diversity of topics pertaining to family life and intimacy.

The striking vulnerability of a body, especially one that belongs to subjects deemed subservient in patriarchal kinship structures, such as children, teenagers, cis women, trans people and gender-non-conforming people, forms a recurring theme in horror written by women. The materiality of existence, long deemed the provenance of women by Western philosophers and social thinkers, is repeatedly revisited in connection to reproduction and reproductive rights, corporeal transformations, intense physical states (agony, ecstasy), sensuality and sex. The sheer number of works that concentrate on how corporeality can be a source of pain and pleasure, fear and comfort, love and hatred, proves that the aesthetic and thematic frames established by 1980s body horror and splatterpunk subgenres,[66] both of which have been associated with a material turn in contemporary horror, may not be enough to understand the complexities of the bodily in horror fiction, especially in reference to the female or feminised body. Although an important thread in feminist criticism of horror cinema and recent film phenomenology concentrates on the representation of female (or feminised) bodies,[67] its conversion to literary criticism is by no means sufficient for my analysis.

Defining Intimacy

Although intimacy is often equated with sex, my understanding encompasses a wide spectrum of personal entanglements, understood as 'acts, states and relationships',[68] both deeply corporeal and intensely emotional, rooted in conventional kinship structures but also exceeding narrow understandings of family or, more generally, personal relationships. Paying close attention to different forms of intimacy can redefine and broaden familial grounds of identification and interpersonal practices.[69] My focus on intimacies in familial settings may strike the reader as counter-intuitive, given that horror fiction is typically defined not by the scope and shape of the relationships that it presents but rather by a mystery to be unravelled, a monster to be vanquished or, in more opaque terms, a disturbing encounter with difference. However, all the novels analysed in this book place relationships at their heart. Some of these relationships are wrapped in mystery (*The Drowning Girl*, *Drawing Blood*), others turn monstrous (*Sineater*, *Black Ambrosia*) and some cause violent disturbance in protagonists' lives (*Within These Walls*, *Come Closer*, *The Cipher*), but all the authors primarily build their narratives around issues of intimacy, bodily autonomy and personal relationships.

Intimacy, in this book, maps various modalities of a relationship: the allocation and distribution of emotional investments, desires, needs and expectations, conflicts and frustrations, betrayals and reconciliations. Intimacy brings social, cultural and institutional conventions that implicitly

14 • House of Horrors

govern personal encounters into focus and helps to identify the appellations that organise relationships, such as mother, son, sister, lover, abuser, survivor, partner, friend, casual acquaintance and subordinate. Conventionally, intimacy delineates domestic spaces or areas hidden from public eyes, as well as safe spaces in which 'a life' can finally thrive, as Lauren Berlant described in the introduction to a special issue of *Critical Inquiry* devoted to intimacy:

> intimacy also involves an aspiration for a narrative about something shared, a story about both oneself and others that will turn out in a particular way. Usually, this story is set within zones of familiarity and comfort: friendship, the couple, and the family form, animated by expressive and emancipating kinds of love. Yet the inwardness of the intimate is met by a corresponding publicness. People consent to trust their desire for 'a life' to institutions of intimacy; and it is hoped that the relations formed within those frames will turn out beautifully, lasting over the long duration, perhaps across generations.[70]

Such a fantasy of an intensely private and thus 'real' life, supported by the flourishing of good and proper intimacies, does not account for the way that intimacy can be deployed to silence people in public through domestic and sexual violence, shame them into compliance through heteronormativity and universalised whiteness, or deny other forms of closeness that exist outside the traditional forms and spaces of intimacy, such as celibacy, singlehood and queer families of choice. Feminist and queer critiques of normative family models[71] are joined here by Indigenous critiques of the racist and colonialist foundations of sexualities, relationships and kinship.[72]

Echoing Deleuze and Guattari's notion of minor literature, Berlant has defined 'minor intimacies' as 'desires for intimacy that bypass the couple or the life narrative it generates'[73] and thus find themselves adrift, without an accepted archive of feelings or designated space in Western culture to grow and solidify in peace. These minor 'glances, gestures, encounters, collaborations, or fantasies'[74] reverberate deeply through the twelve horror novels here, whether taking the form of a queer family of choice, heteronormative nuclear families cracking under capitalist, racial and patriarchal pressures, toxic monogamy, matriarchal and female-centric kinship or radical singlehood.

Biolegal familial relationships are commonly and culturally deemed to be the most durable and relevant of one's life. This is reinforced by the vast range of 'customs, rituals, and laws that privilege familial relationships over non-kin ties and determine who may be defined as family'.[75] The image of a heteronormative nuclear family underpins the 'constitution of and regulation of the normative citizen subject, which encompasses western, white, middle-class, Christian values and morals, and is the foundational structure of western societies'.[76] As Jacqui Gabb has noted, studies on transformations in family life and intimacy since the millennium that have brought new patterns of intimacy to light, have somewhat paradoxically also tended to 'reinforce the underlying status of families as a social unit in which affects and emotions reside (Morgan 1996)'.[77]

Davis and Robinson have described family as 'a discursively constituted space, which is dynamic, unstable and historically and culturally located, encompassing a variety of social, cultural, economic and symbolic meanings'.[78] Interestingly, they link discourses concerning the nuclear family to Butler's performativity, as it is through 'the repetitiveness of the performance of family' that this category is constituted and naturalised.[79] Butler's handy definition of kinship, also referenced by Davis and Robinson, is worth quoting in full:

> If we understand kinship as a set of practices that institutes relationships of various kinds which negotiate the reproduction of life and the demands of death, then kinship practices will be those that emerge to address fundamental forms of human dependency, which may include birth, child rearing, relations of emotional dependency and support, generational ties, illness, dying, and death (to name a few). Kinship is neither a fully autonomous sphere, proclaimed to be distinct from community and friendship – or the regulations of the state – through some definitional fiat, nor is it 'over' or 'dead' just because, as David Schneider has consequentially argued, it has lost the capacity to be formalized and tracked in the conventional ways that ethnologists in the past have attempted to do.[80]

Butler argues that kinship is not distinctly divided from communal or friendship-based relationships; rather, it is institutional practices that enact and legitimise forms of togetherness, such as the passing of a law prohibiting same-sex marriage, the provision of financial aid to only certain forms of cohabitation, or the selection of only conventionally defined friendships for a study on contemporary friendship, thus ignoring queer friendships and friendships containing sexual/erotic elements. In a seminal work on the family arrangements of gays and lesbians, *Families We Choose: Lesbians, Gays, Kinship*,[81] Kath Weston moves away from the dominant kinship framework, delineated by David M. Schneider in his 1968 *American Kinship: a Cultural Account* and predicated 'on the basis of genetics and procreative sexuality',[82] and shows how her interviewees have reconsidered and reorganised kinship, biology, friendship and intimacy. Thus, families can be queered not only through the non-normative sexuality of their members, but also through choices concerning gender roles and expression, the number and roles of people involved in a kinship arrangement, the ages and occupations of family members, technologies of reproduction and cathectic attachments. Anna Muraco has also explored the metaphorical use of family language to describe non-biolegal relationships, as social scripts concerning such ties are often insufficient or non-existent.[83]

As I seek to question the validity, idealisation and predominance of the heteronormative nuclear family in the United States, my working definition of 'family' follows inclusive and intersectional feminist approaches. My use of 'kin' echoes Colleen T. Johnson's essay, in which, while defining kinship as extended family, she acknowledges that the very word 'family' can refer to many different social units, including 'an ideal view of what the family should be like'.[84] This metaphorical usage of 'family' is especially pertinent for my analysis, as the models and familial structures in the novels that I discuss are intended to be perceived less as mimetic representations of sociological reality than as the idealised or imagined types of kinship and intimate relationships that inhabit popular imagination and imaginary socius. However, I remain wary of how words such as 'idealised' and 'imagined' can mislead and denote a reflective relationship between art and life.

I view broadly understood kinship as a multifaceted lens, capable of shedding light on such diverse social issues as gender roles, gender binarism, femininities and masculinities, sexualities, heteronormativity, reproductive rights, domestic abuse, patriarchal culture, family dynamics, parent-child relationships, same-sex couples and alternative kinship, romantic love, close friendships and support networks not based on blood ties, voluntary childlessness and singlehood. Kinship is thus employed as a social script to describe postmodern forms of personal relationships and the ways in which these relationships bear the brunt of changing socio-economic and cultural transformations.

Introduction • 17

Overview of Chapters

I have decided against structuring my work according to themes that would, at least superficially, better correspond with discussions about kinship and intimacy. Thus, instead of focusing on horror narratives that explicitly deal with parenthood, childcare or marriage, I have opted for the more 'stereotypical' themes of haunted houses, monsters, vampires and ghosts. This thematic division stems from my unwillingness to fashion a 'sub-canon' or 'counter-canon' of women's horror fiction by replicating the attitude in which their contribution is subsumed under a nebulously defined 'domesticity' or private sphere. Instead, I examine how narratives thematically associated with conventional horror fiction deal with familial relationships and the bodily.

My choice of four principal theoretical tools – the uncanny, the grotesque, the abject and the spectral – is similarly predicated on my desire to engage with popular investigations of horror literature and resist constructing literary criticism in terms of linear progression. Thus, I combine classic critical approaches with their contemporary reformulations and critiques. In doing so, I acknowledge the enormous impact of the uncanny, grotesque and abject on the study of horror and the Gothic, but at the same time critically assess how these tools have been deployed. In the final chapter I consider the far more recent theoretical development of spectrality studies, which remains closely related to the first chapter through both the pre-eminent ties between hauntology and the uncanny and the thematic closeness of haunted houses and ghosts. My analysis is supplemented by theoretical tools drawn from critical race studies, queer theory and literary criticism.

The haunted house, the main theme of Chapter 1, brings personal relationships marked by extreme loneliness, fear of intimacy and the exclusionary expectations of normative family life into sharp relief. The uncanny, as used here, functions not only as an expression of the bourgeois fear of the lower classes but as a form of twentieth and twenty-first-century social alienation and disorientation. The uncanny marks instances of estrangement, perhaps economic, postcolonial, political or psychological, or, in horror fiction terms, moments in which intimate relationships are violently defamiliarised by the disclosure of familial/familiar secrets. All three novels selected for this chapter revolve around characters attempting to create personal relationships in deeply unsettling and unwelcoming spaces: spaces that act as barriers rather than incentives to establishing intimate relations. In Nancy Holder's *Dead in the Water* (1994), a group of shipwreck survivors must cope with not only a supernatural threat but also their own inability to let go of the past. In Kathe Koja's debut novel from 1991, *The Cipher*, the main character is both unable and unwilling to end two toxic relationships: one with his girlfriend, the other with a mysterious hole that appears in his apartment block. Finally, in Poppy Z. Brite's/Billy Martin's *Drawing Blood* (1993), a pair of young lovers are locked in a spectral loop that drives them to re-enact one of the boys' gruesome childhood traumas. In all three novels, the traditional distribution of power and prescribed gender roles of the traditional nuclear unit clash with less conventional forms of intimacy, including patchwork families, extended families, same-sex couples and straight couples whose very viability is problematised by hostile external forces. Haunted houses – the uncanny heterotopias of postmodernity – function as spaces of the Other, where transgenerational hauntings, family traumas, secrets and anxieties emerge and threaten the individual self, the familial intimacy and the new kinship structures that have formed within.

Chapter 2, devoted to monstrous embodiment, focuses on female and/or feminised subjects, reproduction and its possibly transgressive and oppressive potential, and the replication of family trauma. Caitlín R. Kiernan's *The Drowning Girl: a Memoir* (2012) investigates the complexity of mother-daughter relationships, female sexuality and lesbian desire. In Elizabeth Massie's *Sineater* (1993), a small-town community is torn apart when unorthodox religious rites clash with people's need for intimacy, acceptance and respect. The chapter ends with a close reading of Gwendolyn Kiste's *The Rust Maidens* (2019), in which young girls' monstrous bodies become both the focal point of gendered surveillance and disciplining and a twisted reflection of the disintegration of their working-class community. A critical tool employed in this chapter – the grotesque – is introduced via the writings of Mikhail Bakhtin and feminist criticism by Mary R. Russo. The concept of the grotesque, employed in this chapter both as a set of cultural tropes and as an aesthetic sensibility, reveals the problematic nature of gender dynamics and sexual difference as experienced in intensely private familial and communal enclaves. The grotesque resides in the act of crossing clearly defined borders between spaces or subjects, which, in the process, are de-territorialised and re-territorialised via monstrous becomings.

In Chapter 3, I turn to vampire fiction and its long history of deeply intimate relationships, alternative kinship and negotiation of sexuality, non-normative sex acts and embodiment. Jewelle Gomez's *The Gilda Stories* (1991) charts the life of a Black lesbian female vampire, from escaping slavery and consenting to becoming a vampire in the mid-nineteenth century, through witnessing pivotal moments in the twentieth-century United States, to leading a group of vampire outcasts under a futuristic totalitarian regime. In Melanie Tem's *Prodigal* (1991), each member of a white, suburban, middle-class family is destroyed by a social worker, a psychic vampire gnawing at the already frayed edges of the household. The strangest and most unsettling vision of vampirism can be found in Elizabeth Engstrom's *Black Ambrosia* (1988). In contrast to typical vampire fictions, this novel, which contains no single definition of vampirism, rejects communal and/ or familial ties and presents an entirely alienated and adrift vampire heroine. What links these three novels is their shared concern with the falterings and failings of normative sexuality and a middle-class lifestyle, thus suggesting the erosion of the nuclear family mythos. The abject, which informs the study of vampirism, effectively reveals the constraints of white, middle-class kinship with its emphasis on strict gender roles and a dangerous slippage between social status, (gender) normativity and whiteness. While the abject may be unwelcome, repulsive and frightening, it can also emerge in a burst of *jouissance*, an erotic and eroticised eruption of the counter-politics of pleasure and intimacy, of which the vampire continues to provide the perfect vehicle. While work on the abject by Julia Kristeva, Deborah C. Covino and Katherine J. Goodnow have proven invaluable for my analysis, I also look to critiques of abjection as a prescriptive rather than descriptive formation.

In the final chapter I return to ghosts and hauntings, but rather than approaching this subject via its spatial dimension, I address the temporal displacement engendered by a spectral presence. Spectral visitors in the selected novels function as helpers, messengers, uncanny doubles, enemies and liars, but, most importantly, all signify a violent disruption of temporal linearity. In all three cases, spectral disturbance is relocated from the house onto the bodies of people who are visited, possessed or otherwise affected by spectral visitors. Interestingly, rather than replicate a restorative model of the ghost story, the spectres analysed in this chapter frustrate both the traditional hierarchy in which ghosts exist only in relation to the living, and a typical West-centric binary in which the ghosts (the no-longer human) and the living (the fully human) belong to separate categories. This critique of West-centrism is most compellingly taken up in Tananarive Due's *The Between* (1995), in which the figure of a half-spirit, inspired by the Igbo *ogbanje* and the Yoruba *abiku*, is used to investigate the combined toll of normative masculinity, racism and bourgeois ideals on African-American family life. In Sara Gran's satirical novella *Come Closer* (2003), a demonic possession presents the main protagonist with an escape from her boring and stifling white, upper-middle-class existence. This intensely sensual and sensuous possession not only signals a breakdown of barriers between different selves of the same individual but also between the different realms of the human and the spectral. The final novel, Ania Ahlborn's *Within These Walls* (2015), focuses on a newly reconstituted family of a father and his teenage daughter who fall victim to the intricate manipulation of a cult leader; a manipulation that rests on an elaborate ritualistic haunting. Spectral intrusions weave together a number of analytic threads: queerly inflected disruptions of heteronormative temporality (Jack Halberstam, Terry Castle), consequences of transgenerational trauma (Nicolas Abraham and Maria Torok), questions of social in/visibility and passing (Avery Gordon) and the intricacies of hospitality and hauntological inheritance (Jacques Derrida).

The continuing relevance of the Gothic preoccupation with home, family and the body in contemporary horror fiction proves that the homely, the familial and the intimate remain the locus of horror for female and/or feminised subjects. While some of the novels that I analyse engage with external rather than internal threats, home rarely offers a respite from monstrous figures, spectral disturbances or the social and personal consequences of an abject or grotesque embodiment. Even when a protagonist wishes to protect their family, the home is replete with threats to bodily and mental integrity. In most cases, the familial structures – whether straight marriages, heteronormative nuclear families, same-sex couples or queer families of choice – either actively encourage and enable potential violence and abuse or offer little, if any, protection.

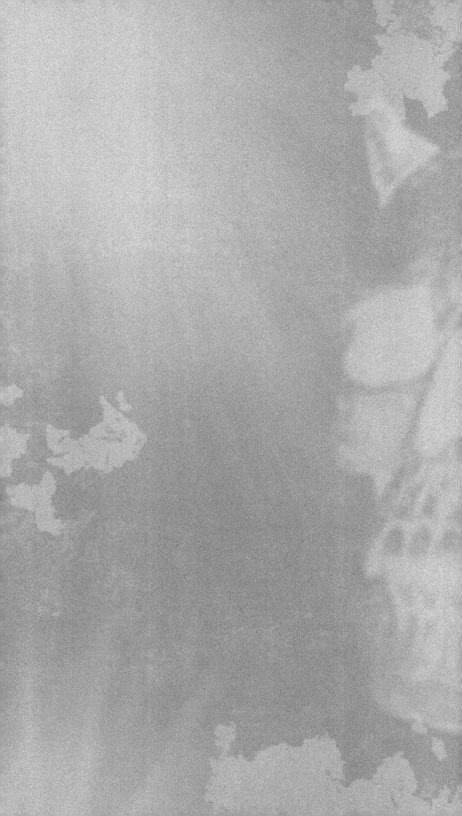

1

Uncanny in the House of Fear

Introduction

IN THIS CHAPTER, I look at novels in which the ominous nature of a house is not connected to ghosts or supernatural threats, 'but stems instead from its very own self'.[1] Nancy Holder's *Dead in the Water*, Kathe Koja's *The Cipher* and Poppy Z. Brite's/Billy Martin's *Drawing Blood* all exceed the ramifications of a classic ghost or possession story and profoundly instrumentalise their houses. These buildings are not extensions of malevolent spirits or theatricised sites of conflict, but rather acquire a presence of their own, thus reflecting, exacerbating or participating in the protagonists' mental deterioration. Crucially, all three revisit the well-known haunted house formula from a feminist and queer standpoint, placing emphasis on relationality, (queer) families of choice and body autonomy in an increasingly hostile, late-capitalist reality. Haunted space becomes the centre stage for a tug of war between old and new kinship structures, but the spaces themselves are no innocent bystanders.

Lived-in spaces are not empty vessels, but sites lit by a dense grid of power relations, social hierarchies and dominant cultural imageries. Sites specifically devoted to private lives are communal arenas in which the traditional distribution of power and prescribed gender roles of the classic nuclear family unit clash with alternative relationship forms, such as patchwork families, families of choice or, in fact, any form of marginalised kinship. Admittedly, feminist theory, with its focus on social relations and power distribution, and psychoanalytical criticism, focusing on the internal processes externalised in art, run the risk of reifying the house as either 'a metaphor signifying gender politics' or 'an extension of the subject's psychodrama'.[2] Wary of this, I look to Andrew Hock Soon Ng's critical approach to Gothic space, which emphasises the materiality of lived space, its physical presence and the way in which protagonists experience that space as '*real space*'.[3]

The uncanny, possibly one of the most clichéd critical tools of the twenty-first century, remains one of the finest for examining the haunted house motif in relation to the anxieties associated with establishing and sustaining family life and participating in various forms of intimacy. The uncanny, the critical career of which began as an essentially bourgeois fear of the proverbial barbarians at the gate, has grown to encompass fears of the recesses of the human psyche *and* of personal failure, often understood in terms of financial or societal breakdown. Families being unable to leave their newly bought decrepit or suspiciously cheap houses due to a lack of money is a common theme. Nicholas in Kathe Koja's *The Cipher* cannot escape the impoverished state that plunges him into depression and a highly self-destructive relationship with his girlfriend, Nakota. Lacking the safety net of middle-class financial comfort, the protagonists in Poppy Z. Brite's/Billy Martin's *Drawing Blood*, Trevor and Zach, are unable to shrug off transgenerational trauma through expensive long-term therapy and/or medication. It is no coincidence that so many contemporary haunted house narratives centre on dilapidated, ex-middle-class houses or rundown, inner-city flats. In fact, following the premise that modern architecture is becoming increasingly uncanny, we see how the contemporary family home unveils 'the repressed truth concerning the alienating results of private ownership'.[4] As bourgeois aspirations and expectations become increasingly unsustainable and unattainable in late-capitalist societies, the middle class has become its own worst enemy. The protagonists of Nancy Holder's *Dead in the Water*, despite being more economically secure than Nicholas, Trevor and Zach, all want to escape their existence on a cruise ship, the quintessential middle-class symbol of affordable luxury and exotic travel, offering a suspension from daily routine and an illusory promise of reinvention in a short-lived microsociety. Ultimately, all three novels illustrate how obsolete representations of picture-perfect family life continue to thwart attempts to escape haunted familial space or establish new familial structures.

Eighteenth and nineteenth-century Gothic fiction sealed the relationship between architecture, secrets and family for subsequent Gothic and horror narratives.[5] The haunted house formula harks back to the earliest examples of late eighteenth-century Gothic romances, to the mysterious castles of Horace Walpole's Otranto and Anne Radcliffe's Udolpho: these estates were not only haunted by the threat of external violence but by the intimate familial cruelty that could erupt within their walls at any moment. As Susanne Becker in *Gothic Forms of Feminine Fictions* has noted, 'feminine gothics are haunted houses, not only in the contextual sense of "experience" but also in the intertextual sense of continuation and deconstruction of feminine textuality'.[6] Given the centrality of the heroine's relationship with her own corporeality and the body of her mother, houses in early Gothic fiction frequently function as maternal spaces, dark and winding, uncanny in their associations with the womb/tomb.[7] Yet for all the maternal associations, the 'typical Gothic mother is absent: dead, imprisoned or somehow abjected',[8] and thus cannot provide her daughter with help or solace.

The related Gothic narrative feature of 'the specter of father-daughter incest' coincided with 'the emergence of the nuclear family with its attendant intimacy and privacy'.[9] The despotic father or paternal figure often acts as a tyrannical guardian of the familial past or a usurper employing secrets to manipulate and control the household. In this sense, the Gothic vestigiality establishes a strong link between ancestral guilt and the house, understood metonymically as a family line, or metaphorically as a supposedly safe haven. The Gothic house often retells and revises the biblical Fall, during which the original family unit was established and almost immediately marked by the darkness stemming from a desire for knowledge.[10] That the pursuit of knowledge is dangerous not only becomes clear to every Gothic heroine but to every horror protagonist.

In the decades following the rise of the Gothic, two middle-class inventions aligned: the novel and the bourgeois family house. In fact, the narrative in English domestic novels coils around the house and quite often genders the building itself as female.[11] Changing economies that moved production away from the home prepared the ground for the creation of separate social spheres. While men led nations, worked and spoke out in the public (hazardous) sphere, women maintained households and raised children in the safety of the private. The white middle-class house came to symbolise a refuge from both the hatred directed at the conspicuously luxurious, upper-class mansions and the infectious grime associated with the lower classes and their miserable dwellings. In the North American context, the house became the essential ground for exercising the cults of both domesticity[12] and true womanhood,[13] underlining the role and importance of white, propertied women in shaping the young American nation through their pious, obedient and domestic existence. Black feminist scholars such as Venetria K. Patton,[14] Evelynn M. Hammonds[15] and Patricia Hill Collins,[16] have identified and underlined the role of whiteness in moulding the dominant forms and expressions of middle and upper-class American femininity.

Arguably, whiteness is a specifically American materialisation of the uncanny, linked on the one hand with the idealised middle-class household and its classist and racist assumptions, and on the other hand with American Gothic fiction in its emphasis on the struggle between the forces of light and darkness, freedom and enslavement, democracy and tyranny, often literalised through what Toni Morrison has theorised as the 'Africanist presence'.[17] While the three novels analysed in this chapter do not theorise whiteness directly, the promise of safety associated with a middle-class existence is heavily imbued with the promise of racial privilege. In contrast, racial history, costs of racialisation for both individuals and communities, and acute lack of racial privilege play a central role in haunted house novels by Black writers: Toni Morrison's *Beloved* (1987), Tananarive Due's *The Good House* (2003), LaTanya McQueen's *When the Reckoning Comes* (2021) and British author Helen Oyeyemi's *White Is for Witching* (2009).

American Gothic, as a fiction of silent displacements, curious exclusions and yawning gaps in familial history, lends itself easily to psychoanalytic readings. A case in point, two American Gothic haunted house classics, Edgar Allan Poe's 'The Fall of the House of Usher' and Nathaniel Hawthorne's *The House of the Seven Gables*, dwell on anxieties surrounding family bloodlines, the potential impurity and/or impropriety of familial relationships and, significantly, property.[18] Additionally, both 'displace the supernatural focus of the text from the figure of the ghost . . . to the house'.[19] Thus, the matrix on which future American horror writers would rely was established, one in which the house stands for more than a mere vessel for supernatural disturbance.[20]

Interestingly, haunted house cinema has recently had a revival, with films featuring anxieties relating to land/property ownership and the paramount importance of this for American cultural imaginary. Central to this is the mythos of the American Dream and its increasing unavailability to large swaths of people, moral ambivalence and guilt towards the hostile

Uncanny in the House of Fear • 27

takeover and occupation of Indigenous land, and slavery and the political and economic disenfranchisement of Black people.[21] Many mainstream haunted house narratives decontextualise ancestral violence and reduce specific moments of America's ultraviolent history to such tired clichés as 'Indian burial ground' and 'witch trials'. However, a slate of recent publications do in fact lean into the discomfort and connect with this distressing past, for instance, Tananarive Due's *The Good House*, Matt Ruff's *Lovecraft Country* (2016), Stephen Graham Jones's *Mapping the Interior* (2017), Silvia Moreno-Garcia's *Mexican Gothic* (2020) and Tiffany D. Jackson's *White Smoke* (2021).

Uncanny Houses

The following introduction to the uncanny is heavily indebted to Anneleen Masschelein's monograph, *The Unconcept*, in which she outlines an elemental bifurcation in the critical reception and distribution of the uncanny in the twentieth century: 'the "postromantic/aesthetic" tradition [which] emphasizes the semantic kernels of transcendence, the supernatural, and the occult' and 'the "existential/post-Marxist" semantic line [which focuses on] alienation, strangeness, and angst.'[22] The former 'sticks' easily to related aesthetic/critical tools such as abjection and monstrosity, and has found a fertile niche in studies of the fantastic. The latter explores the uncanny in more general terms and 'attaches' to philosophical and sociopolitical examinations of the modern condition.[23] While Masschelein's neat division helps keep track of the many materialisations of the uncanny, the concept functions on three interconnected levels in this chapter: that of the narrative, in which conventional examples of the uncanny, first collated by Freud, are deployed to heighten the readers' experience of fear and unease; that of space, in which three places – a haunted ship, a haunted room and a haunted house – cohere as heterotopic sites of familial discomfort and danger; and finally, that of literary analysis, which is always implicated in the uncanny processes of citing, echoing and referencing, but also in deconstructing, defamiliarising and destabilising the familiar and the given.[24]

Obviously, Freud did not invent the uncanny, but as the father of psychoanalytic discourse he is credited with developing a sub-discourse on the issue. In a psychoanalytic reading, the uncanny ('*Das Unheimliche*') is psychic content that should have remained hidden but returned, or was returned, to the plain of our conscious existence.[25] Freud played the part of a literary critic and amateur linguist, dissecting the uncanny by assembling and then examining several examples of events that might evoke or provoke this feeling. Overall, these fall into two categories: materials repressed during infancy and atavistic beliefs inherited from earlier and more primitive times. Thus, 'the uncanny is that class of the frightening which leads back to what is known of old and long familiar'.[26] Freud did not view the adjectives *heimlich* and *unheimlich* as total opposites: rather than denoting a contrasting notion, the latter, through the prefix *un-*, indicates something repressed. David Farrell Krell has noted that the prefix *un-* not only operates as a marker of repression and concealment, but in purely semantic terms is 'utterly superfluous': the German 'heimlich', understood primarily as *homely* and *familiar*, already encompasses its very negation, namely *secret*, *hidden* and *occluded*.[27] Despite its semantic futility, *un-* becomes a defining feature of the uncanny by underlining its narrative structure, understood as a movement from incomplete repression to unfinished materialisation.

In his landmark study of the uncanny, Nicholas Royle has elaborated on Freud's essay and defines the uncanny as a crisis of that which is deemed proper and natural.[28] In his engaging and rather cleverly designed study, the uncanny becomes a nomadic concept, leaking into Marx's work on alienation, mechanical repetition, and 'a specter haunting Europe', and later reappears in Derrida's hauntology and deconstruction, which could be read as uncanny philosophy in itself. The uncanny suffuses Heidegger's philosophy of being not-at-home (*Unzuhause*) and of perpetual homelessness, as well as Wittgenstein's fixation on the strangeness of everyday existence. From a literary perspective, Royle perceives Russian formalism and *ostranenie*, Brecht's alienation effect and Todorov's investigation of the fantastic as all working within the realm of the uncanny. However, Freud's 'The Uncanny' retains its central position.

In contrast, Terry Castle locates the birth of the uncanny far earlier. As Freud's 1919 essay began as a re-examination of Ernst Jentsch's 1906 essay, 'On the Psychology of the Uncanny', perhaps Jentsch was grandfather of the uncanny and Freud a true Gothic usurper. In *The Female Thermometer* (1995), Castle argues that the uncanny emerged in the eighteenth century as a peculiar side effect of the elevation of reason and rationalism during the Enlightenment.[29] The uncanny, thus, became 'a sort of theme-index: an obsessional inventory of eerie fantasies, motifs, and effects, an itemized tropology of the weird',[30] providing safe haven for every item, experience or feeling cancelled or obfuscated by the Age of Reason, as Castle explains:

> What I argue here . . . is that the historic Enlightenment inter-
> nalization of the spectral – the gradual reinterpretation of ghosts
> and apparitions as hallucinations, or projections of the mind –
> introduced a new uncanniness into human consciousness itself.
> The mind became a 'world of phantoms' and thinking itself an act
> of ghost-seeing. Literature allegorized the change: in late eight-
> eenth-century Gothic fiction . . . the self-conscious debunking of
> stories of ghosts and apparitions coincides with an uncanny 'spe-
> cialization' of human psychology.[31]

The uncanny as a by-product of the Enlightenment also appears in Fred Botting's *Limits of Horror*, in which he suggests the premodern uncanny 'had a religious and social place and retained sacred and untouchable asso-ciations'.[32] Whatever was repressed, cloaked and lost along the way during the eighteenth and nineteenth centuries re-emerged under the guise of the uncanny. In the broadest possible sense, it was this sense of the *numinosum* that had to be suppressed for rationalism to reign. Therefore, the super-natural, the weird and the unexplained were relegated to the backroom of the human mind, where they have resided ever since alongside unspoken desires, taboos and other 'ghostly' manifestations of the numinous and the unconscious.[33]

Modernity also manufactured its own hysterical by-products, such as an irrational fear of fragmentation, mechanisation and dissolution of the self; a dread of losing the certainty of uniqueness and control over one's life; and a terror of new scientific and medical developments that threat-ened the integrity of the body with invasive and involuntary transforma-tions. While the first metaphorical home of the architectural uncanny was the house, Anthony Vidler has argued that its second was 'the city, where what was once walled and intimate . . . has been rendered strange by the spatial incursions of modernity'.[34] By the beginning of the twentieth cen-tury, the cityscape had emerged as a wholly new and frightening space, capable of terrorising urban dwellers with its labyrinthine structures, dark alleys, off-limits zones, suffocating tenement flats and menacing edifices. Importantly, in Vidler's formulation, the uncanny was first associated with the fears of the rising bourgeoisie, not quite at home in their freshly built or newly acquired residences. Many emerging middle-class anxieties cen-tred on the house precisely because this was the place that reminded the new class of their apparent rootlessness and lack of time-honoured family traditions. As Vidler reminds us, space as a 'threat, as harbinger of the unseen, operates as medical and physical metaphor for all the possible erosions of bourgeois bodily and social well being'.[35] Thus, the neo-classicist principles of transparency, order and light in both architecture and life, devised to sweep away secrets and shadows, were inevitably complemented by 'the invention of a spatial phenomenology of darkness'.[36] This perhaps explains the continuous popularity of (neo)Victorian aesthetics in haunted house stories. Although these distinctive houses are quite spacious, they are visually weighed down by dark and heavy furniture, as well as the assorted clutter that is quickly generated through diligent consumption. These portentous buildings appear to be doubly insulated: by unyielding bricks on the outside; on the inside by thick draperies, sombre paintings and dark wallpaper. One wonders who needs so much protection, and from what/whom?

Like Vidler's architectural uncanny, Paulina Palmer's queer uncanny merges aesthetic exploration with broader social analysis. In her pivotal study, *The Queer Uncanny: New Perspectives on the Gothic* (2012), Palmer returns the uncanny to the realm of intimacy yet never loses sight of the political dimension of one's identity. As the uncanny is witnessed tangentially rather than directly and explores the interplay of familiar and unfamiliar, as well as the homely and the secretive, it is a perfect tool for investigating the experiences and representations of queer subjects living in a heteronormative society.[37] Following Rosemary Jackson's definition of the uncanny as an agent for unveiling and rediscovering anxieties rendered invisible in a cultural field, Palmer points to the issues of invisibility, transgression and excess represented by queer experience.[38] Palmer argues that the uncanny, understood precisely as 'a signifier of excess', is able to 'uncover the unfamiliar beneath the familiar and, by challenging the conventional view of reality as unitary, to prompt the subject to question mainstream, "common-sense" versions of it'.[39]

On the following pages, the queer uncanny will primarily indicate attempts to interrogate normative and exclusive notions of kinship through and by spatial structures. In Poppy Z. Brite's/Billy Martin's work, rather than a safe haven, the house becomes contentious space, dangerous and fraught with anxieties delineating the limitations of not only a conventionally conceived family, but a modern-day queer one, whose queerness is predicated not only on the sexuality, sexual orientation or gender expression of its members, but also on their non-compliance with (hetero)normative social expectations. In the novels by Nancy Holder and Kathe Koja, the uncanny primarily emerges in connection

Uncanny in the House of Fear • 31

with spatial arrangements, a crushing estrangement of lived-in space bringing anxieties related to femininity and female desire, intimacy, emotional dependency, economic precarity and the decline of a white bourgeois family into focus.

Void Dreams in *Dead in the Water*

Nancy Holder's winner of the 1994 Bram Stoker Award, *Dead in the Water*, presents us with a reconstituted family formed by strangers bonding on a holiday cruiser, the *Morris*, and, after it sinks *en route* to Hawaii, the ghost-ship that rescues the holidaymakers.[40] Referencing the tradition of American sea Gothic,[41] Holder portrays the ocean as yet another frontier, an uncanny space where the unknown must be faced and demons fought, and from which, after undergoing brutal trials, heroes can triumphantly emerge. Replacing the haunted house, the *Pandora* – aptly named in a passenger's dream – is staffed by a ghostly crew still serving an eighteenth-century buccaneer and necromancer, Captain Reade, in return for temporary oblivion, revealed in short hallucinations of their past lives. Existing in this hellish limbo comes at a high price and over time the survivors have been transformed into zombie-like slaves forced to cannibalise the crews and passengers of other ships.

With each new sunken ship and ghost-slaves, *Pandora* acquires not only more 'passengers', but also furniture, trinkets, rooms and even entire decks, thus transforming the ship into a decaying bricolage of styles and fashions. The accumulation of memorabilia and assorted furnishings mirrors the way household objects are collected over several generations. Yet, on *Pandora*, the accumulation of economic and social capital usually associated with such costly possessions is offset by a permeating deep-rooted decay. The initial splendour of furnishings gives way to horrifying glimpses of shattered glass, tattered walls and dreary decorations. Donna, a no-nonsense policewoman haunted by past trauma, dreams of swimming through the decaying ship:

> Bobbing and drifting, she swam within the ribs of the ship like something that had peeled away from it. A piece of living tissue, floating inside a prison of rib bones. No, no, the ship wasn't alive. Its ribs were wood, rotting wood. She narrowed her eyes. Rotting, and impregnated with worms. The ribs were a writhing mass of them. (p. 193)

32 • House of Horrors

Even within her dream, the ship switches between different planes, never allowing a final understanding of what is happening. Déjà vu and repetition compulsion, Freud's iconic examples of the uncanny, reverberate through *Pandora*'s passageways and challenge the stability of reality. Some of the shipwreck survivors even begin to question whether they are dead or alive, and whether the ship is in fact real:

> [Elise] had walked down this same section a dozen times. But she had never noticed – never seen – the royal red carpet, the flocked walls, the elaborate crystal lamps hanging from the ceiling. She had never seen how dirty it was, with cobwebs dripping like diamonds from the teardrop coronas of the fixtures; the green mold on the thick oak baseboards. (p. 228)

The ontological rifts that are destroying *Pandora*'s reality trigger deep sensorial disorientation: characters are plagued by intense visions, their senses overwhelmed by smells, lights, textures, flavours and physical sensations such as arousal, panic and nausea.[42] It is unclear whether the monsters and ghosts populating *Pandora*'s decks are Reade's enslaved victims, extensions of his dark magic or emanations of an ancient power. The *Morris* survivors eat lavish meals, have sexual encounters with mysterious strangers and are enveloped by silky bedcovers and designer clothes that disturb their bodily autonomy in intensely unsettling ways. Instead of protecting the survivors, the ship invades and manipulates their bodies.

Pandora is a perfect vehicle for the uncanny: every object, person and name, though eerily familiar, is simultaneously alien and treacherous. Even memories prove to be unreliable, constantly evolving to fit Reade's agenda. Shadowy movements materialise in the peripheral vision of survivors, invariably *abseits* ('from afar'), thus echoing Freud's opening paragraph of 'The Uncanny'. In these moments, *Pandora* unveils her true face, albeit only for an instance. Each shipwrecked passenger struggles with their own disturbing glimpses of two illusory realities: one filled with death and decay, the other based on their innermost desires. Donna is the only one capable of withstanding the siren song, and only to an extent. Her levelheadedness and apparent immunity to the creature keeping *Pandora* alive, which also granted Reade his immortality and power, position her as Reade's object of desire, the catalyst for a mutiny and an alternative maternal figure to the motley crew of survivors.

Protagonists constantly tread out of rotting sea depths and onto the lavishly decorated decks of a picture-perfect holiday cruiser. Their sensory modalities – visual, auditory, olfactory, tactile – are perverted as they move in and out of their fantasies and nightmarish visions. Such a disorienting and unsettling space suggests a centuries-long fascination with *horror vacui*. On *Pandora*, recurring sensations of ice-cold water and visions of impenetrable darkness and drowning evoke a dread of spaces devoid of boundaries and a clearly defined end. Baroque architects attempted to alleviate such fears by filling empty space with an infinite number of spirals, mirrors and spectacular ornaments. Similarly, *Pandora* is filled with a plethora of eye-catching knick-knacks, rarities, curiosa and contraptions intended to distract passengers from the dark engulfing water. However, baroque space – or any space crammed with eerie trinkets and optical illusions – provides only a reflection of the paranoid, irrational and splintered self that finds no solace in this architectural cornucopia. This example of baroque space suggests there are places that can cause people to experience actual physical or mental discomfort, even psychosis.[43]

Ontological uncertainty is also linked to what Samuel Weber has described as the 'crisis of perception and of phenomenality' that accompanies 'a mortal danger to the subject'.[44] Weber has noted that a feature of the uncanny rests on the 'desire to penetrate, discover and ultimately to conserve the integrity of perception: perceiver and perceived, the wholeness of the body, the power of vision'. This requires a rejection of the 'almost-nothing,' of figures fleetingly glimpsed *abseits*.[45] Such denial, Weber tells us, presupposes a kind of narrative that actively perpetuates this repudiation.[46] Horror narratives customarily employ this tactic, refusing to yield the final piece of knowledge and delay the moment of comprehension. In *Dead in the Water*, this delay relates to Captain Reade's past crimes, his inconceivable pact with the mythological monstress Scylla and awareness of the creature herself.

Scylla emerges late in the novel and remains a deliberately indeterminate character to the end: '[s]he was a gray, floating mass, like silvery clouds, like lumpy fog; pieces reached at him like shaking eager hands. Sometimes they were tentacles, and sometimes they were pincers, and sometimes they were fingers' (p. 389). In line with her varied representations in Greek and Roman art, her body is a monstrous hybrid, at times presented as 'a belching whirlpool', a half-woman with 'a sea serpent's long tail, and six slavering dog's heads at her waist' and as a many-limbed monster with a profusion of teeth.[47] As her body continues to alternate between

34 • House of Horrors

various forms, she is forced into the female stereotypes of scorned woman, unforgiving witch and horrifying sea-monster, occasionally all at the same time. Scylla reunites two easily recognisable female *topoi*: the monstrous feminine – 'Scylla the devouring whirlpool', the terrifying castratrix[48] – and the goddess. On the one hand, her mythological origin, tentacled limbs and pincers confirm her status not just as a monster but as an archaic mother, one 'who conceives all by herself, the original parent, the godhead of all fertility and the origin of procreation'.[49] On the other, her identity as a godlike, all-powerful creature longing for love/worship places her on the side of the *sacrum*, where 'fantasies of the divine feminine [can be celebrated] . . . driving all notions of monstrosity aside'.[50] Scylla oscillates between these two images – sacred goddess/enchanting lover and profane hybrid monster – fusing her lovers' fears and desires, inviting the male gaze and obliterating it in a single gesture.

While Scylla acts as a vengeful, but largely absent maternal figure, it is Captain Reade who moves to the fore as the despotic patriarch. The reconstituted family of shipwrecked passengers are successively destroyed by this possessive father figure. By openly courting the uncanny monsters residing in the dark, Reade, originally condemned to death for sexually abusing and killing a cabin boy in an occult ritual in 1797,[51] embodies the irrational content thrown outside the order of things in the Age of Reason. Having set him adrift, his crew had thrown the cabin boy's disembodied head into his boat. As the days passed, Reade had eaten the head and died. Then, in a plot reminiscent of the Flying Dutchman legend, he sold his soul to the mysterious female power of Scylla. In his madness, Reade betrayed Scylla, stopped feeding her and trapped her deep within the bowels of *Pandora*, where, ironically, she is locked inside a metal box. Because her generative power runs through Reade and, by extension, through *Pandora*, Scylla partakes in their shared creation: the ghostly ship, their haunted house. Enraged by her companion's betrayal, Scylla calls to Cha-Cha, a Vietnam veteran and hippie, who eventually takes Reade's place as her lover/instrument/captain. Only then is it revealed that it was Scylla who orchestrated the events leading to her escape and the exchange of her lovers.

Although Scylla lives in water, any potential associations with a life source and reproduction are negated by her uncontrollable disorderly femininity. Rather than giving life she devours it frantically. From a strictly psychoanalytic view, her offensive body, fabricated from fog, tentacles, teeth and human hands, is the uncanny sight/site of female genitalia, from which the male gaze wants to escape and yet to which it yearns to return. In

Uncanny in the House of Fear • 35

a more contemporary reading drawing on Mikhail Bakhtin's theory of the grotesque and its subsequent feminist reformulations, hers is the female grotesque body, repulsive and monstrous, fecund and open to intrusions, abjected but also elevated in a carnivalesque spirit through connotations of reversed power and sovereignty.[52] Scylla's hybrid body – leaking, contaminating, erratic – belongs to the lower order of things, as it literally resides at the bottom of the sea, struggling to leave her Pandora's box. The ship, acting as an extension of Scylla's body, mirrors her hybridity: '[h]er hull was a pastiche of metal vessels from which wooden masts and bowsprits extended helter-skelter like spears stuck in a carcass; a propeller at least a story tall; half a steamboat paddlewheel, the wheelhouse of a tug' (p. 399). Copious references to dripping water, leaks and wet surfaces feed into a theme of corporeal contamination: sudden shifts in the structure of the ship mean no one is safe from Scylla's intrusions, whether manifesting as icy water or as dreams filled with Captain Reade's Faustian propositions.

In this familial melodrama, the quarrelling parents Captain Reade and Scylla are fighting over their 'house' and their children, the shipwrecked survivors. They want the newcomers to feed and sustain them the way children are expected to take care of their elderly parents. In this sense, the story is one of toxic familial relations, in which separated parents compete for their children's attention and nourishment. The only way to remain on *Pandora* in a state of blissful reverie is by eating the flesh of new passengers and devouring their dreams. Cannibalism, thus, stands for incestuous relations, as it translates into a metaphorical consummation of the flesh of people within one household in order to perpetuate familial relations in an unchanged form. Ultimately, only Donna and one other crew member manage to resist being lulled or forced into staying and escape the collapsing *Pandora*. The others, unable to leave the familiar space of their relived memories to (re)create their own familial space elsewhere, are turned into living-dead monsters, feeding off one another in a grotesque houseboat of illusions.

This short-lived patchwork family rapidly disintegrates, due not only to Reade and Scylla's mind games and squabbles, but also to their repressed fears and desires resurfacing with magnified force on the *Pandora*. John, an ever-anxious doctor who cannot believe his son will recover from cancer or that a potential relationship with Donna could succeed, ultimately succumbs to despair and death; Elise and Phil, a *nouveau riche* couple, plunge deeper into a caricature of entitlement and passive-aggressive toxicity; Ruth, a warm-hearted elderly woman, cannot let go of her dead husband and move on with life; Ramón, the first officer and former criminal, is consumed by dreams of masculine power; and Donna, haunted by the memory of a drowned boy, is too afraid to act on her feelings for Glenn, her police partner. The protagonists' inability to cope with death and mourning eliminates the possibility of establishing new or repairing existing families. Still, this inability to move on could also relate to fairly formulaic and limited character development. While some manage to evolve to some degree, including Donna, the tough, white, working-class, street-smart cop, others are confined in clichés that allow little to no flexibility. Ramón, the sole non-white character, starts out as a sympathetic first officer, but is soon revealed to be an ex-gang member who cannot resist returning to his criminal ways.[53]

Back on land, Glenn finally leaves his family for Donna. However, after his wife and children die in a freak pool accident, Scylla's insidious presence is confirmed and Donna decides to leave Glenn and face the monster once more. Whether Cha-Cha is unable to soothe Scylla's pain or she has been irreversibly broken by the abusive relationship with a mentally unstable captain, or the proverbial Pandora's box has been ripped apart by the events aboard the ghost-ship, is no longer relevant. Although it is clearly suggested that the driving force behind Scylla's actions is her longing for a man's love and affection, men have minimal influence on her behaviour. The final confrontation, suggested on the very last page, will take place between two women fighting to end their loneliness. Solidarity and mutual understanding are unthinkable. As the madwoman in the basement rather than the attic, Scylla acts as Donna's unwelcome double, 'an uncanny harbinger of death' who can voice Donna's own ambivalence and anxiety.[54] Scylla is thus a woman who is enraged by men who lie to her and refuse to commit; she hates other women for the perceived freedoms she has been denied and hates herself for needing the male companionship that has both defined and scarred her.

The uncanny properties of the ghost-ship – its architectural hybridity, ontological indeterminacy and corporeal invasiveness – help create a transgressive Gothic drama, in which a mad, possessive father imprisons the archaic mother, and their adopted children are devoured by their shared fury and strange obsessions. A confusion of orders reigns in *Dead in the Water*, as *Pandora* not only functions as a ghost-ship but also as a haunted family house and an extension of Scylla and Reade's revolting powers. Simultaneously organic and inorganic, dead and alive, the ship manipulates, entices and consumes its inhabitants.

Uncanny in the House of Fear • 37

Unhomely Funhole in *The Cipher*

In her 1991 debut novel, *The Cipher*, Kathe Koja transgresses conventional horror fiction mechanisms by avoiding the usual approaches to plot structure, style and characterisation.[55] Following Jeff VanderMeer's insightful analysis, Steven Shaviro has situated Koja's early prose squarely in the New Weird rather than horror tradition.[56] He notes that a curious form of emptiness resides at the centre of Koja's early prose in that she rejects both 'the social and the personal' dimension of horror fiction, and leaves her readers 'only with the *affects* of the genre'.[57] Thus, horror fans' expectations are frustrated on several levels: readers cannot easily cast the novel in terms of a struggle between good and evil; there is no Freudian 'return of the repressed' and no secrets waiting to be revealed; the novel does not yield itself to an allegorical reading; and no final catharsis awaits the patient reader.

Negating potential social interpretations appears rather hasty to me, and even Shaviro has conceded that all Koja's early characters have obsessively individualistic natures, a feature that he attributes to the neoconservative and neoliberal climate of the 1980s. The fact that the characters 'narcissistically shrink into themselves, because any broader engagement with the world would put them in danger'[58] does not necessarily preclude readings in which their narcissism, self-imposed exile and alienation from social networks are part of a larger critique of late-capitalist society. The fact that all the characters are white – a fact unstated is a fact confirmed – speaks volumes about the privilege of a 'narcissistic shrinkage into oneself' and the possibility of opting out of a comfortable if commodified middle-class lifestyle without such repercussions as police harassment, lower wages (even for already lowly paid temp jobs) or stymied access to the art scene they all frequent. It could also be argued that Koja does not entirely forgo the uncanny or the return of the repressed, as Shaviro suggests, but knowingly engages with the modern understanding of the uncanny, which encompasses not only defamiliarisation and the homely/unhomely dichotomy, but also homelessness, estrangement and economic precarity.[59]

Strikingly, *The Cipher* does not present a traditional discovery plot with likeable protagonists and clearly defined antagonists/monsters. In Noël Carroll's classic formula, developed most fully in *The Philosophy of Horror: or, Paradoxes of the Heart* (1990), human curiosity and a morbid fascination with 'cognitively threatening' monsters function as a *raison d'être* for all horror texts. While totalising theories of this kind are relatively

38 • House of Horrors

easy to refute, it is true that a great many horror texts follow the discovery plot and revolve around a monster figure of some kind. However, speculative fiction novels in the vein of Koja's early output challenge Carroll's theory by problematising monstrosity and discarding the need for explanations and linear progression from the very beginning. Indeed, Koja's characters are curiously uncurious and immensely unlikeable.

The main protagonist and first-person narrator of *The Cipher*, Nicholas, together with his on-again, off-again girlfriend, Nakota, stumble on an abandoned room in their apartment building, in which they find a strange-smelling and sinister-looking hole in one of the walls. The Funhole, as christened by Nakota, constitutes an ontological impossibility: a non/presence, a pulsating intensity, a living blackness. Almost immediately, Nakota sets forth to experiment. Her fascination is the driving force behind each test, every attempt to engage with the Funhole, as Nicholas remains involved only to keep Nakota happy. When her obsession escalates and she becomes frustrated by Nicholas's lack of enthusiasm, she leaves him in search of more pliable and eager followers. The novel ends with a series of inexplicable events and Nicholas finally succumbing to Nakota's desire to explore the dark potentialities of the Funhole.

Rather than a need to quench the cognitive unease generated by the hole, Nakota's tests represent a quest for thrills and desire for transformation. Nakota is less interested in understanding the phenomenon than in witnessing its power and undergoing some form of corporeal conversion. The boundaries between life and death are suspended when a severed hand is briefly animated inside the Funhole. Inorganic matter, such as Randy's sculptures and Malcolm's death mask, come to life when placed nearby. The line between human and non-human is crossed when Nicholas pushes Malcolm's head into the hole and half his face is transformed into a viperfish monstrosity. The distinction between oneself and the Other is also questioned, as Nicholas accidentally places his hand in the hole and develops a miniature Funhole on his right palm. Finally, during the last session with the phenomenon, Nicholas is able to move his hands freely through closed doors, thus crossing the last physical barriers between himself and the un/reality of the Funhole.

The novel draws our attention to the strange materiality of the bodily, although the body in question may not necessarily be considered fully human, alive or even recognisably organic. And yet, the protagonists ignore the stark impossibility of the Funhole's origins. Their off-hand manner may be a consequence of being exposed to a reality in which clear-cut

Uncanny in the House of Fear • 39

distinctions between organicism and inorganicism have collapsed in the wake of radical medical interventions and the profound technologization, even cybernisation of life. Vidler reminds us that 'the body, itself invaded and reshaped by technology, invades and permeates the space outside, even as this space takes on dimensions that themselves confuse the inner and the outer, visually, mentally, and physically'.[60] The Funhole may thus be read as a manifestation of organic matter's assault on inanimate matter, thereby challenging various spatial and environmental divisions but not surprising Koja's blasé protagonists.

As a site of the uncanny, the Funhole enacts an unwanted return of corporeality and materiality, repressed by protagonists who refuse to participate in the never-ending cycle of accumulation and consumption in which their bodies take central stage as both objects and subjects of the consumerist gaze.[61] Koja's characters emphatically reject the fantasy of everlasting consumerism and instead embrace death, pain, denial, and isolation 'as a form of transcendence' and solace.[62] This material turn could explain the profusion of smells and odours emanating from the Funhole: scents often trigger micro-uncanny events in which solid objects or memories of such objects and connected situations are recovered through highly specific, yet transient aromas.

It should be emphasised that the materiality that is returned – or returns – to Nicholas and Nakota does not belong to a pre-consumerist, pre-lapsarian order, in which corporeality remains innocent and free from market forces. On the contrary, the Funhole brings forth *unhuman* matter. Following Dylan Triggs, I perceive the unhuman as a conceptual tool that is reminiscent of the Freudian uncanny, in that the prefix 'un' marks that which 'haunt[s] the human without it being fully integrated into humanity'.[63] The Funhole thus stages this process, the return of the unhuman, 'the human becoming unhuman',[64] as Nicholas's body is assaulted by the very materiality that he wishes to forget: the dark recesses of his own body. As the novel ends, a gooey substance flowing from Nicholas's stigmatised hand coats his body and he readies himself for the final experiment of entering the Funhole: 'I was becoming a process . . . But to become your disease? To become the consumption itself?' (p. 323). Ironically, a character who pointedly rejects a commodity-obsessed lifestyle is transformed into the very process of material(ist) consumption that he wishes to escape. In the last few sentences of the novel, Nicholas hints that the Funhole may actually be a physical representation of his own personal void. Dispassionately, he muses: 'what if it *is* me? What if somehow I'm crawling blind and

40 • House of Horrors

headfirst into my own sick heart, the void made manifest and disguised as hellhole, to roil in the aching stink of my own emptiness forever?' (p. 355). Although this reading is neither particularly favoured nor repudiated, it is the only hint of an explanation that readers receive throughout the novel.[65] The origin, substance and meaning of the Funhole are never openly addressed. The phenomenon is simply described as 'that negative place' (p. 4). However, its connections with darkness are emphasised:

> Black. Not darkness, not the absence of light but living black. Maybe a foot in diameter, maybe a little more. Pure black and the sense of pulsation, especially when you looked at it too closely, the sense of something not living but alive, not even some*thing* but some – process. (p. 3)

Sight, privileged within the Western cognitive regime, is repeatedly invalidated in *The Cipher*, as characters struggle with the Funhole's status as an absence, a void, or, at best, video static. The transient and volatile nature of odours emanating from the Funhole further accentuate the process as its main, and perhaps only characteristic. For Nakota the Funhole embodies 'an avenue to change. To transcursion' (p. 292). For Nicholas, however, the Funhole merely amounts to emptiness: 'a negativity, and absence, a *lack*. A depression, that's what a hole was, no matter how dark and lively, no matter how ultimately full' (p. 138).

At some point it is revealed that Nicholas functions as a conduit, a catalyst who 'activates' the Funhole: without him, there is no Funhole, only an ordinary hole in just another decrepit tenement flat. In sharp contrast to the ever-passive and apathetic Nicholas, Nakota actually welcomes and appreciates the prospect of transformation and therefore resents his centrality: 'We all know it's me who should be in there . . . I'm a perfect candidate for a change. A becoming' (p. 339). But when the Funhole finally lets Nakota into a locked room, Nicholas inadvertently kills her in an attempted rescue. Nicholas prevents her from entering the hole because he knows that 'for her there would be no transformations, no ultimate transcursion to fulfilment: she was just another insect, just another fucking bug' (p. 352).

The Funhole, presented as the abyss incarnate, inspires both panic and desire by projecting images of hell and heaven, suggesting unnatural configurations and inviting a penetrative gaze onto itself. The fact that Nicholas has a cheap reproduction of Hieronymus Bosch's *The Garden of*

Earthly Delights hanging in his otherwise depersonalised flat functions as a satirical counterpoint to the 'delights' offered by the Funhole, the sexual nature of which is established when Nicholas either masturbates or has sex with Nakota in its vicinity. In one of the more disturbing encounters, Nakota, still in the initial phase of experiments, places a living mouse in the hole. The rodent explodes leaving only a foot and mutated head. This excites the couple, and when they finally have sex in Nicholas's apartment, they use the mouse head in their fondling and kissing. The head is merely a substitute for the true third participant, the Funhole, which becomes a vagina-like organ in Nicholas's 'fleshy dreams' (p. 29). Nicholas, initially happy about reuniting with Nakota, comes to realise that rather than fucking each other, they were having sex with the Funhole.

As previously mentioned, the emptiness of the Funhole is figuratively mirrored through Nicholas's self. Following an aborted suicide attempt, Nicholas dwells on his own cowardice and worthlessness: 'It's so easy to be nothing. It requires very little thought or afterthought' (p. 121). The nothingness professed by Nicholas may account for his unique relationship with the Funhole: the manner in which he accepts everything life throws at him and floats with the current of his mundane existence make him a perfect receptacle for whatever negativity the Funhole may convey. Nicholas becomes the one true disciple of the Funhole, unwilling yet loyal, someone who will not turn away or escape because, paradoxically, unlike Nakota, Malcolm and other devotees, he desires no enlightenment, no secret wisdom. Although other characters eagerly declare their readiness for the ultimate sacrifice, their offerings are tainted by a burning desire to be transformed or gain something from the Funhole, be it fame, knowledge or enlightenment.

The words used to describe those gathered around the Funhole – followers, devotees, disciples – suggest a sectarian model. And this is precisely the mode of choice for almost all relationships in *The Cipher*. It is well known that religious cults utilise familial language, and words such as 'brothers' or 'children' are used to cloak a wide range of abuses and manipulation. The miraculous Funhole functions as a temple, around which a number of power relations form; as in a typical cult, these are largely toxic or fake. While Nicholas reluctantly plays the part of stigmatic prophet, Nakota appoints herself high priestess, gathers new acolytes and eventually forms her own alternative clique. Within this dysfunctional family, Nakota appears to be in charge, manipulating both Nicholas and Malcolm through the bestowal of attention and sexual favours. It is entirely possible to read Nakota as a *femme fatale*, self-absorbed, egoistic and manipulative, while the other two female characters – Nora and Vanese – are nurturing, maternal figures. However, Nakota's cruelty, fierceness and pronounced disregard for anything culturally constructed as feminine, such as clothing, intensive body care and makeup, suggest a reversal of traditionally defined gender roles. This becomes clear when we contrast her 'unfeminine' behaviour with Nicholas's utter – and culturally coded as feminine – passivity. Rather than remaining a submissive female victim, Nakota takes control and propels the narrative. Nicholas accepts his fate until the very end: it is only when the Funhole physically abuses, taunts and pushes Nicholas to breaking point that he attempts to save Nakota, and he can only 'save' her from the Funhole by killing her in the process.

Although Nicholas is the key to the Funhole, it is Nakota, about whom little is actually revealed, who appears to be key to the story. The overabundance of names that she goes by – Jane, Nakota and Shrike – suggest a multifaceted personality, one to which Nicholas has only limited access. Nicholas's first-person narration depicts her as an antagonistic presence, 'a leech' (p. 269) and 'a queen of heat and brutal desire, of everything crooked and twisted and wrong' (p. 342). Our awareness of her avaricious fixation on the Funhole, plus her jealousy and insensitivity, originate from Nicholas's narration. As her voice is muted throughout, Nakota is unable to counter these characterisations. And yet Nicholas desperately clings to her and is even willing to assume some kind of responsibility for the Funhole in order to keep an eye on Nakota and her followers.

Their self-destructive, toxic relationship stands in sharp contrast to that of Randy and Vanese. Although also failed artists with dead-end jobs, the other couple manage to make their relationship work. Nicholas admits that even their flat has 'a home look to it', with pictures of friends, Randy's art, decorations and old 'friendly furniture' (p. 277) – something he will never have. At one point in the narrative, as Vanese shows concern for his well-being, Nicholas half-jokingly asks her to be his mother. A part of him appears to long for solace and support, despite his disinclination to reach out to anyone. The only person he asks for help or, to be more precise, to return a favour, is his old acquaintance Nora, at whose place he crashes for a few days when contemplating suicide. Ultimately, just as he is unable to let go of Nakota, he is unable to end his life. While Nora and Vanese prove that being in a relationship can be pain-free, Nakota frankly declares '[i]f it doesn't hurt, you're not doing it right' (p. 146).

Rather than middle-class protagonists, whose banality and cultural recognisability makes them easy to identify with, Koja imagines characters that subsist on the fringes of society: self-avowed outcasts living in poetic squalor, constantly scrambling for money to buy fast food, cheap beer and cigarettes. Yet, judging by their education and use of obscure art references, they have evidently benefitted from middle-class privilege at some point and have chosen borderline poverty as the only available avenue of opting out. As Koja's protagonists are a self-styled white underclass of alternative artists and art groupies, the uncanny operates in a different way. No longer unease and anxiety associated with a bourgeois house, the uncanny surrounding the Funhole denotes the homesickness and homelessness associated with the modern human condition. Thus, a cosy middle-class haunted house is transformed into an abandoned storage unit in a decrepit tenement building, while the traditional family unit haunted by Gothic vestigiality and the unresolved past is replaced by unlikeable individuals hounded by their own inadequacies, nihilism and an emptiness that refers to the future rather than the past. Thus, *The Cipher* dwells uncomfortably in the desert of the neoliberal self.

Hantke is right to draw attention to the objectification of relations in *The Cipher*: faced with a profound lack of commodities, the characters perceive one another as objects to be exploited rather than subjects with whom they can communicate or co-operate. As communication enables consumption, characters who are 'perverse, suicidal, or antisocial' cannot partake in the late-capitalist reality.[66] As Mark Fisher has stated, 'people work by communicating' in post-Fordist capitalism: thus, one must swiftly learn how to navigate an incessant flow of information or drown.[67] While the novel is set in the early 1990s, a time when the flow of information was still a trickle, Koja's protagonists correctly intuit that the way out is silence and stillness. Despite having no interested in monetising the Funhole, the pseudo-artistic cult generated by Malcolm and Nakota speaks of a hunger for power that cannot be contained by a purely metaphysical yearning for transcendence. They may reject money but, at least to some of Koja's characters, social capital does matter.

The Queer (Uncanny) Desire in *Drawing Blood*

Due to her selection of social outcasts and disaffected youth as protagonists, Koja's early fiction has often been bracketed with the horror work of Poppy Z. Brite's/Billy Martin. Certainly, the two authors were lauded as among the best female voices of the short-lived splatterpunk movement of the early 1990s.[68] Martin, who began his transition in the early 2000s, initially abandoned both the 'Poppy Z. Brite' identity and his writing career, considering both to be finished. In recent years, however, he has returned to writing and is once again using 'Poppy Z. Brite' as a literary pseudonym, evidenced by his Patreon webpage. As Brite's/ Martin's early work remains an essential part of early-1990s women's horror fiction, I have chosen to include his second novel. Similarly to Koja's, Brite's/Martin's *Drawing Blood* (1993) also features young people attempting to eke out an existence beyond normative middle-class expectations. In contrast to *The Cipher*, however, Brite's/Martin's novel explicitly deals with queer desire and families of choice and, as such, directly taps into the queer uncanny.

Drawing Blood is perhaps the most generically obvious of the three novels chosen for this chapter: it takes place in an actual haunted house and the novel begins and ends with the main hero and young comic illustrator, Trevor, travelling to his family home. It is here, when Trevor is five years old, that his mother and younger brother are butchered by his father, Bobby, who later commits suicide. Two decades later, Trevor is back on Violin Road, near the town of Missing Mile, where he meets the computer hacker Zach, another boy from an abusive household. This is the first serious relationship for both boys, one that shatters their defences and allows them to form an alternative family unit. As Zach has been too afraid of becoming too dependent on his lovers and Trevor too afraid of wanting to hurt them, both have previously avoided falling in love. Interestingly, neither boy ever discusses their sexuality or identity; in the somewhat naïve universe of Brite's/Martin's early novels, homophobia is relegated to the margins and characters are free to act on their desires.

The universe of *Drawing Blood*, as with all Brite's/Martin's early prose, is almost exclusively populated by striking androgynous men, disenchanted rebels and angsty Gothicky teens on the run.[69] Almost every character is white, the notable exceptions being Eddy, an Asian-American female stripper hopelessly in love with Zach, and Dougal, a Black Jamaican man who joins her quest to warn Zach about the federal agents closing in on his location.[70] The only other non-white person of consequence in the story is the renowned Black jazz artist Charlie 'Bird' Parker: having heard his father listen obsessively to his music, Trevor draws a comic panel about Parker. An episode of police brutality from Parker's life becomes fuel for the vicious mind games of the house, christened Birdland by Trevor after his father's acclaimed comic book. Via Trevor's comic strip, Birdland gives Parker's story a different ending, in which the white racist cops are crucified and burned for their brutal murder of Parker and his colleague, who later return as revenge-seeking zombies. However, this superficial reference to actual trauma is not used to advance any significant commentary on racial politics and proves to be only a foreshadowing of Trevor's destiny.

Brite/Martin composed a classic haunted house tale, albeit with a distinctly queer twist. By juxtaposing images of a haunted house with queer desire, culturally marked as alarming and excessive, Brite/Martin effectively collapses distinctions between the positive and negative connotations of both concepts. The house is depicted as a somewhat disturbing, yet still romantic backdrop for a fairly homonormative love story of redemption and forgiveness.[71] Uncanny space, previously literally covered in blood and darkness, is thus reclaimed and redeemed by Trevor and Zach, who come to represent a living example of the benefits that queer families of choice can provide. The centrality of a conventional nuclear family is challenged by queer desire, which functions not only as a destabilising agent but also a counterweight to traditional family ethos and, in Brite's/Martin's fiction, as its visibly better and healthier alternative. Brite/Martin contrasts a number of families of choice with the traditional family model, represented by the two lovers' terrifyingly dysfunctional parental homes. As well as Eddy, Zach's best friend from New Orleans, we are introduced to an extended family of straight and gay teenagers who gather in a local music shop, and in the local rock pub, Sacred Yew, young outsiders are not only welcomed but also frequently helped by an older generation of hippies and ex-members of 1960s and 1970s countercultural movements. All these groups help Zach and Trevor, at no point questioning the boys about their situation. In fact, in a naïve and idealistic gesture, every character (except the federal agents tracking Zach) is portrayed as either an open-minded queer or a liberal straight.

The openness and freedom with which queer desire and queer love function in the novel seems at odds with Palmer's queer uncanny and its connotations of secrecy, invisibility and Gothic transgression. Zach and Trevor are not secretive about their relationship and, as far as they are concerned, are not breaking any significant taboos. Just as the queer uncanny can be used to disclose or identify queer themes in texts that are ostensibly indifferent to LGBTQ+ subjects, it can also emphasise the ties between the uncanny and queerness, their shared familiarity with phenomenological alienation and repression. In this sense, the queer uncanny may disclose how queer desire functions in popular imagination and, rather than only describe how a given text manages its own queerness, point to the imaginaries used to delineate its borders. In Brite's/Martin's novel, the motifs shared by both the uncanny and queer desire are excess, doubling and repetition compulsion. Excess is primarily associated with the house itself and the way it fails to contain both the supernatural spillage and emotional devastation it brought to Trevor's family. Doubling and repetition compulsion control Trevor's interactions with both the house and Zach, thus underscoring issues of recognition, visibility and self-awareness.

The abandoned run-down house on Violin Road is steeped in Gothic clichés: there are dense shadows, rusty blood stains, eerie green light from the overgrown kudzu and even a ghost in the bathroom where Bobby hanged himself. Electricity still flows despite being long disconnected. In one particularly blood-curdling moment, the house presents Trevor with the very same hammer that his father used to kill his mother and brother. From the moment Trevor steps into the Violin Road house it manipulates his behaviour, at times taking full control of his mind and body. In a telling episode, the house influences Trevor to change the comic story that he has been developing, then proceeds to rip his story to pieces:

> Holding each other like a pair of twins in the womb, [Zach and Trevor] were able to sleep. Sometime just before dawn, a slow shimmering began in the air near the ceiling just above the bed. It deepened into a vaguely circular whirlpool pattern something like the waves of heat that swim above asphalt in the heart of a Southern summer. Then tiny white fragments of paper began to fall, appearing in the air and seesawing slowly down. Soon a funnel-shaped cloud of them was swirling like a freak snowstorm in the hot, still room. (p. 189)

The small portal opening above is proof that the house has hidden depths. Terry, the middle-aged owner of the Missing Mile record store, recalls what he and his childhood friends had witnessed inside the house:

> Terry had seen a city street around him, a boarded-up slum, wavering like a mirage but definitely there. R.J. had seen a dark deserted bar with shattered glass on the floor and cracked mirrors on the walls so dusty that he could not see his face in them. And Steve would never say what he had seen, except that it had legs like a bug. (p. 376)

Uncanny in the House of Fear • 47

These urban spaces may have been a mystery to the children who witnessed them, but to Trevor these are the familiar mean streets of Bobby's alternative comic book, Birdland, in which the titular *Birdland* – named after one of Charlie Bird Parker's songs – contains 'the slums and beat sections of New York or New Orleans or Kansas City' (p. 109), junkies, jazz musicians and lost souls of the counterculture.

Birdland is also a phantasmagorical hallucinatory reality fuelled by art *and* blood. For a younger Trevor, it was a place of artistry and creativity, a creative plane 'where you could work magic, the place where no one else could touch you' (p. 18), but he also witnessed his father's reactions as his own access to Birdland was restricted: it was when drinking no longer opened the doors to Birdland that Bobby resorted to murder-suicide. Two decades later, through hallucinogenic mushrooms and intense penetrative sex, Trevor can slip into Birdland. He finds the parallel version of Violin Road house and asks Bobby why he killed his family and, more importantly, why he chose to spare his eldest son. This is where *Drawing Blood* jumps head-on into a time-travel paradox: at the age of twenty-five, Trevor is also the ghost that visited his father twenty years earlier, a ghost that saved five-year-old Trevor from his father's hammer. The origins, localisation and real purpose of Birdland are lost in conjecture: is it a place that provides artists with inspiration in exchange for their blood, sweat and exertion, or a place sustained by artists' pain and violence, a vampiric universe that keeps drawing Trevor in, 'filling his mind with images and icons till he overflowed like a pitcher of dark liquid' (p. 140)? Bobby confides in Trevor that 'Birdland is a machine oiled with the blood of artists . . . [it] is a mirror that reflects our deaths. Birdland never existed' (p. 349). This suggests that Birdland, understood as a plane of pure creativity and inspiration, was never there to begin with; there has always only been Birdland, the negative space, the mirror to the tortured soul of Bobby, and now Trevor.

Both Trevor and Zach, who soon follows his lover into Birdland, experience its reality as grotesque, distorted and unsettling, a place that manifests their deepest fears and traumatic memories. Fear, shame, guilt and anger are fuelled by Birdland, which leads them into terrifying encounters with their parents, would-be lovers, random strangers and characters from Bobby's comic book. As mentioned, the universe of *Drawing Blood* is uncharacteristically devoid of homophobia or queerphobia, leaving the characters free to explore their sexuality and desires. Birdland, however, turns these desires into nightmares: Zach is led into a cinema in which couples watch brutal, pornographic, all-male *giallo* movies and where he is accosted by a rotting amalgamate of his ex-lovers. This episode, with its emphasis on gay sex and physical disintegration, taps into homophobic and AIDS-phobic anxieties and proves that (internalised) homophobia and queerphobia are very much present in the world of *Drawing Blood*, albeit subconsciously. It is during his final trip to Birdland that Trevor fully realises how interwoven his sexual arousal and desires are with violent urges and a yearning for self-annihilation. While not specifically linked to homosexual desire – Bobby was, after all, straight – the negativity associated with non-reproductive sexuality in *Drawing Blood* does bring to mind Leo Edelman's figure of the homosexual/queer on whom heteronormative culture projects a death drive. Birdland is revealed as a place where reproductive futurity is most violently rejected: in the hellish cinema, Zach watches in horror as an actor's penis is first sheathed in a condom and then, in a clear reference to his own masturbatory practice during which he always wears a condom, is amputated with a pair of scissors. The masturbation and casual sex that Zach previously engaged in are thus coded as not merely fruitless but dangerous, if not fatal.

Similarly, Bobby's obsession with the 'puzzle of the flesh and blood and bone' (p. 323) speaks to an eroticised desire that does not simply avoid reproduction but actively seeks total annihilation. When Trevor visits the Birdland version of the Violin Road house, he comes face to face not only with his past but also his own potential un-futurity. As a fellow artist and his father's successor, he feels obliged to explore Zach's totality by breaking it apart:

> 'I just want to know how you're made,' Trevor breathed in his ear. 'I love you so much, Zach. I want to climb inside you. I want to taste your brain. I want to feel your heart beating in my hands.' 'It can only beat in your hands for a few seconds, Trev. Then I'll be dead and you won't have me anymore.' 'Yes I will. You'll be right here. This place preserves its dead.' (p. 326)

Ultimately, both Zach and Trevor reject the feverish dreams of ecstatic extinction in Birdland, ignore Edelman's call to embrace queer negativity and choose a rather blissful homonormative future.

The excess associated with Birdland, both in its nested baroque form – Trevor visits the house near Missing Mile and enters Birdland, in which he finds the 1972 Violin Road house – and the promise of all-consuming queer negativity, is supplemented by recurring themes of doubling and repetition compulsion. To Zach, Trevor's personal hell – Birdland – functions like a computer program on a continuous loop:

> He's taking me to his hell . . . and he's going to eat me there, he's going to rip me apart looking for the magic inside me, and he won't find it. Then he'll fulfill the condition of the loop, he'll kill himself. What a stupid program. (p. 328)

Similarly, Trevor feels that he cannot escape the circle of violence initiated by his father and has feared this legacy – 'the violence inherent in his genes' (p. 112) – throughout his life. In a care home at the age of twelve, he had reacted with intense violence when a boy had touched him in the shower: the merest hint of erotic pleasure had triggered a vicious response. More than twenty years later, Trevor comes extremely close to succumbing to the same strange compulsion that destroyed his family. When he hits Zach, initially by accident, Trevor fears he may not be able to stop as 'the softness of Zach's lips spreading and splitting open against his hand felt *so damn good*' (p. 205, original emphasis). Although, at least in theory, repetition compulsion should override the pleasure principle, in Trevor's case the two appear to be intertwined, just as they had been for his father.

Doubling, a powerful Gothic theme associated with same-sex desire, is clearly visible in how the two boys mirror each other, through their traumatic childhoods, violent fathers, negligent mothers and anxieties regarding intimacy, as well as in the remarkable ferocity of their relationship. Yet another less obvious doubling is that of life and art, which permeates Birdland and results in a profound crisis of perception; a crisis that, as Weber has noted, is bound with experience of the uncanny. Bizarre two-dimensional cartoon creatures populate the black and white streets of Birdland, and the spatial arrangements of the place defy the laws of physics, adding to its disorientating texture. Importantly, Birdland tries to lure Trevor into becoming his father's double and switch from art to murder. Bobby had turned against his family when his inspiration had vanished. No longer able to provide for his loved ones, he decided to break their liminal borders to discover how they operated, how their hearts beat, how their blood flowed. Only after killing them was he finally able to sketch his wife, tracing every broken bone and wound he had crafted with a hammer. Predictably, as he associates artistic failure with his father's descent into madness, Trevor exhibits an obsessive-compulsive need to constantly draw.

50 • House of Horrors

Comic book drawings acquire uncanny overtones as they gradually take over Trevor's life. Although his artwork is initially rooted in the actual world, as his Parker and Brown story indicates, Trevor's drawings become increasingly alienated from reality: the closer he gets to Missing Mile and Birdland, the darker, less realistic and more visceral his illustrations are. Art is described as an uncontrollable and treacherous force, which Trevor only manages to subjugate at the very last moment. He fights the temptation to reduce Zach's whole being to mere physicality, to be experimented with, studied, dissected and then artistically recreated. Trevor's dramatic gesture – the breaking of his drawing hand – symbolises his rejection of the transgenerational haunting passed down by his father. The talent for and addiction to drawing that he inherited from his father are countered by Trevor's decision to spend the rest of his life slowly and respectfully discovering Zach's wholeness. Intimacy is embraced and the dark eroticism of death is unambiguously rejected.

Conclusion

The naïveté of Brite's/Martin's representation of queer desire and the exclusively positive aspects of the queer uncanny in *Drawing Blood* have rarely been displayed in novels by other authors that include lesbian, gay and queer characters. Brite/Martin himself experimented with far darker depictions of queer sexuality and taboo desires in the much more extreme *Lost Souls* (1992) and *Exquisite Corpse* (1994), which address incest, cannibalism, serial killers, monstrous births and vampirism. Still, his early novels emphasise the importance of physical intimacy and queer desire as the foundations of alternative forms of kinship. His early fiction differs from Koja's and Holder's, neither of whom appear to trust the 'puzzle of the flesh and blood and bone' in the same way as Brite's/Martin's characters. Zach and Trevor manage to escape the haunted house and restrictive conventionalities of middle-class family life, even though they still opt for a normative monogamous relationship, cushioned by Zach's lucrative hacker work. In contrast, neither Donna nor Nicholas leaves their haunted spaces: the former returns to sea to confront Scylla, who continues to haunt and hurt the survivors and their families; the latter begins a curious transformation, becoming a haunted space himself.

What these three novels share is a conviction that escaping haunted familial space comes at an extremely high cost. The protagonists must deal with their own baggage of family secrets, social expectations, guilt and personal failures, as well as fears of the new and unknown. What is more, haunted space as such is distinguished by its own peculiar character and the difficulties that it poses for those who cross its threshold. Manuel Aguirre has delineated three common configurations of the Gothic or Gothicised space: the labyrinth, the concentric journey and *mise en abyme*.[72] These models are employed in the novels discussed here: the labyrinthine structures appear in Birdland; the *mise en abyme* can be found in *The Cipher*; and the concentric journeys take place aboard *Pandora*. Aguirre has described how Gothic novels consistently and consciously break the balanced pattern of entering and leaving the two realms: that is, it is far easier to enter the irrational sphere than to leave it. This asymmetry is also underlined by the fact that the Other, denoting the *numinosum*, colonises the seemingly safe province of human understanding.[73] In such asymmetry, adds Aguirre, Gothic space reveals its propensity towards anisotropy, through which internal Gothic geography acquires different spatial characteristics, even measurements, depending on the perspective adopted by protagonists. Contemporary horror writers readily employ this device, perhaps most famously in Mark Z. Danielewski's *House of Leaves* (2000). Holder, Koja and Brite/Martin use this technique to emphasise the instability of haunted space, its dangerous nature and the feeling of 'not being at home' endured by its inhabitants: *Pandora* expands and contracts, changing its borders, design and furniture at will; the Funhole appears to spread indefinitely, despite finite wall measurements; and an entire new level of reality is unlocked in the Violin Road house.

The uncanny effects of spatiality delineate the disintegrating perimeter of traditional family structures. Because these houses lack stability and authenticity, they cannot provide their residents with the safety and security associated with conventionally understood home and family life. All three spaces pretend to be something they are not – a luxury cruise ship, a vacant storage room, an abandoned house – and in each case, it is the gradual intensification of the uncanny – as estrangement, repressed trauma coming to light, repetition compulsion and weird materiality – that reveals these to be mere facades.[74] Their artificiality notwithstanding, all three spaces interact with their inhabitants through materiality. It is the smells, the textures, the shades of light, the feel of furniture, the geometry of walls that the protagonists use to orientate themselves while exploring *Pandora*, the Funhole and the Violin Road house. As domesticity and familiarity are not just immaterial configurations of feeling and affect but also manifest as physical features of a lived-in space, they need to interact with these spaces. Still, familiarity is often a double-edged sword for protagonists who are lulled into a false sense of security. Trevor's mattress in his old room, the only one unstained by blood, functions as both a reminder of a childhood as yet untouched by death and carnage, and an enticing vision of future happiness with Zach. But the mattress is merely another tool for Birdland, an empty vessel of faux warmth designed to trap him deeper in his own conflicted needs and dark desires. *The Cipher*, in contrast, leaves its protagonists in a barren reality, devoid of material comforts or any tangible markers of warmth and communality. Weary of being homesick, Nicholas clings to Nakota because her body offers a modicum of familiarity, but Koja makes it abundantly clear there can be no comfort in the flesh, at least not in its human form.

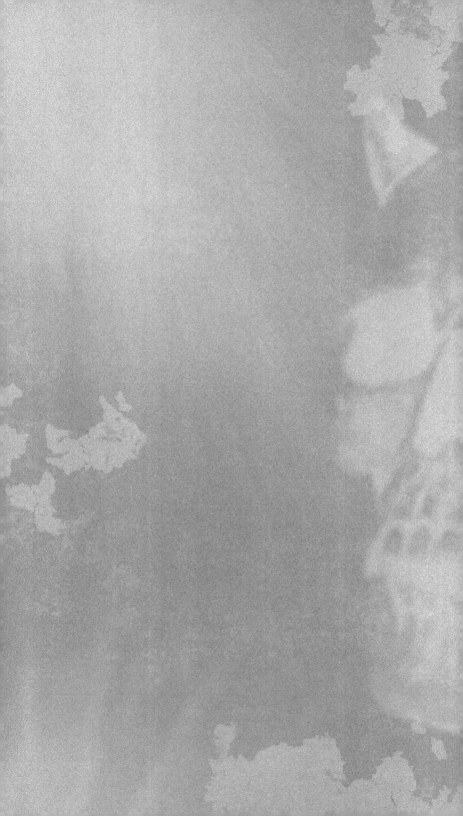

2

Grotesque Monsters and Hybrid Subjectivities

Introduction

WITH MARY SHELLEY'S *Frankenstein* marking the shift from Gothic mode to horror, Frankenstein's creation demonstrates that the grotesque has been an integral part of the genre from its very inception. The monster's beautiful 'lustrous black' hair and 'teeth of pearly whiteness' are juxtaposed with 'watery eyes', a 'shrivelled complexion and straight black lips'[1] – it is in this collision of feminine beauty *and* monstrosity that the grotesque most clearly emerges.[2] While the monster's grotesque nature underlines his pitiable status as a victim of Victor's hubris, responses invoked by other grotesque figures encompass the whole emotional gamut, from revulsion and terror, to fascination and a humorous awareness of life's absurdity.[3] The grotesque is, first and foremost, an aesthetic category used to describe a corporeal disturbance or, to be more precise, a disturbing body that for some reason frustrates normative bodily expectations. In classic Western thought, corporeality is metonymically and metaphorically linked with femininity and women, and thus a grotesque body is read through and alongside excessive and dangerous femininity and/or destabilising processes of feminisation. Of course, not all horror texts rely on grotesque aesthetics and, conversely, many works that feature the grotesque do not fall under the horror or Gothic jurisdictions.

56 • House of Horrors

In contrast to earlier traditions of the Gothic and the medieval carnival, sympathy for the grotesque monster is now the norm.[4] This sympathy goes beyond the typically Romantic fascination with dark brooding anti-heroes and is underpinned by understanding and empathy, as well as a certain willingness to identify with the monstrous and unwanted. As Spooner has stated when referring to Fred Botting's *Making Monstrous* (1991), the more obvious identification choice for twentieth and twenty-first-century subjects is the monster rather than its creator. The contemporary fascination with monstrous bodies and the popularity of modern-day sideshows, neo-burlesque and *nouveau cirque* reflect profound transformations in 'the traditional relationship between employment, property, and the body' generated by 'new systems of production, consumption and distribution' over the last half century.[5] The 'bodily turn' in horror texts may also reflect wider cultural shifts in late twentieth-century Western societies; the new ways of experiencing one's corporeality in the technologically mediated, increasingly medicalised and economically precarious structures of late capitalism require new critical idioms capable of bridging gaps between the physical and the cerebral. One could also argue that this renewed interest in the material and corporeal in, for instance, continental philosophy and feminist critical theory, reveals a need to go beyond social constructivism and the Cartesian body-mind split when exploring subjectivities. The grotesque, with its emphasis on physicality, irregularity and changeability, is thus an ideal critical tool with which to analyse the freedoms granted to, and the limitations imposed on, the female and/or feminised body.

Two characteristics that encapsulate the grotesque are its multiplicity and the ability to create conflicting or peculiar mergers and hybrids, always within the realist framework that makes the grotesque legible. With the notable exception of Mikhail Bakhtin, who wrote extensively on the body politic and the carnivalesque, the grotesque and its various registers are routinely employed to debate the bodily rather than the social and the communal; most critics interpret the grotesque as a mode of individuation rather than a tool to discuss social interactions. Even Mary J. Russo, when discussing the potential of the female grotesque to dismantle patriarchal structures, perceived the grotesque as a collection of individual affects, stylisations and experiences. In the three novels that I have selected for this chapter, however, grotesque aesthetics are always relational, and although inscribed onto the female or feminised body, the bodily is inexorably interlinked with the social. Here we can find alternative matrilineal models of subjectification and lesbian desire in Caitlín R. Kiernan's *The Drowning Girl: a Memoir* (2012); the unwanted feminisation of male subjects and a community's collective guilt in Elizabeth Massie's *Sineater* (1993); and the disintegration of a community staged on/through the bodies of young girls in Gwendolyn Kiste's *The Rust Maidens* (2018).

In this chapter, I purposefully focus on the protagonists' corporeality: how they experience their own bodies; how their families and communities react to their bodily transgressions; and, reciprocally, how communal transgressions impact on female and feminised bodies. Reflecting on the familial structures portrayed in these novels, I explore the practices of reproduction and sexuality permitted within the confines of these relationships. The text that, in particular, deals with feminised bodies, reproductive freedom and reproductive work is Massie's *Sineater*, although the novel primarily discusses the reproductive potentialities of men. Focusing on women-centred relations, both familial and erotic, the hybridisation and hysterisation of lesbian bodies, and ways to counter homophobic and transphobic depictions of lesbian desire, Kiernan's *The Drowning Girl* presents alternatives to the traditional patriarchal family. Kiste's *The Rust Maidens* shifts focus to the corporeality of teenage girls as they wrestle with the external control to which their bodies are subjected and to the dissolution of the traditional white, working-class community enacted through and by their bodies.

While scholarship on the grotesque – female or otherwise – disregards family dynamics, I find it interesting that these three authors opted for grotesque aesthetics to highlight the more disturbing or unusual aspects of familial relationships. In Massie's *Sineater*, the focus is interactions between parents and children, and between siblings, with the grotesque underlining the entrapment of female (or feminised) bodies within the conservative narrative of reproduction. Kiernan's *Drowning Girl* follows adult women striving to establish new relationships beyond the rigidly defined boundaries of 'normal', yet haunted by the painful shadows of their childhoods and family lives. Here, the grotesque brings the supposedly 'unnatural' nature of their adult relationships into focus. In Kiste's *The Rust Maidens*, the grotesque 'affliction' that transforms the bodies of five teenage girls into post-human monsters demonstrates the weight of normative gender expectations, a weight that has corroded their community long before the story begins.

58 • House of Horrors

Grotesque Bodies

The physicality implied by the word 'grotesque' harks back to its etymological beginnings: the Italian *grottesca* from *grotto*, and *pittura grottesca*. The latter denotes ancient Roman murals excavated from cave-like structures or rooms.[6] Theoretical studies of the grotesque can be traced back to nineteenth-century art criticism in the vein of Ruskin's work on art and architecture, but it is possible to look back further to the ancient and medieval fascination with monsters and monstrosity, a springboard for later formulations of the grotesque. For the benefit of this discussion, I will limit my critical overview to texts from the twentieth century and later. The most well-known contemporary analysis is Mikhail Bakhtin's discussion of the grotesque body and the carnivalesque in his *Rabelais and His World* (1941). Bakhtin examined 'the acts of the bodily drama' carried out by Gargantua and Pantagruel, such as defecating, copulating, eating and burping,[7] through which 'the body transgresses here its own limits: it swallows, devours, rends the world apart, is enriched and grows at the world's expense'.[8] The grotesque body is thus incomplete and open to invasion, in sharp contrast to the classical body; smooth, whole and separate from other bodies, environments or politics: a body controlled and guided by the mind.

The grotesque challenges body-mind dualism by emphasising – and exaggerating – those moments when the bodily escapes rational thinking and control. Only by accepting what has been made private, shameful and degraded can one hope to eradicate this dualism: 'to enter into the carnival body, to experience grotesque realism and its laughter, exuberance, and joyful abandon is to recover that which has been lost.'[9] The liberating potential of the grotesque reappears in Bakhtin's assertion that a grotesque body is 'a body in the act of becoming. It is never finished, never completed; it is continually built, created, and builds and creates another body'.[10] Significantly, those body parts that extend the body and breach its boundaries – such as the bowels, the genitals, the mouth and the nose – lend themselves most easily to exuberance and excess.

Although Bakhtin's theory of the grotesque body and the carnivalesque has continued to exert influence, it has also received criticism, most notably for his unproblematic treatment of gender dynamics when describing grotesque female bodies.[11] A more in-depth critique by Alison Milbank concentrates on the 'drama of demystification' that Bakhtinian theory appears to provide, 'as the orthodox, the decorous and the

Grotesque Monsters and Hybrid Subjectivities • 59

authoritative is "uncrowned" by the carnivalesque energies of the grotesque'.[12] Milbank rightly notes that such an analytic model is appealing to researchers schooled in deconstruction, as 'it mimics their own critical procedures'.[13] The model also 'imitates the gesture of the Gothic heroine herself, whose flight from tyrannical imprisonment defies patriarchal authority and decrowns the power of the supernatural'.[14] Ultimately, this ostensibly subversive act only upsets rather than dismantles the status quo, and thus, rather than being dismantled, the borders of respectability and normativity are merely affirmed.

The medieval and Renaissance grotesque, as described by Bakhtin, ultimately gave way to the Romantic grotesque, a reimagining that introduces us to 'a terrifying world, alien to man', who no longer understands or controls his surroundings.[15] Although laughter remains an essential part of the Romantic grotesque, it is bereft of the joy and power to rejuvenate that characterised earlier incarnations.[16] For Spooner, the two traditions are united through the Gothic-Carnivalesque: some of the vulgar merriment of Bakhtinian grotesque bodies returns, fusing with the Romantic emphasis on the individual and alienation deriving from one's own peculiarities.[17] Spooner claims the Gothic theme of liminality finds its expression within the Gothic-Carnivalesque, where 'the sinister is continually shading into the comic and vice versa'.[18] With its 'preoccupation with the "folk" grotesque of the circus, with freakish heroes and heroines and with the celebration of bodily excess', she sees a return of the original spirit of Carnival in contemporary Gothic.[19] Of course, just as the medieval carnival was institutionalised by authorities as an effective vent for people's frustrations, contemporary grotesque bodies can quickly be consumed and commodified by mainstream cultural production.

Within the framework of medieval teratology, monsters were carriers of God-given signs. As the Latin root *monstrare* suggests, they were intended to show, to de*monstra*te fearsome and awe-inspiring messages inscribed on their bodies by the Maker himself. On a superficial level, contemporary monsters continue to be blank spaces on which new cultural messages can be recorded. No longer solely theological signs of wonder, monstrous bodies have been and are activated to help establish national identities, regulate and enforce gender normativity, medicalise non-normative physicality, and institutionalise prescribed norms and standards. Historically, the 'categories of otherness', whether relating to race and ethnicity, sexual difference or the non-human, have traversed an upward or downward path, with monsters becoming either saintly,

60 • House of Horrors

angelic beings or animals, mutants or deviants.[20] Monstrosity is a cultural construct rather than an objective given, and monsters are not simply born; they are carefully constructed and performed in order to fit certain narratives.

As the interplay between motherhood and monsterhood has gained critical import in recent years, I concentrate on links between monstrosity and the regulation of womanhood and female reproduction for my analysis. A case in point is Erin Harrington's 'monstrous-maternal', through which she analyses the inherent transgressive and socially tabooed contradictions in dominant constructions of motherhood.[21] Essential motherhood, Harrington argues, is a double-edged sword, simultaneously proclaiming the required qualities to be innate, obvious and biologically unshakeable, *and* suggesting that the said requirements are indeed impossible to fulfil: failure is certain. Referencing and moving beyond Barbara Creed's abject motherhood, the monstrous-maternal articulates the cultural dis/ease surrounding motherhood, delineating the tension between 'the idea that the specific demands of motherhood make one monstrous' and 'the suggestion that somehow monstrosity is there, nascent and deeply embodied, stitched firmly into the very construction of "essential" motherhood itself'.[22]

Following Julia Kristeva, and employing psychoanalytic theories to investigate the social implications of the monstrous feminine, sociologist Jane M. Ussher has argued that art has replaced religion as the 'force of purification and catharsis' in increasingly secularised societies.[23] The female body is idealised – and thus neutralised – through artistic or pseudo-artistic representations: its dangerous orifices are closed, its 'fecund corporeality removed' or, better yet, caught momentarily in a nakedness that invites the male gaze while offering no troubling concerns for the assumed-to-be male viewer.[24] Against a backdrop of negative tropes and themes, from the iconography of *vagina dentata* to the spurned psychotic lover in *Fatal Attraction* (1987), women's bodies continue to be the locus of desires and deep-rooted anxieties. The key to this desire/anxiety dyad is the female reproductive body, which, as Ussher has argued, 'is central to the process by which women take up the subject position "woman"; central to the performance of normative femininity'.[25] 'The embodied changes' that accompany pregnancy, menstruation and menopause are discursively positioned as sites of 'danger or debilitation', while 'signs of fecundity' are 'signifiers of feminine excess'.[26] Drawing from both Butler's performativity theory and Foucault's work on self-surveillance,

Ussher has explored how the 'natural' female body is regulated, controlled and, when necessary, punished within a rigid social and cultural framework. The pathologisation, sexualisation and medicalisation of the female body, described by Michel Foucault in the first volume of *The History of Sexuality*, chart the historical and sociocultural trajectories along which the female body has been positioned as unruly and in need of expert (male) attention: to borrow Ussher's expression, it is a 'potential site of madness, badness or weakness'.[27]

Historically, both normative and deviant performances of (white) womanhood have been enabled and sustained by the racist and colonialist politics of regulating the non-Western, non-white Other. Foucault, like Russo, remained silent on that topic; however, Sander Gilman (1985),[28] Evelynn M. Hammonds (1994, 1997),[29] Loraine O'Grady (1994),[30] Beverly Guy-Shefthall (2002)[31] and, more recently, Kaila Adia Story (2010)[32] and Sabrina Stings (2019),[33] have clearly identified the legacy of eighteenth-century racist and sexist ideologies of white male supremacy and the horrifying ways in which Black women's bodies have been instrumentalised, not just as carriers of metaphors but as objects of abuse and exploitation often masquerading as scientific enquiry. Thus, spectacles of grotesque femininity must also be read against racist discourses of womanhood, in which, by default, the non-white woman violates social decorum and bodily norms. In the US context, the dominant white culture fabricated a spectre of Black femininity as terrifying *and* grotesque: oversexualised, animalistic, angry, big, loud, non-maternal and non-feminine. Paradoxically, in racist imagery, Black women simultaneously occupy two spaces: of lack and of excess. '*Not* feminine *enough* and yet *too* female' is a refrain that structures eighteenth and nineteenth-century pseudo-scientific discourses on Black women. In the three novels that I analyse here, this lack-excess paradox marks the bodies considered to be grotesque, but the axes shift depending on the protagonist in question and the social context of their transgression: they might be too feminine, not feminine enough, or feminine in a way considered threatening; they might be *too* female in that their bodies go beyond the typical transformations of bodies assigned female at birth; or not female enough in a transphobic or essentialist sense.

Mary J. Russo is the most renowned feminist critic to have investigated the inner workings of grotesque aesthetics. Published in 1994, Russo's *The Female Grotesque: Risk, Excess and Modernity* was a welcome intervention in this critical corpus, which had previously skirted the issue

62 • House of Horrors

of gender dynamics or, at best, deployed concepts of femininity and womanhood that lacked critical awareness. Russo has examined this subject in the history of art criticism, which has consistently deemed the grotesque to be peripheral and superficial, and thus metaphorically linked to Western notions of femininity.[34] By the late nineteenth century, the post-Romantic grotesque was not only being used to describe tangible – and often purely decorative – objects, but also interior states and experiences, and thus intersecting with other aesthetic and cultural categories gaining relevancy, such as the uncanny, the strange and the abject.[35] Both these perspectives, whether centring on the rejuvenating carnivalesque spirit or Romantic individualism and the uncanny, rely on the body and the bodily; while the Bakhtinian approach to the grotesque addresses the social body or body politic, the latter relates more to 'the psychic register and to the bodily as cultural projection of an inner state'.

Russo adds a perspective that returns to the body, not in terms of the psychic register or body politic, but through a specific, material female body portrayed in contemporary art. She reads 'the female grotesque' as a crucial category in 'identity-formation for both men and women as a space of risk and abjection'.[37] Interestingly, rather than arguing for a distinct male counterpart, Russo contends that the 'male grotesque' constructs male subjectivity 'through an association with the feminine as the body marked by difference'.[38] Following Russo, Creed has described how the male body is marked as grotesque in horror cinema by being feminised: '[the male body] is penetrated, changes shape, swells, bleeds, is cut open, grows hair and fangs.'[39] The female/feminised body then functions as a site on which the lines separating culture from nature and the human from the non-human are drawn and redrawn.

Clearly, Russo's description of the female grotesque as '[l]ow, hidden, earthly, dark, material, immanent, visceral'[40] runs the risk of gender essentialism. But she is fully aware that connotations ascribed to the female body, grotesque or otherwise, are culture-dependent and should be analysed as such. The female grotesque can thus be deployed in a critical mode, subverting the socially constructed divisions between nature and culture, mind and body, male and female. At the same time, the spectacle of the female self – enabled by the grotesque – may swiftly be reabsorbed into hegemonic discourses of femininity, especially if this spectacle rests on the exploitation of female/feminised bodies.

Hybrid Lesbian Bodies in *The Drowning Girl*

The hysterisation of female bodies lies at the centre of Caitlín R. Kiernan's 2012 novel, *The Drowning Girl: a Memoir*,[41] with the female grotesque challenging stereotypes of lesbian monstrosity and perversion in various hysterical narratives of women. Kiernan imagines potent matrilineal and women-centred alternatives to monstrous representations of same-sex desires and relationships. Although female homosexuality has been less historically visible than male homosexuality in both legal and medical arenas, with the emergence of sexology and psychology, and the increasing medicalisation of sexuality and control over female bodies in the second half of the nineteenth century, lesbianism became represented in ever more monstrous terms in *fin de siècle* art and literature. The very spectre of lesbianism doubled the danger of female sexuality, already perceived as unstable and precarious. The predatory lesbian stereotype found fertile cultural soil among late nineteenth-century poets and novelists. The *femmes damnees*, immortalised by Toulouse-Lautrec and Emile Zola, were created for the pleasure of male viewers/readers, and the image of a dangerous, albeit heteronormatively eroticised lesbian has persisted through countless iterations in Western culture. Kiernan's novel explicitly comments on this late nineteenth-century cultural obsession with monstrous female sexuality through a subplot concerning the fictional painter Philip George Saltonstall and his unnerving paintings of mermaids.[42]

In conventional horror narratives, the female body is either a monster to be exorcised and destroyed or, more frequently, a victim to be sacrificed and/or avenged, thereby advancing the male protagonist's storyline. The thin line between monstrosity and victimisation is often blurred, especially when the bodies of female victims turn monstrous during mutilation, or when a monstrous body mirrors the uncanny mutability of a female body. These two modes – female monstrosity and female victimisation – are both deeply scopophilic and solely constructed to invite the male gaze. Linda Williams, in her classic essay 'When the Woman Looks', argues that whereas:

> The male look expresses conventional fear at that which differs from itself . . . the female look – a look given a preeminent position in the horror film – shares the male fear of the monster's freakishness, but also recognizes the sense in which this freakishness is similar to her own [sexual] difference.[43]

64 • House of Horrors

Freakishness and aberration, words that Williams uses to define monstrosity in her essay, belong to the same register as the grotesque and refer to bodies deviating from the norm, thus suggesting hybridity, hyperbole and excess, or, conversely, conspicuous absence and lack. Of course, the association between monstrosity and womanhood is perennial, dating back to antiquity: for Aristotle the normal human body was male; the female an anomaly, an aberration, a male gone wrong.[44]

I focus on how Kiernan explores both this association of women with monstrosity and/or victimhood, and the image of a predatory lesbian. I also note how the grotesque functions as 'a corollary to queerness' by questioning 'the dominant discourses of what is inherently normal or abnormal'.[45] In narratives exploring queer desire, such as Kiernan's work, the queer body is often posited as a hybrid, but it is also a grotesque body in the sense that, first, it is consciously stylised as unfinished and 'in the making', and second, it embraces a hopeful and deeply sensual kind of non-normativity. The radical body transformations described in *The Drowning Girl* illustrate how queer subjects resist the normative scripts targeted at their bodies, desires and the texts they produce.[46] The grotesque aesthetics of *The Drowning Girl* are deployed largely in connection to the often historically linked concepts of female madness and lesbian corporeality. Kiernan's skilful use of both affirmative and reactionary modes of the grotesque brings the generic limitations of horror fiction into focus: it is unable to convey the intricacies of women's experiences without resorting to the age-old tropes of female monstrosity, victimhood and abnormality.

Kiernan adamantly rejects the 'genre horror' label and, while no fan of literary categorisation in general, prefers to have their work included in the weird fiction category.[47] Although weird fiction and the New Weird, with which Kiernan is now most readily associated, could be considered tumorous outgrowths of horror fiction, especially when examining the entangled roots of most genre fiction, the majority of critics see it as a whole new strand of the fantastic.[48] Humanity's infinite ignorance and powerlessness in the face of cosmic horror and the horrors of modernity, as explored by the original weird fiction writers, including H. P. Lovecraft, Arthur Machen and Robert W. Chambers, and the eerie world of radical embodiment and electrifying corporeal transformations at the centre of the New Weird wave, from authors such as China Miéville, Caitlín R. Kiernan, Livia Llewellyn, Thomas Ligotti and Laird Barron, are not exclusive to weird writing and appear in other genres of the fantastic. In other words, the narrative and stylistic conventions, mood, tonality and goals of weird fiction may differ from those of horror fiction, but this is often a difference of degree, not of kind. In the case of *The Drowning Girl*, horror literary conventions, together with motifs and characters originating in fantasy fiction and fairy tales, are *en-weirded* by Kiernan. En-weirding emphasises the processual character of New Weird fiction, which distorts, manipulates and reframes other genres of the fantastic, including the original weird fiction. Rather than follow more conventional generic conventions to their logical, if predictable, conclusion, en-weirding pushes at the limits of genre fiction to maintain dis/ease, discomfort, anxiety and fragmentation. From this perspective, Kiernan's weird fiction expands on genre horror, reveals its limitations, plays with its borders, but never leaves its territory completely. Importantly, en-weirding can also be understood as a process of queering: working against established models and freeing genre conventions from normative literary expectations.[49]

Kiernan's novel presents two types of family, both structured around ties between women and thus set apart from conventional nuclear family units: lesbian and exclusively matrilineal relationships. Both these alternative kinship forms are marked by deep ambivalence, separation anxiety and toxic interdependence, yet they also anchor the main protagonist, Imp, in her struggles to shield herself from a schizophrenic breakdown. Men are conspicuously absent from the story; there are no fathers, male lovers or brothers to influence the main protagonist in any way. Kiernan's novel does not engage with Gothic threats to a woman's bodily integrity from such generic characters as mad patriarchs or evil tyrants; rather, the threat primarily comes from within, the result of crossing problematic boundaries in relationships with other women.

The Drowning Girl: a Memoir is a fictionalised memoir by India Morgan Phelps, also known as Imp, a fitting nickname that brings to mind a mischievous magical, non-gendered creature, and echoes Edgar Allan Poe's story 'The Imp of the Perverse'. Imp weaves together two narratives in which she recalls how she met and fell for Eva. The heart of the novel and its main source of mystery lies in a temporal paradox: Imp has met Eva for the first time . . . twice. Early in her account, Imp refers to being a schizophrenic, and readers may assume that, like Poe's narrator in 'The Imp of the Perverse', she is unreliable and her words are fiction disguised as fact. At the same time, Imp declares her desire to write a ghost story, albeit one located within the framework of a memoir. This ghost story will be true but may not be factual. Thus, Imp signals her conscious instrumentalisation of genre fiction to tell a real story of her life. This gesture

66 • House of Horrors

mirrors Kiernan's penchant for metafiction: they too use familiar generic conventions – horror, fairy tale, memoir and ghost story – but these are ultimately springboards for a larger conversation about memory, trauma and the place of fiction and literary genres in storytelling.

Imp recalls how she found Eva naked on a riverbank in July, while also finding her in November, lying naked on the side of the road by the woods. In the first narrative, the seductive Eva becomes a mermaid-like creature whose story draws inspiration from Imp's favourite fairy tale, the Little Mermaid, and mermaid paintings by Philip George Saltonstall. As Imp has long been obsessed with Saltonstall's paintings, his biography and the folk and fairy tales that inspired his work, the July Eva appears as a siren-like figure. In the second story, the November Eva becomes a she-wolf in need of rescue. This reflects Imp's intense dislike of the Little Red Riding Hood story, a dislike that intensifies following an exhibition by a contemporary artist who, in a series of deeply disturbing artworks that capitalise on trauma porn, juxtaposes the medieval Little Red Riding Hood stories with the Black Dahlia murder of 1946.

As Imp desperately attempts to make sense of the two meetings with Eva, her mental condition deteriorates and the reader discovers that Imp fabricated the second story as a coping mechanism after the traumatic outcome of the first (and the only real) meeting with Eva in July. With the help of her new girlfriend, Abalyn, Imp learns that Eva's mother died in the mass suicide of a water-worshipping cult in the early 1990s. Having stalked Imp and learnt about her obsession with Saltonstall's paintings, mermaids and sea snake folklore, Eva proceeded to seduce Imp and manipulate her into assisting her own suicide, a duplication of her mother's twenty years earlier. Imp's subsequent breakdown triggers the need to compose a new narrative, one in which, rather than helplessly watching her die, she saves Eva. As Imp slowly spirals into mental breakdown, she attempts to drown herself in the bath to stop the intrusive thoughts triggered by Eva. Later, through a chance meeting with Abalyn, who left Imp soon after the suicide attempt, Imp is forced to accept that there was always only one Eva. In response to this information from a third, objective party, Imp stops taking her medication and has a psychotic breakdown. Abalyn stays with Imp to help her recover.

This crude summary hardly does justice to the intricate web of literary references, styles and textual devices employed by Imp in her memoir. Letters, short stories, fragments of reference books, folktales, meta-fiction, self-referential jokes, false memories and real events all intermingle in an attempt to make sense of the two Evas and, if possible, dispose of one.

A clear theme of doubling and the double emerges in the way that the narrative is structured. For instance, Eva, as Imp's doppelganger, is also the mentally ill daughter of a mentally disturbed mother. Even Eva's original name – Imogene May – suggest a deeper affiliation with Imp, whose full name is India Morgan. Not only are there two Evas and two distinct hauntings in Imp's mind, but also two Evas in real life: the mother who was a member of the water cult in the early 1990s and the daughter who insinuated herself into Imp's life. More importantly, Imp herself is doubled. She continually steps away from the first-person narrative in order to chastise her narrative persona for tardiness or avoiding the main issue:

> And that's the day I met Abalyn Armitage.
> 'I think I've been telling lies,' Imp types. (p. 20)

The doublings continue in subplots: two mermaid paintings by Saltonstall exist, not one, as Imp has hitherto assumed. And there are two versions of Abalyn's past: she carried a doubleness within herself for almost twenty years, before her AMAB (assigned male at birth) body was aligned with her female gender through surgery. Even Imp recognises the importance of '[d]uality. The mutability of the flesh. Transition. Having to hide one's true self away. Masks. Secrecy. Mermaids, werewolves, gender' (p. 43), as well as the way that doubling impacts on her own life. This series of doublings confuses the traditional Western dyads of subject/object, active/passive, male/female and, by doing so, undermines the heterosexual order that rests on such binary oppositions. As Marilyn Farwell has argued, it is precisely her refusal to stay within binary logic that ensures the lesbian protagonist will be 'gendered female but an excessive or grotesque female'.[50] In Kiernan's novel, doublings also indicate a refusal to engage in traditional horror fiction, in which the narrative is either propelled through monstrous deaths of women or enacted by grotesque, feminised monsters. All the deaths of women in *The Drowning Girl* are suicides, and Imp, rather than searching for answers or culprits, accepts the decisions that her loved ones have made. Imp places the suicides of her mother and grandmother alongside those of Virginia Woolf, Anne Sexton and Diane Arbus, thus emphasising the creativity, strength and self-determination associated with these iconic figures. Curiously, the only violent female death described in the novel is that of Elizabeth Short, aka Black Dahlia. Her horrific murder, an infamous explosion of misogyny, becomes mere fodder for an artist searching for a cheap combination of titillation, trauma porn and the

68 • House of Horrors

grotesque. The fact that the artist is a man is intended to highlight how instrumentally women's deaths are treated within a male-dominated art: women's mutilated corpses are deployed to both excite the audience and instil a fear of female transgression.

Kiernan consistently constructs a 'lesbian narrative space'[51] by refusing to use female bodies in manners associated with a typical horror narrative. Thus, rather than using a sideshow or circus aesthetic for Eva's hybrid body, which would inevitably raise questions about the gaze and gendered economic relations, they gather alternatives to the patriarchal narratives of monstrous lesbians from folk culture. The realistic sex scenes in *The Drowning Girl* are designed to thwart scopophilic intrusions and frustrate the expectations of readers accustomed to either heteronormative lesbian sex scenes or soft-core intimacy:

> Eva Canning laid me out on my bed, filleted me, and she buried her face between my thighs, and her tongue sang unspeakable songs into me . . . She lapped between my legs, and filled me to bursting with music few have ever heard and lived. She made me Ulysses. She made me a lyre and a harp and flute. She played me (two meanings here). And songs are stories, and so she made of me a book, just as I became a song. (pp. 287–8)

Their encounters lose none of their erotic impact as the depictions become increasingly unreal and fantastic: this in turn could be read as a parodic commentary on the grotesque 'unnaturalness' of two women having sex:

> Eva writhed in the vermiform coils of eels and sea snakes, hagfish and lamprey. She fastened that ravenous, barbeled mouth about the folds of my labia, rasping teeth working at my clit. She writhed and coiled about me, wrapping me in a smothering, protective cocoon of slime, thick translucent mucus exuded from unseen glands or pores. Across her rib cage were drawn the gill slits of a shark, out of water and gasping, opening and closing, breathless but undying. Her breasts had vanished, leaving her chest flat except for those gills. I gazed into black eyes, eyes that were only black and nothing more, and they gazed into me.
> She flowered, and bled me dry.
> She took my voice, and filled me with song.
> Unloving, she left me no choice but to love her. (p. 295)

Using sensual rather than explicitly horrific descriptions of Eva's grotesque hybrid body, Kiernan precludes attempts to 'normalise' the lesbian body or to prove that she fits the Western cultural norm of a white, able-bodied, heteronormative woman. The grotesque aesthetics that Kiernan applies to hybrid subjectivities and embodiment, effectively interrogate the discourse of monstrous lesbianism. At the same time, Kiernan does not shy away from the ambivalent nature of hybrid mergers, and they manage to both subvert and recover lesbian and queer femininities through engagement with quasi-mythical, animal-like and grotesque beings. The undetermined nature of Eva's body is also investigated, as her hybrid incarnations are approximations rather than finished creations. While she is mermaid-like or resembles a sea snake or a she-wolf or a female dog, none of her bodily transformations ever reaches completion. One could argue that the irony embedded in Eva's grotesqueness resurfaces in the very idea of the lesbian monstrous body that Kiernan challenges and transforms. With her body locked in a perpetual state of becoming, Eva could be placed in the Bakhtinian order of the grotesque, yet rather than laughter, her body incites awe and wonder:

> I cried when Eva told me this, and she wiped my tears away with flickering hands unable to decide if it was best to be paws or hands. She was all of a splendid metamorphosis . . . She was first this one thing and then that other, right before my eyes. She was a kaleidoscope chrysalis of shifting skeletons and muscle and marrow, bile and the four richly appointed chambers of a mammalian heart . . . She was never for an instant only a single beast, as I will not accept the deceit that there was only ever one of her, that I must choose between July and November. (p. 211)

Hybridisation and radical openness also emerge in the very structure of the narrative, as Imp is unable to follow through with just one story, one identity of Eva, or one identity of herself. Her longing to maintain two conflicting accounts reveals her desperate desire for an impossible blend of identities. The way that Kiernan structures the novel is also hybrid in that Imp refuses to follow the traditional rules of writing. Scorning Aristotelian mimesis and decorum, she discards the three-part plot structure and questions the arbitrariness of beginnings and ends. She also playfully promises to be a reliable narrator and not lie: 'Which is not to say every word will be factual. Only that every word will be true. Or as true as I can

70 • House of Horrors

manage' (p. 6). At times Imp switches to the third person, especially when reproving herself for stalling or digressing, or to provide a metafictional comment on the structure of narrative: '"And what about this business with chapters?" Imp typed. "If I'm not writing this to be read – which I'm most emphatically not – and if it's not a book, as such, then why is it that I'm bothering with chapters?"' (p. 28). This refusal to follow traditional narrative paths constitutes yet another break with the phallogocentric regime. Language and stories are unreliable, unstable and unpredictable, and one's own memories cannot be trusted, as evidenced by the many false recollections in Imp's diaries, such as finding a seventy-five-dollar bill in the street. Imp's research into the two painters, Saltontall of the mermaid creatures and Perrault of the Black Dahlia she-wolf, also reveals the hybridity of their lives and creations, a *bricolage* of news reports, folktales, dreams, visions, memories and figments of imagination. Kiernan refuses to uphold the rigid border between the factual and the fictional and allows Imp to investigate her own versions of the past and employ imagination to fill in the gaps.

Imp muses over the idea of haunting, which for her encompasses the instances of being haunted not only by ghosts, but also poems, intrusive thoughts, her relatives' suicides, her own schizophrenia, paintings, sculptures, even fairy tales: 'Sirens are intrusive thoughts that even sane men and women have. You can call them sirens, or you can call them haunting. Doesn't matter' (p. 103). It is being haunted by a siren that initially inspires Imp to write her own 'ghost story':

'I'm going to write a ghost story now,' she typed.
'A ghost story with a mermaid and a wolf,' she also typed.
I also typed. (p. 1)

Imp sees writing as the best tool for facing and exorcising ghostly memories from her past, and in the course of relating her own narrative(s), writes fictional short stories about the two painters to lay her obsessions to rest. However, she remains aware of the twofold potential of art to expulse spectres yet replicate the original haunting:

Hauntings are memes, especially pernicious thought contagions, social contagions that need no viral or bacterial host and are transmitted in a thousand different ways. A book, a poem, a song, a bedtime story, a grandmother's suicide, the choreography of a dance, a few frames of film, a diagnosis of schizophrenia, a deadly tumble from a horse, a faded photograph, or a story . . . Or a painting hanging on a wall. (p. 12)

Whether her memoir is as successful as her fiction is debatable. Imp admits her 'stories don't care what I want from them. Stories do not serve me. Even my own stories' (p. 104). The two fictional stories appear to help a little, but the burden of Imp's recovery rests on her memoir, which she calls 'a pocket full of stones' (p. 27). This reference to Virginia Woolf suggests that Imp's narrative is not only her way of drowning intrusive thoughts, but also of drowning a part of herself, yet unlike Eva, without sacrificing her life.

The portrayal of Imp's suicidal heritage is not entirely desolate and depressing. She describes her mother's suicide pragmatically: 'So, yeah. My mother, Rosemary Anne, died in Butler Hospital. She committed suicide in Butler Hospital, even though she was on a suicide watch at the time. She was in bed, in restraints, and there was a video camera in her room. But she still pulled it off . . . She said she was sorry, but that she was glad I understood, that she was grateful that I understood' (p. 3). Thus, it is not Eva's suicide *per se* that causes Imp's breakdown but the fact she had been emotionally and psychologically manipulated into falling in love with Eva, then helping and witnessing her death.

Imp represents the fourth generation of women whose behaviour has been considered abnormal by medical professionals and society in general: 'My family's lunacy lines up tidy as boxcars: grandmother, daughter, the daughter's daughter, and thrown in for good measure, the great-aunt. Maybe the Curse goes even further back than that' (p. 5). Inherited madness transcends the confines of transgenerational haunting to become a transgenerational bond. Past suicides and her foremothers' madness are not shameful secrets that threaten Imp's integrity, but sources of guidance to inspire her life choices. When describing her great-aunt Caroline, who collected dead birds and mice and labelled their jars with Bible passages, she provides her psychiatrist with alternative explanations for this behaviour, such as a keen interest in natural history and an attempt to establish agreement between specific species and scripture. However, 'Dr. Ogilvy said, no, she was likely also schizophrenic. I didn't argue' (p. 4–5). Imp accepts the medical diagnosis of her own schizophrenia, but counters ableist medical discourses by describing her 'disease' as her own sentience: just like her mother, grandmother and great-aunt Caroline, Imp has her own special way of seeing the world.

Female madness is thus redefined to include non-normative behaviour and neuroatypical character traits. It is also a family gift, and when Imp recalls her meeting with the wolf-Eva, she acknowledges that '[m] adwomen can see such apparitions, and our touch can render them corporeal' (p. 215). Her madness makes Imp better attuned to the uncanny, despite her awareness of the constraints of the narratives underpinning her perception of the supernatural and the bizarre:

> When moving through fairy tales, one must obey the laws of fairy. When moving through a ghost story, Gothic and Victorian law applies. Here I creep my footpath through both at once and the dictates are unclear, winding together in greenbrier snarls I'll have to prick my fingers on spinning wheel spindle-shanks to comprehend (p. 216).

Kiernan's novel also references Adrienne Rich's lesbian continuum, in which a lesbian is a woman seeking other women for support, understanding and love, not necessarily in erotic or sensual terms. It is clear that Imp longs for the company of women. Her childhood home, with her father and grandfathers all dead, gone, non-existent, was in all respects a matriarchy. This may explain why the word 'lesbian' never appears in the book and 'gay' is used only three times, by Abalyn when referring to her past and the impracticality of contemporary terminology.[52] One could argue that both Eva and Imp are searching for a lost maternal/feminine connection. Whereas Imp finally finds comfort in her art and her relationship with Abalyn, Eva decides to join her mother in death by drowning. Imp chooses exogamous kinship and reaffirms the importance of women-only relations, while Eva chooses endogamy in the sense she would rather follow her mother than establish a new connection with someone else. Importantly, Imp's matriarchal and matrilineal family is never ridiculed: the world without men in which she lives is stable and loving, never grotesque or incomplete.

Despite emphasising matrilineal connections and women-centred relationships, Kiernan steers clear of the crude essentialism that would posit cis-women as 'real' women, as demonstrated by the unconditional acceptance of Abalyn's womanhood. In addition, Kiernan addresses the potential subversiveness of lesbian eroticism and sexuality. Lesbian subjects are still haunted by their perverse shadows and doppelgangers in contemporary popular culture, evidenced by the unremitting popularity of, for example, lesbian vampires and butch aggressors. Kiernan counters these stereotypes through the siren, a figure often used 'to represent the monstrosity and degeneracy of lesbian and the "new woman"' by late nineteenth-century (male) writers and artists.[53] Thus, by using the mermaid/siren theme and creating a fictional nineteenth-century painter obsessed with sirens, Kiernan counters this heritage. The images of fantastic female bodies that haunt, fascinate and repulse Imp are all created by male artists and, over time, she collapses under the weight of these interventions in the female and/or lesbian body. By underlining the creative autonomy of Imp, revealed to be both a talented writer and a painter capable of envisioning fantastic worlds and alternative realities, Kiernan suggests the new lesbian textuality and imagery can function as an effective counterpart to traditional male-orientated and male-generated texts of the fantastic. Accentuating the communal qualities of artistic work, Imp unearths intricate webs of references, allusions, mythologies and folktales that nurture each piece of art, including her own creations. Therefore, paintings, novels *and* bodies are queerly grotesque as they participate in a rapid and ongoing series of mergers, fusions and coalitions, as well as violent severances from other cultural texts. The end results are never stable, sleek and closed off, but open, disturbing and captivating.

Lesbian and/or female monstrosity, represented by the imagery of mermaids and she-wolves, ceases to be a site of disgust, passive victimisation or castration anxiety. Instead, Kiernan re-colonises lesbian desire and transforms it into a field ripe with ambiguities, sensuality and creative possibilities for radical reimaginings of one's selfhood and one's familial relations. Exclusive matrilineality offers an escape from laboriously oedipalised kinship and its toxic emphasis on law, language, hierarchy and neurotypicality. After all, Imp deploys the master's tools to dismantle his house, but her semantic puzzles, inter-textual and meta-textual games, compulsive repetitions, literary echoes and general textual instability suggest a different kind of language, one closer to Cixous's *écriture feminine* and the maternal white ink.[54] Interestingly, by crafting such an unusual ghost story (or perhaps we should say two stories), Kiernan probes the very boundaries and generic foundations of horror fiction with grotesque hybrids and material entanglements that hint at a new type of dark fiction, one moving towards ambivalence, subtle subversion, and the embrace of the sexual and feminine in all their guises.

74 • House of Horrors

Male Grotesque in *Sineater*

At a glance, Elizabeth Massie's *Sineater* is the most generically conventional novel of the three books discussed in this chapter. The winner of the 1993 Bram Stoker Award, *Sineater* follows Southern Gothic traditions closely, as its plot revolves around an intimidating matriarch, an isolated backwater community, an explosion of violence, '[a] mansion that will be destroyed, a declining family, a genealogical secret, revenge and murder'.[55] Massie's novel also seems the most traditional in the way that it presents kinship. At the same time, *Sineater* is the most non-conventional novel of the three, because it applies the grotesque aesthetics to men and boys rather than women, and therefore calls into question the gendered structure of the grotesque and its associations with femininity and womanhood. On the one hand, the unwanted feminisation the male bodies undergo in *Sineater* does not really affect gender binary and the conceptual structures of the two genders remains largely intact. On the other hand, however, the radical potential of Massie's novel could be found in its symbolic break with cis-gendered structure of human reproduction. The female grotesque, as employed by Massie, points to the dangers of obsessive attachments, limited personal freedoms accorded to individuals (of all genders) within fundamentalist communities and the troubling entanglement of two families, all set within broader community dynamics.

Although the story alternates between different viewpoints, the main focalisation belongs to a ten-year-old boy, Joel, who lives in a small southern town of Ellison, in the Beacon Cove community, in the early 1990s. Joel is special, as he is the youngest of the Barkers, a family feared and shunned by the whole community because Joel's father, Avery, is the local sineater – a person responsible for cleansing dead bodies of their sins.[56] Yet, in contrast to the earlier sineaters of Ellison, when Avery was forced to become one, he decided not to forgo his plans to have a family, thus becoming the first sineater to have a wife and children. Not allowed to talk to them or even look at them, he visits his home at night, when his children are asleep, and spends his days roaming the forest. The father's abject position spills onto his entire family – his wife, Lelia, never leaves their little dilapidated farm, his two older children, Petrie and Curry, have never learnt to read or write and have never gone to town by daylight. It is the youngest son's (Joel's) going to school that threatens to tear the whole community apart.

When the story begins a new radical sect starts to coalesce in opposition to Avery and to what is perceived as his growing wickedness (i.e., his decision to have a family). Missy Campbell (Aunt Missy), who hails from a respected family of lay preachers, leads her flock of believers to turn their backs not only on Avery and his sineating practice, but also on everyone who has helped or interacted with Joel or any of the Barkers. Cruel pranks and little acts of violence escalate and lead to a bloody finale, in which it is revealed that Missy killed her twelve-year-old daughter during a failed exorcism and as she was unable to cope with the guilt she projected her despair onto Avery. Meanwhile, the person responsible for the carnage turns out to be Curry, who felt slighted by the community's increasing lack of faith in his father's hallowed role, which he was supposed to take over in the future. It is Curry who kidnaps Missy, her nephew (Burke) and a local postman who wanted justice after losing his hand in a bomb explosion. Both Avery and Curry die at the end, and it is the youngest, Joel, who takes over the family business of sineating, vowing, however, to change the grotesque rituals and dispel at least some of the air of abjection that has hitherto enveloped the sineater.

Crucially, it is not Avery's abjection that troubles the Beacon Cove community, but his grotesque nature and, to be precise, his decision to have children, which is seen as incompatible with the sineating service to the community. As Missy explains it to Burke, the sineater having a wife and kids is 'a sign of the evil growin' in the Cove' (Part 1, Chapter 9).[57] Consequently, it is Avery, rather than Lelia, who is burdened with the stigma of illicit and transgressive reproduction. The prologue (set in 1979) shows a very Bakhtinian tableau of Lelia giving birth to Joel, with terrified Petrie and Curry forced to watch, because 'a new baby was the family's business, and it was not a private thing' (Prologue). This is the only scene in the entire novel focalised by Curry and can be read as a pivotal moment in which his future is defined. His younger sister, Petrie, as a woman, will be exempt from the burden of being the next sineater, and it will be Curry's duty to take up his father's mantle at some point. His younger brother, however, will have independence unimaginable to Curry. In fact, it was Joel's freedom to do as he wanted, to go to school, to interact with other people, that hurt Curry the most. Curry, as the future sineater, and Petrie, as another irrelevant female household member, were not allowed to go to school or socialise with others. Joel, however, was exempt from these restrictions, as his role at the Barker household was limited to being just a child, rather than his father's successor (Curry) or his mother's aide (Petrie).

76 • House of Horrors

Because of the ban on looking at the sineater, the descriptions of Avery's body veer towards the fantastic, even the phantasmatic. Seven-year-old Curry muses that if their mother died during childbirth, their father would come 'ravenous with hunger, slobbering and seething with the heat of sin' and maybe even his saliva would be poisonous (Prologue). When Curry goes outside to yell to his father the sex of a newborn, he notices a form cautiously moving in the shadows – '[s]omething huge, thick, and dark. The sineater' (Prologue). Already at the very beginning, Avery is presented as some*thing* rather than some*one*, as if his very role in the Beacon Cove community has automatically removed him from the human into the non-human territory, into the realm of horrifying hybrid beasts. Later, when Joel is trying to imagine his father, he is able to see only 'shadows [that] hint at the shape of a man . . . A void fills that shape, a void that holds all the vileness and evil that has ever been Beacon Cove. A void not empty, but full of blackness' (Part 1, Chapter 9). His father is no longer kin but a supernatural force that makes the trees part 'for this man-shape' (Part 1, Chapter 9). He is the local bogeyman, as Burke cruelly reminds Joel at one point (Part 1, Chapter 9).

When Joel steals his mother's old photograph of Avery, he does not know whether it was taken before or after Avery's transformation into a sineater, and this makes Joel extremely anxious and afraid to look at the picture. Instead, he succumbs to yet another grotesque phantasm of his father:

> And then the crack of light in his mind pulls open, and the fissure of his imagination widens . . . and Joel sees the sineater's boots, the large, threatening curve of taut and angry legs, the large torso, the shoulders, broad and thick and hardened, with arms and hands spread outward, clawed and ready to swipe the face off an intrusive boy . . . He sees a neck, large and dark, sweaty and pulsing with rage. A chin, hair on it dense and spiked like the vicious thorns of a sword brush tree. A mouth snarled with crazed anger. Deformed cheeks of leather, flat flaring nose, and eyes. (Part 2, Chapter 15)

On one occasion, when Joel is seriously ill and is lying in bed with high fever listening to Avery's heavy steps, he cannot help imagining his father's fantastic body in terms of its grotesque largeness and non-human features. The triad mentioned by Edwards and Graulund – exuberance, exaggeration and excess – outline the grotesqueness of Joel's fantasies concerning Avery's body: 'He is tall, oh Dear God, yes. Almost as tall as the kitchen

Grotesque Monsters and Hybrid Subjectivities • 77

ceiling. And his arms are like tree trunks, knotted with muscle, with hands of leather and nails as sharp as fish hooks. Legs thick and hard' (Part 2, Chapter 5). References to animals form the second tier of Joel's imaginings: 'boots of glistening reptile skin and toes painted with metal caps. His neck like a bear's and his face' (Part 2, Chapter 5). A similar description of Avery is presented when he attends a wake at which he is refused access to the deceased's body. First, Avery sends in one of Joel's goats with a message tied to its neck. Missy's followers, however, interpret the unfortunate messenger as the devil's familiar and set it on fire. The goat escapes into the forest and the blaze of the fire lights up the trees so that everyone can see 'the shadow of a man, forty feet tall, his arms outstretched in anger and his hands clutching out at the air like giant claws, thrown against an enormous spruce tree. The black head looms. The arms raise higher, the hands coming together into monstrous, deadly fists' (Part 2, Chapter 25). Joel is paralysed with fear and watches a silhouette suggesting 'the image of the sineater. The claws, the thick and brutal arms, the spiked beard and cruel, twisted, inhuman mouth' (Part 2, Chapter 25). While Avery's very humanity is called into question, references to beastly animality and larger-than-life blackness beg the question of racial stereotypes at work. The projection of the Other's perceived monstrosity onto supernatural monsters is a common narrative convention in horror and considering that Beacon Cove is conspicuously devoid of any BIPOC citizens, their absence transforms into a disturbing presence through Avery, the local bogeyman, dressed in shadows, 'wild' and unkempt, squatting in the forest.[58]

It is only at the very end, when Joel finds his dying father, that he is no longer afraid to look into Avery's face, which 'is bearded, the whiskers crudely cut with sort of dull knife. His hair is unkempt, uneven locks framing his forehead. There are lines on the face, although the lines do not so much speak of age as care. And his eyes are blue. Curry's blue. Petrie's blue. And yet not. There is a vulnerability there, and fear, and sorrow' (Part 4, Chapter 2). Joel finds a sad, fragile man whose life had been taken from him by the very community that then ostracised him. We also learn that Avery has been living in the cabin in which his own father was burnt to death almost thirty years before. This is where Burke discovers a stash of farm magazines, popular weeklies, all carefully wrapped in a plastic bag. There are also birthday cards and photographs of Lelia concealed in there. Avery's horrifying aura begins to crumble, as we realise he was a deeply unhappy, lonely man, who spent most of his time remembering the happy days before he was forced to become a sineater.

78 • House of Horrors

Avery's grotesquery fits the order of Russo's female grotesque, as he is marked by the sign of difference on several levels. He is forced to sacrifice his happiness and his dreams for the sake of his community, but his sacrifice is not considered noble and heroic, as in male-centred narratives. On the contrary, it is a sacrifice that belongs to the sphere of reproductive (rather than productive) work, as his work is considered a duty and a vocation that requires no compensation. He is associated with soil and dirt, as he lives alone in the forest, moves stealthily at night and resembles a wild beast rather than a human being. He is also connected to the dark side of procreation and reproduction, because of his brazen decision to reproduce, the decision that simultaneously disgusts and fascinates the Beacon Cove community. After all, he is a monster, who has been allowed to breed and his children are thus marked by his monstrous nature. His body is feminised also in the sense that it is open to intrusions (through the symbolic eating of human excrements – their sins) and leaks (as in the poisonous drool that Curry imagines in the beginning of the novel). Lastly, his is a body that undergoes drastic physical changes, when, for instance, he seems to grow forty foot tall. Such dramatic bodily transformations in horror suggest a feminisation of the monster, whose body grows, extends and crosses new barriers just like a female body does during its liminal phases, such as pregnancy.

Other male protagonists also partake of the female grotesque, most notably Burke, a boy a few years older than Joel, sent by his parents to help his Aunt Missy. Once in Ellison, he is forced to join Missy's sect. While carving a crude star on Burke's arm to mark his entrance into their congregation, she implores him to '[t]hink of the sineater and his evil. He is filled with more sin than can be held. He will rise up like the devil and chew us up' (Part 1, Chapter 2). Afterwards, he is given drugs and taken to a shed where he witnesses his aunt's failed attempt at exorcising her daughter by driving nails into her eyes. This traumatic experience is, however, blocked from his memory and it is only when he is being tortured with nails by Curry at the end of the novel that he remembers what happened in Aunt Missy's shed. Through Burke we learn that Aunt Missy has merged several distinct themes in her crusade against the sineater: 'People going to listen to false preachers. Changing rituals to suit themselves . . . Women dressing in men's clothes. Kids getting taught about their bodies at school. The sineater getting married and having a family' (Part 1, Chapter 13). Missy believes there is too much sin for the sineater to handle and he has changed into the Devil himself by refusing to follow time-honoured traditions. Of

Grotesque Monsters and Hybrid Subjectivities • 79

course, Burke does not really believe in Missy's teachings and what truly fascinates him is the power that Missy exerts over her congregation, as well as the sway that the sineater seems to hold over the entire community, including his aunt.

As more inhabitants of Ellison join Missy's congregation, her cabin swells with new devotees, and her garden is filled with tents of people who decide to live near their charismatic prophetess. Burke is reminded of a carnival with '[t]he smells of fatty meats cooking over the backyard fire . . . Sweat. Grit' (Part 2, Chapter 17). He sees Missy's rituals as one big 'monstrous farce', albeit a carnivalesque farce, in which real power resides (Part 2, Chapter 22). In a truly grotesque turn, Missy comes up with a new sineating ritual in which the whole congregation is expected to drink the blood and eat the flesh of the dead person, whom they want to cleanse of their sins. Burke is forced to follow his aunt's example, even though he is shaking and gagging on the cadaver's blood and skin:

> The crowd swarms over the corpse, making cuts and hunching down to suckle the body like a frantic gathering of obscene hairless kittens over a wrinkled, decaying mother. *Fucking coward!* Dave's [Burke's] face buries into the sharp cedar needles on the ground. His body spasms, and without knowing or caring, he wets himself. (Part 2, Chapter 24)

Ultimately, Burke is just a child, too weak to confront his Aunt Missy and the sineater, and is thus forced to partake in a cannibalistic ceremony that manages to simultaneously mock the Christian sacrament of communion *and* the community's sineating rituals. The visceral image of his broken leaking body lying face-down on the ground is yet another image of the female grotesque applied to a male subject. Burke's humiliation at the wake is what drives him into the forest where he is kidnapped, humiliated and crucified by Curry.

While Burke and the postman are tortured, Missy is left outside the abandoned cabin chained to a tree. Joel finds the three and runs to town for help, but is turned away by another man, Fitch. He then solicits Curry's help and together they help the three, although Curry decides to leave the postman behind as they are unable to take all three into town at once. He even reproaches Joel for his childish desire to save the postman: 'He ain't your friend. You're a Barker. You know your place' (Part 3, Chapter 18). Curry admits that he manipulated Fitch into helping him,

80 • House of Horrors

as he wanted to respond to their father's diminishing importance in the community and wanted to make sure that he, as his father's successor, would 'have the fear that is due [him]' (Part 3, Chapter 19). Even as a small child, Curry knew that 'he was born to keep Avery from God's holy and terrible burning lake when he dies', and that his role in the community was to be glorious and terrifying (Prologue). Seeking power and respect for his family is, however, inexorably connected to his jealousy of Joel: 'If I can't have what my spoiled little brother has, then I want what I can have. If I can't go into town, if I can't go to school and learn to read and write or walk in the daylight where other people talk, then I'll be feared like nobody was ever feared in Beacon Cove' (Part 3, Chapter 19). Begrudging his little brother's freedom to do as he pleases, Curry wants to set up an example with the people he kidnapped. He slits Missy's throat but is stopped by his own father. Still, before he dies Curry manages to mortally wound Avery.

The twin bodies of the father and his firstborn son are grotesque in that they become figures of displacement, perhaps also a metonymic representation of the community. As the body politic of the crumbling community – their bodies are frightening and frightened in equal parts, filled with a glorious purpose and lacking agency, belonging simultaneously to the *sacrum* and the *profanum*, chosen by the community and clearly abandoned by their people. In fact, the shop owner acknowledges the communal responsibility for what is happening, as he curses both the Barkers 'for being who they were and . . . Ellison and Beacon Cover for making them who they were' (Part 3, Chapter 10). In a truly Southern Gothic conclusion, the vestiges of the community's past destroy its present. Unsurprisingly perhaps, the story of the community's involvement with charismatic evangelical practices dates back to the Civil War.[59]

Missy has tolerated the local Baptist church but considered their religious standards far too slack, and so when her daughter died, she turned to Avery's to look for a scapegoat.[60] Speaking as God's prophet, Missy tries to persuade the Beacon Cove community to turn away from Avery: 'We must seek a new tradition. We cannot do as we have always done. The blister has grown to a head. The face on that head is the devil' (Part 1, Chapter 7). Thanks to Missy's admonitions and apocalyptic warnings, few people take any interest in Joel. Those who do try to help – his third-grade teacher, the postman, the owner of a shop where Curry leaves his woven baskets for tourists – are punished sooner or later: the teacher is locked with a rats' nest and suffers a stroke, the postman's hand is blown away by

Grotesque Monsters and Hybrid Subjectivities • 81

a home-made bomb attached to the Barkers' postbox and he is later left to die in the woods, the shop owner's beloved dogs are killed and then his wife dies in a church explosion. And the school principal is brutally murdered after he refuses to expel Joel.

Witnessing the destruction that he has inadvertently triggered, Joel realises the depressing truth that '[f]or his whole life, Joel will have only his family to be with him. Only his family to attend him. And together, they will cower in the dark and be shunned by day and will cry and shiver and pray' (Part 3, Chapter 1). As his mother reminds him: 'We are the least of all, Joel. We got our place, our duty . . . you have no choice in being a Barker. We was assigned of God, Joel' (Part 1, Chapter 3). Only his sister, Petrie, seems to long for an escape from such a dreary existence, and she is the only one who chooses to live elsewhere at the end of the novel. Lelia and Curry are, however, resigned to their fate, and Joel 'alone, longs for his world to be bigger' (Part 3, Chapter 13).

The novel's division into five parts – 'Joel and Lelia', 'Joel and Petrie', 'Joel and Curry', 'Joel and Avery' and 'Joel' – speaks to Joel's relationships with different family members and marks his ultimate separation from them. The final part, simply titled 'Joel', describes his self-avowed isolation. Petrie has left Ellison and is now working as a cleaner in a motel. Lelia has withdrawn from life and is mourning the Barkers' violent breakup. Joel no longer goes to school. He has taken over the sineating from Avery and has started wearing Curry's woollen coat, thus symbolically establishing a connection with his male kin. He has gone to Missy's funeral and eaten the potatoes that he first placed on her coffin, but he made sure to make eye contact with everyone present. He has decided to let everyone know that 'the ritual will not be the same. The sineater will eat in full view. The people may not welcome him, but their caution will be respect, not fear . . . Joel will look at the mourners and they will look at him. They will see the good there, not the evil. They will see the salvation, not the damnation' (Part 5). Ultimately, *Sineater* is also a novel about missing fathers, who are either dead (Missy Campbell and her daughter) or are forced to leave their families (the Barkers) or are helpless (his best friend's father, the ex-pastor and the fatherly school principal). In this reading, the grotesque representation of male bodies lacks any substantial potential for the subversion of patriarchy. Instead, broken families of the Campbells and the Barkers mirror the general breakdown of community ties in Ellison.

Monstrous Girlhood in *The Rust Maidens*

Gwendolyn Kiste's debut novel, *The Rust Maidens* (winner of the Bram Stoker Award for Best First Novel in 2019) alternates between two timelines: 1980 and 2008. Phoebe, a white middle-aged woman returns home to Denton Street, Cleveland in 2008 to help her mother pack their belongings before bulldozers raze their almost-abandoned neighbourhood. This prompts a painful reckoning with Phoebe's past and her role in the events of 1980, when five neighbourhood girls, including Phoebe's best friend and beloved cousin, Jacqueline, began transforming into the titular Rust Maidens, slowly shedding their organic selves to reveal harshly lined bodies made of rust, steel and glass.[61] Their metamorphosis coincided with the strike action at the local steel mill, followed soon by its closure; a place where many of the Denton Street fathers worked, and which had glued the community together in a tight web of stifling gender roles, deep-cut maternal control, overlooked parental abuse and abandoned teenage dreams. The novel implies both a literal connection between the girls' 'sickness' and the steel mill (manifested as a post-human correspondence of bodies) and a more metaphysical one in which their rust bodies reflect (or perhaps take upon themselves) the actual decay and disintegration of their community. In both readings, however, the grotesque nature of their bodies emphasises the girls' ambiguous and volatile status in the Denton Street community: they are to be cherished and protected but also surveilled and subjugated, displayed as ornaments but quickly hidden if found guilty of transgression, celebrated for conforming to white femininity ideals but also punished and belittled for being their mothers' daughters. Among all these competing and often contradictory reactions triggered by the girls, it is their embodiment that stands at the centre: what they do with their bodies and what is done to their bodies are two most important topics for the Denton Street community, and that is even before the girls start leaking strange silvery water from open wounds and turn to rust.

The novel comments on the girls' objectification by literally turning them into non-organic objects; however, this metallic 'objectification' actually bestows on them a degree of agency, unthinkable in their previous human-girl lives. Their girlhood, of which they were already dispossessed by a white working-class culture in which they grew up, is thus returned to them, albeit in a completely new form. On the one hand, their girlhood is defined by a set of particular circumstances – geographical location, historical moment, social organisation and cultural production – and Kiste carefully delineates the constraints of living in a patriarchal working-class community, with its emphasis on nuclear families and traditional gender roles and with the looming collapse of an industry that enabled their community formation in the first place. On the other hand, however, the social and physical restrictions imposed on these girls and the surveillance they are constantly subjected to reveal a familiar pattern of cultural mistrust of young girls. The unceasing popularity of possession horror in the last few decades is the best evidence that adolescent girls and their embodied selves generate acute cultural anxiety, specifically targeting their changing bodies, sexuality but also their fraught position in the heterosexual matrix. In Western cultural narratives, young girls' supposed instability is often presented through hysterical and/or obsessive behaviours, heightened emotionality, childishness alternating with sexiness, but also, especially in horror, through grotesque embodiment: bodily fluids, contortions, open wounds, tumours, sickly looking skin. Russo points to bodies-in-transformation such as 'the pregnant body, the aging body, the irregular body' as paradigmatic examples of grotesque and unruly bodies, especially 'when set loose in the public sphere',[62] and the girl's is an irregular body precisely because of its liminal status – no longer a child, yet no adult woman either.

Girls, as Catherine Driscoll argues, became 'highly visible in twentieth-century Western cultures-mostly as a marker of immature and malleable identity, and as a publicly preeminent image of desirability',[63] and, I would argue, it is this very combination of immaturity, pliability and desirability that generates both fear and suspicion of adolescent girls and a compulsive need to control them. Carla Rice adds that '[i]n contemporary Westernized cultures, social and scientific constructions cast puberty as a precarious period that poses particular challenges for girls',[64] and the supposedly premature development of young girls' bodies sparks debates about dangers that the girls both attract and constitute themselves. Kiste presents us with a whole array of group and individual attempts at containing the girls – physically hurting them, locking them in their rooms/houses, gaslighting them, publicly shaming them, blaming them for the community's misfortunes, controlling their reproductive rights, spying on them, choosing partners/friends for them. As Phoebe recalls bitterly:

> [the parents] were desperate to take hold of them, to do their best to stop the blossoming insurrection, even if they weren't sure they could win . . . There was decorum to maintain, a sense of authority over our

84 • House of Horrors

own. Because what kind of men would our fathers be if they couldn't control five little girls? And what kind of women would our mothers be if they didn't stand behind their husbands? (p. 124)

One of the normative discourses triggered by the girls' condition is that of an 'unfit mother' or a 'disabled mother', which is exemplified by Dawn's story. Her baby, Eleanor, is taken away just after birth, as Dawn's young age and her 'sickness' make her doubly unfit to mother the child.[65] Eleanor is spirited away to Clint, her negligent and alcoholic teen father, whose suitability for parenthood is never questioned by the neighbourhood, even though it soon becomes clear that he is the one unfit and wholly unprepared to take care of a child. In a couple of heart-wrenching scenes, Phoebe facilitates brief meetings between Dawn and baby Eleanor, which prove beyond doubt that Dawn's steel fingers and glass-shard fingernails are dangerous only in the eyes of others; Dawn never hurts her baby. Still, when Dawn breast-feeds her wailing baby and the community sees the rusty liquid dripping from her nipple and smearing the infant's lips red, they are only further convinced of Dawn's monstrosity. The fact that the baby is fine or that the rusty 'milk' might be good for Eleanor is conveniently ignored. Dawn's disability is constructed through ableist inscriptions on her body, which define her 'condition' as physical deterioration and potentially contagious sickness. As Rosemarie Garland Thompson argues, '[c]onstructed as the embodiment of corporeal insufficiency and deviance, the physically disabled body becomes a repository for social anxieties',[66] but in Dawn's case these anxieties stem not just from bodily difference but sexual difference too. Dawn's embodied experience channels community's sense of pessimism and loss – being denied her motherhood by the community generates both a physical and an emotional anguish for Dawn, alleviated only by the physical presence of the other four Rust Maidens.

While the rise of social media has opened girls' private spaces (that is their bedrooms) on an unprecedented scale, the novel's historical setting allows Kiste to present Phoebe and the other girls' world as deeply private and mostly unknown, even to their parents. Driscoll notes that '[g]irls often seem to be not only produced in relation to the nuclear family but to live their adolescence closely contained within its territory'.[67] It is at home that the girls learn how to navigate patriarchal heteronormative rules and it is the domestic space that becomes their primary place of belonging or disbelonging (that is a place where they can practise both conformity to and rebellion against their families). Rather than stage their rebellion in the

Grotesque Monsters and Hybrid Subjectivities • 85

public sphere, as is often the case with adolescent boys (or rather how their rebellion is often portrayed and analysed), the girls in Kiste's novel rebel against their community by going inward and by establishing intensely private spaces of their own.[68] Phoebe and Jacqueline regularly sneak into an abandoned building on their street, and later on, the five rust maidens claim this very house as their commune-cum-cocoon. Phoebe, always the black sheep of the community, has a tree house turned bug house, where she and Jacqueline escape their parents' prying eyes. In the end, the five girls fuse with a giant foundry furnace at the now defunct steel mill, Phoebe being the only witness to their disappearance. Their decision melds a public male-dominated space (exclusive to their fathers and community father figures) with an isolated female-only space associated with secrecy, friendship and femininity.

Kiste describes a bleak reality in which the strict division of spheres does not translate into tighter bonds between adult women. Friendship is frown on – the mothers do not have friends and their daughters are not supposed to have ones either. Even though the matrons of Denton Street meet regularly to plan events and make decisions for all their families, their solidarity works only to protect the men and the community from perceived threats such as unwanted pregnancy or a potential scandal caused by domestic violence. That is why Aunt Betty (Jacqueline's mother) hates Phoebe and her mother so much – she cannot imagine being friends with another woman, especially not the one who 'stole' her older brother from her, which is why she tries to sabotage her daughter's friendship with Phoebe. Phoebe and Jacqueline keep their own friendship on the lowdown, while the other four girls, snobbish Helena (the pastor's daughter), artistic Violet (the doctor's daughter), strange Lisa (the abused girl) and scared Dawn (the teen mother), all are solitary figures. Rust Maidens break with this imposed solitude by forming their own family unit, one based on true friendship and companionship. The price for that is breaking other connections: with their parents, Dawn's child (Elizabeth), Phoebe herself. Throughout the novel, Phoebe imagines herself as a valid alternative to the Denton Street community for her cousin, which is why she schemes to steal her college fund and escape with Jacqueline. Her non-conforming behaviour and the sheer determination to leave distinguishes her from the other girls who are all resigned to stay in the community, which perhaps explains why she is the only girl not turning into a Rust Maiden. Still, the bond that develops between the five girls is stronger than Phoebe's friendship with Jacqueline, if not better. Phoebe, for all her love for Jacqueline, sees her cousin as an extension of herself ('we were practically two halves of one girl' (p. 17)), and, however unconsciously, she tries to impose on Jacqueline her own dreams and aspirations. The Rust Maidens, in contrast, accept Jacqueline for who (and what) she is, and do not expect her to change or leave Cleveland. Jacqueline quite rightly points out that Phoebe treats her as a damsel in distress, someone to save to make herself feel better but in reality '[w]e haven't been the same for a long time' (p. 106), and maybe, just maybe, Jacqueline has been a Rust Maiden for much longer than Phoebe realises, and the shedding of her organic self was just a way to reveal her authentic self.

As a potent, if simplistic, metaphor, the Rust Maidens' bodies stand for the disintegrating body of their community. Steel is the foundation on which the Denton Street community has been built. Men's work is what defines not just their own roles as breadwinners, but also their wives' roles as homemakers and their children's roles as dutiful would-be-steelworkers and would-be-housewives. The girls' bodies shed their human organic selves to reveal not just steel, iron and glass but also the process of decay that has been eating away at their community. A case in point, the Rust Maidens constantly ooze silvery water, which facilitates the rusting and reveals their true selves, while the community is slowly dissolved by liquor, with Phoebe, her mother, Lisa' father, and Dawn's boyfriend all described as alcoholics (or on their way to become ones), and with large quantities of alcohol ever-present at community functions and family dinners.

Rust, an iron oxide, forms when iron and oxygen react in the presence of water or moisture. Given enough time, rust will envelop the entire iron mass – and while the chemical process is neither intrinsically good nor bad, for humans utilising iron products, rust signifies decay. Similarly, while the Rust Maidens' transformation seems neither scary nor appealing to the girls, the rusting that their bodies undergo is read through teratological lens by their community. A little while into their transformation, the girls begin to fuse with metal and move through it. Once the community sees them doing it, the girls become 'something else' and their status as non-human monsters is confirmed. This also marks the moment that their power is seen: 'All five of them, gorgeous and fearsome and not at all the girls we thought we knew. We remembered them as quiet, as sweet, as familiar. We didn't remember them as powerful' (p. 123). Phoebe struggles not to think of them as monsters but as girls, especially when during a midnight excursion into their cocooning residence she finds discarded chrysalises and realises they have shed their organic-human selves. Still, she understands that in doing so they have become not only powerful and self-sufficient, but also beautiful and close to one another.[69] Thus, their monstrosity alternates between various functions: revealing the sins of the community, being a grotesque form of punishment, serving as a violent but undeserved blow and performing a wondrous spectacle of feminine power.

The 1980 narrative ends with the entire community divided not just along the picket lines but between the Rust Maidens' protectors and their opponents. Phoebe and her parents are leading those who want to protect the girls from being taken away by secret government agencies or, worse, dragged and punished by the other group, controlled by Aunt Betty, and hellbent on punishing the Maidens for the wrongs suffered by the community. When the Maidens' cocoon house collapses, the community stands shattered. Phoebe knows, however, the Rust Maidens' true destination: the closed mill. In an ominous ending, the girls, now in their ghostly metallic bodies, merge with the very place that used to define their lives:

> One by one, starting with Lisa, the girls fused into the rust that made them. Their bodies contorted into the shadows and metal, popping and writhing in ways that made my own bones ache. But the girls didn't cry out. Instead, they smiled. Their fingers and arms went first, the glass cracking through the steel, and then their legs and torsos twisted into the dark until only their faces remained. Even once their lips and ears and cheeks melded into the furnace, I swore I could still see those eyes looking out at me, dark and strange and somewhere too distant to fathom. Jacqueline was last. (p. 209)

Phoebe realises that the correspondence between the girls and the mill runs deep: 'This mill had given us life. Food on the table, roofs over our head, a shape to our everyday existences. Now it was closed up, bound for rust, and soon to be forgotten. The girls were the same, and they understood that. They would take this place and repurpose it for themselves' (p. 180). The collapse of the Rust Belt industrial cities, the shame and sadness that accompanied it, but also cultural erasure suffered by these communities is bound with the fate of forgotten girls from abandoned mill, factory and mine towns, shamed and rejected for their transgressions, unable to fit in a post-industrial world. Phoebe intuits this sense of a lost future early on when attending her high school graduation:

> Us girls knew this better than most. If there was limited space in the world, then we were the first ones on the team to get cut. No room for us at the steel mills, the boardrooms, the operating rooms. No room for us anywhere. We'd become wives and mothers, and only if we were lucky – and smart enough to do it in that order. (p. 22)

Moving away from a literal correspondence between the Rust Maidens' transformation and the demise of the Denton Street community, we might think of their grotesque bodies as a series of commentaries on the ecological devastation brought by unchecked industrialisation and the way that damage can be contained, challenged, even reversed. Early on, the neighbourhood matrons fearfully reject the possibility that the mill and the pollution that it generates might have something to do with their daughters' condition. Aunt Betty cuts this conversation short by admonishing others: 'Don't blame the men. They didn't do this' (p. 70), as if the men and the mill were one entity, exempt from any social or personal accountability. *The Rust Maidens* can be read as an eco-cautionary tale of post-industrial wreckage, in which the social, the individual and the ecological consequences of heavy industry are woven tightly together. Still, if Kiste's novel is read as an ecofeminist and ecocritical narrative, female monstrosity and grotesque bodies do not necessarily signal tragic demise of a community but might be in fact recovered as instruments of a nomadic post-human subjectivity that flourishes in the Denton Street literal and metaphorical ruins.

As readers, we have no access to that subjectivity, we see only glimpses of it caught by Phoebe, an eighteen-year-old girl who barely understands herself, let alone others. What becomes clear to Phoebe, however, is the girls' interconnectedness. They share thoughts; they instinctively know if any of them is in danger and can materialise at each other's side in a blink of an eye. While their final form, or at least the one witnessed by Phoebe in 1980, seems to consist of metal and glass, the way they manipulate glass shards, decaying walls or a car radio suggests an ability to transcend the confines of their new bodies. The only barrier mentioned in the novel is a newly installed steel door, which lacking any rust or signs of decay, cannot be manipulated by them. Decay is then redefined as both a catalyst and a carrier of post-human nomadic subjectivity. Spread everywhere, unnoticed and forgotten, considered a nuisance and a sure sign of decline, decay becomes a line of flight used by the girls to avoid sedimentation and calcification, to invoke a Deleuzian-Guattarian vocabulary of subjectivity.

Braidotti, building on and expanding Deleuze and Guattari's work, reminds us that '[t]he nomad is a transgressive identity, whose transitory nature is precisely the reason why s/he can make connections at all. Nomadic politics is a matter of bonding, of coalitions, of interconnections'.[70] Nomadic subjectivity, which as Braidotti argues persuasively, 'can provide an alternative foundation for ethical and political subjectivity',[71] embraces non-unitary, dynamic vision of the self, radically immanent, and materially embodied and embedded. The Rust Maidens, as 'new kinds of desiring subjects',[72] engage in multiple becomings with the non-human, the non-organic, technological and ecological agents, guided and infused by generative desire. Importantly, the novel effectively distorts conventional definitions of such agents by showing how oxidation of iron, a naturally occurring phenomenon, which simultaneously features prominently in human endeavours to stave off the inevitable decline of alloy properties, acts as a curious catalyst to the non-human becoming of the five girls. Oil, viscous water, Lake Erie seaweed, steel, pewter, sand, glass, rust, dirt are not merely raw materials but co-conspirators, companions and animate chemical formulas rewriting girls' internal wirings. While Phoebe witnesses the Maidens' final transformation at the old steel mill, this is merely the first step in the girls' next chapter, not the end of their journey. The fact that they can manipulate objects from afar in 2008 (including electrical equipment), ride on electric currents, move at will through rust and dirt-infested localisations in Cleveland seems to confirm the theory of their infinite becomings. Braidotti notes that '[t]he nomad enacts transitions without a teleological purpose',[73] which perhaps explains why the Rust Maidens' transformation needs neither goal nor explanation.

The grotesque might be used as a marker of change, a freeze-frame shot of a stage at which Jacqueline, Lisa, Helena, Dawn and Violet are no longer human girls but have not (yet) become non-human Others. The grotesque catches them in the act, at a moment when their open wounds leak viscous water and their organic selves transform into non-organic (or more-than-organic) substances. They are caught not just between different materialities, but also between different states of being, which is evidenced by the heavy emphasis on the way that their bodies smell and sound: 'You could smell it before you were inside. It reeked of stagnant water and earth and something unknown, something that seemed to have passed a threshold and returned. Something not alive' (p. 45). The girls can emit a high-pitched non-human sound to protect themselves, hurt others, or just communicate their anguish. Hearing Jacqueline's inhuman wail, Phoebe considers the scream 'so otherworldly but almost familiar too, like the lullaby of a factory. Like a thousand rusted nails dragged against a plate of steel. The sound shuddered through me, and I wanted to scream too' (p. 90). Smell and sound feature prominently in the regulatory practices of femininity, with the natural female body odours considered increasingly unwelcome in mainstream cultural practices, and raised female voices read as shrill and hysterical (rather than strong and inspiring). In this sense, the grotesque hybridity of their smells ('something not alive', 'of stagnant water and earth') and sounds ('like the lullaby of a factory', 'like a thousand rusted nails dragged against a plate of steel') celebrates a teratological spectacle of the post-human self, no longer defined by the so-called unfeminine or unladylike behaviour but spilling into the non-human and the non-organic territories. The Rust Maidens embody the way the female and the non-human grotesqueries are co-constitutive, and it is the infusion of the non-human that can implode the normative models of femininity and rigid gender roles that weigh down not just the girls, but the whole community.

Conclusion

The three novels utilise the grotesque aesthetics in vastly different ways, but all three authors remain cognisant of the problematic nature of gender dynamics at play. Difference stands at the centre of the grotesque, as this form of aesthetics rests on clearly defined zones, which can then be crisscrossed, mutated, merged or violently reconstituted via monstrous becomings. Since physical changes and un/natural transformations have been historically linked with femininity and womanhood in Western philosophy and art, the grotesque body is a feminised body by definition. Sexual difference itself is further compounded by racialising and naturalising biases that buttress discourses of monstrosity and normativity in Western culture. This means that the grotesque body is read not just in terms of transgressive femininity, but more specifically non-white and/or non-human femininity. The scopic offence committed by the non-normative body is always predicated on more than one transgression: more than just gender roles, more than gender expression or gendered body scripts, more than heteronormativity or hegemonic whiteness, and definitely more than the human.

In Kiernan's novel I looked at how its female protagonist, Imp, handles pain and pleasure, shame and exhilaration connected to her non-normative sexuality (one that is often presented as a spectacle geared towards the cis-hetero male gaze) and her neuroatypicality (which is medicalised as a disorder), and how she explores relationships that fall outside the dominion of traditional kinship. Whereas Kiernan invested the grotesque with dark eroticism capable of destabilising phallogocentric regimes of power, Massie looked at grotesque male bodies whose enforced feminisation destabilised a rural Christian community. With Kiste's novel, I returned to female grotesque and its implicit indictment of strict gender roles. I also analysed how grotesque bodies in Kiste's novel could be turned into generative sites of post-human becomings and offer a foundation for nomadic subjectivity. Faced with constant devaluation of girlhood and intrusive surveillance of female bodies, Kiste's protagonists find succour in a female-only community, in which intense female friendship offers both an insulation from and power over surrounding reality. In contrast, the sineater's family buckles under the combined weight of social ostracism and religious fanaticism, and Massie's novel ends with the surviving Bakers separated, but perhaps finally free.

For Russo, as argued by Braidotti, the female grotesque 'marks the return of the repressed of the political unconscious of late postmodernity through the expression of a carnivalesque culture of the excessive, the risky and the abject'.[74] The renewed interest in the bodily manifests itself in a cultural fascination with the collapse of identifiable and agreed-on barriers and binary oppositions. The grotesque feeds on such conflicts and tensions as well as splits and mergers of incongruous concepts and embodied selves. That is perhaps why the grotesque is readily employed by contemporary horror novelists who, in a way, look back at the original classic Gothic texts and their 'gleeful excessiveness'.[75] In contemporary horror fiction, the grotesque, understood both as a repertoire of cultural tropes and as a particular aesthetics, may be used to critically engage with normative expectations concerning the protagonists, their gender roles, their roles and desires within familial structures and the ways their embodied selves are placed within larger set of intimacies. Still, the powerful pull of the grotesque may also activate a longing for normativity and a nostalgia for non-monstrous, non-transformed bodies. Even though the transformative potential of the grotesque remains debatable, the grotesque may function as a meeting point between different modes of thinking about the body, subjectivity and human relations (both private and communal).

3

Blood(y) Ties in Vampire Fictions

Introduction

MATRILINEALITY, the reproductive body and intense female bonds played central roles in the previous chapter, in which I looked closely at monstrous female and/or feminised bodies. This chapter will in turn concentrate on the ways in which contemporary vampire fictions rewrite the Oedipal plot and how they highlight tensions associated with communality, (self)imposed exile, and processes of abjection and exclusion. Ever since Bram Stoker described Dracula slicing his chest to feed Mina, familial imagery has been eagerly discussed by both vampire fiction authors and critics who have analysed the recurrent images of (monstrous) childbirth and reproduction, suckling and feeding, and taboo sex acts. Unsurprisingly, the most popular representations of vampires portray them as preoccupied with establishing hierarchical kinship structures that are recognised as *families*, and which often attempt to circumvent familial middle-class conventions. In this sense, queer families have been a staple of vampire fiction for much longer than in other types of horror story.

Whether read as a staple of horror literature, a subgenre of the Gothic, or even 'a subgenre of popular fiction',[1] vampire fiction has not only flourished in the past three decades, but also splintered into new subgenres; these include but are not limited to paranormal romance, vampire erotica or young adult supernatural romance. Indeed, vampire fiction also morphed its way into other genres, for instance, detective fiction, science

94 • House of Horrors

fiction and weird fiction. This generic indistinctness mirrors the episte-mological ambivalence of the vampire: they are the UnDead (that is, nei-ther fully alive nor fully dead); in some tales they lack mirror reflection, which obviously violates the basic laws of physics that should apply to both the dead and the living; and some narratives stress vampires' ability to transform into animals, thus crossing the human versus non-human barrier. However, one form of ambiguity that has been reappearing repeat-edly since the early nineteenth century is the vampire's ability to transgress gendered binaries.

Praising the more radical strain of contemporary women's vampire fiction, Gina Wisker argues that these 'women writers explore and enact the practice based in queer theory by defying boundaries, refusing cate-gories and destructively oriented definitions of difference, expressing the carnivalesque'.[2] Still, this begs a question which kinds of queer practices are being used – and maybe abused? – and whether these practices are deemed subversive only on account of being designated as queer. Wisker goes on to suggest that:

> [w]hether used as the worst kind of terror to be exorcised or, in its contemporary form, as potential social/sexual transgressor, cele-brated as troubled hybrid offering eternal love, the vampire disrupts polarized systems of thought. It undermines and disempowers West-ern logical tendencies to construct divisive, hierarchical, oppositional structures. In restrictive, repressive eras, the vampire's transgres-sion of gender boundaries, life/death, day/night behavior, and its invasion of the sanctity of body, home, and blood, are elements of its abjection.[3]

Wisker thus interprets contemporary women's vampire fictions as surpass-ing their bland and repressive predecessors. However, her faith in the vam-pires' subversive potential and ability to transcend 'binaries, boundaries, and divisions'[4] might have been too hasty, judging by the outpouring of gender, race and class-normative vampire fictions in the past two decades. Critical and artistic readiness to position vampires as essentially transgres-sive figures points to the problematic nature of contemporary vampire narratives. With the vampires' generic as well as genetic ability to question the rigidity of normalised and naturalised boundaries, vampires seem to be ideal vessels for confronting what is understood as *normal, natural* and *tra-ditional*.[5] Still, I am less interested in vampires' perceived transgressiveness and more in the very limits of situating the vampire as an inherently queer figure; privileging the margin as a desired place to be and to speak from is an especially tricky gesture in vampire fictions penned by writers, who, because of their gender and/or race, are already operating from a marginalised and precarious position.

Since the establishment of blood and/or alternative families constitutes the main theme of this chapter, the critical lens used to bring into focus the intricacies of vampiric reproduction will be the abject. I am aware that abjection, as a critical tool, runs the risk of becoming a prescriptive rather than descriptive formation and might occlude readings that move past gendered understanding of embodiment. My understanding of vampire fiction is, however, embedded in theories of gendered practices of kinship and reproduction as well as gendered performance of the body. Consequently, I feel abjection cannot and, indeed, should not be sidestepped. In popular understanding, the processes of abjection are located, first and foremost, in rituals regarding corpses, bodily fluids, excrements and blood, all of which appear in vampire fictions, as the vampire performs a number of taboo acts related to the abjected aspects of human physiology. In a classic Kristevan formulation, however, abjection is linked to the repudiation of the maternal, a violent break with the mother that needs to take place before the child can enter the Law of the Father and begin the process of individualisation and socialisation. Themes of (absent) mothers, motherhood and maternity are strongly present in vampire fictions, and while vampiric reproduction often tries to circumvent the mother and deny her role in procreation, the maternal can never be completely rejected and repressed, which mirrors the very process of abjection.

Critics such as Catherine Spooner,[6] Fred Botting[7] and Veronica Hollinger[8] link the contemporary fascination with vampires with larger cultural shifts that have reconfigured the way that we engage with monsters and monstrosity as such. Their writings echo Nina Auerbach's thesis that each new decade gets the vampires it deserves,[9] and the vampires, because of their inherent fluidity, carry and magnify fears prevalent at a given cultural moment. Jack Halberstam in *Skin Shows* argues that the postmodern Gothic is deeply invested in the figure of the monster, as it is through the often tragic monster's fate that the readers and audiences are able to witness the hunters' fall from grace and victims' less-than-innocent entanglement in the hunt.[10] According to Sabine Meyer, contemporary monsters may 'function as a sort of litmus test for the (in)sufficiency of our modes of categorization, representation, and interpretation rather than merely as a metaphor for all things alien to dominant fictions of the norm'.[11] If, as Hollinger argues, one of the consequences of the postmodern legitimation crisis is an ongoing process of deconstruction of hitherto fixed concepts, then the vampire becomes 'a monster-of-choice these days, since it is itself an inherently deconstructive figure':[12] it traverses the boundaries between human and non-human, dead and alive, monstrosity and normality. Meyer notes that the postmodern vampire's ability:

> to cross generic boundaries . . . to be good or bad or somewhere in between, to switch back and forth between being predator and prey, colonizer and colonized, traditional villain and utopian savior, makes her/him a compelling and productive alternative to the idea of the unified, unambiguously identifiable subject encoded and enforced within normative discourse.[13]

Even though the vampire has achieved an 'archetypal status for the representation of queer, social and sexual identities',[14] many of those non-heteronormative representations of vampirism end up reinforcing the idea that homoerotic and homosexual relationships either originate in or result in disorder, moral chaos and corruption. Anne Rice's vastly popular series of novels, *The Vampire Chronicles*, is the quintessential example of such contested and self-contradictory vampire fiction. While Anne Rice was the most popular woman writer associated with vampire fiction *per se*, one can find a number of female predecessors (such as nineteenth-century Gothic authors, Mary Elizabeth Braddon and Mary E. Wilkins Freeman) and a host of Rice's contemporaries who were busy rewriting *Dracula*'s and *Carmilla*'s scripts in the 1970s and 1980s. For instance, vampires populating Chelsea Quinn Yarbro's and Suzy McKee Charnas's novels differ from their earlier incarnations in their relative proximity to human life. Gordon and Hollinger underline the 'domestication' of the vampire, which, according to them, began in the second half of the twentieth century.[15] Similarly, Jules Zanger, in 'Metaphor into Metonymy: the Vampire Next Door', describes two significant changes to the vampire lore: first, the 'new' vampire tends to be more family-oriented and communal, and second, he or she has lost the metaphysical and/or spiritual edge of absolute evil and corruption, which used to be associated with Stoker's Dracula.[16] Zanger writes that the vampire has shifted 'from solitary to multiple and communal, from metaphoric Anti-Christ to secular sinner, from magical to mundane', and has thus moved from the

Blood(y) Ties in Vampire Fictions • 97

realm of metaphor into the realm of metonymy.[17] The vampire no longer represents the Other residing in a completely different semantic order, but is now a figure of an all-too-human outsider who nevertheless has not abandoned the shared human semantic field of recognition. Twenty-first-century vampires continue their climb on the humanisation axis and an increased emphasis on self-reflexivity and irony in contemporary vampire fiction allows these texts 'to contest hegemonic structures of race, gender, and sexuality' much more effectively than earlier texts.[18]

The most interesting attempts at rewriting the traditional vampire mythology took place in the late 1980s and early 1990s, when a wave of newcomers flooded the horror market. Often considered niche and/or low-brow, and printed by small publishing presses, books by Melanie Tem, Elizabeth Engstrom, Poppy Z. Brite/Billy Martin, Jewelle Gomez, Elaine Bergstrom, Jeanne Kalogridis, Tananarive Due, Kristine Kathryn Rusch, L. A. Banks, Nancy A. Collins, Yvonne Navarro, Laurell K. Hamilton, as well as short story anthologies edited by Poppy Z. Brite/Billy Martin, Pam Keesey and Amarantha Knight speak to an enormous popularity of women's vampire fiction (and its various offshoots) among horror and dark fantasy fans. For the present study I have selected three novels published between 1988 and 1991: Jewelle Gomez's *The Gilda Stories* (1991), Elizabeth Engstrom's *Black Ambrosia* (1988) and Melanie Tem's *Prodigal* (1991). Even though today's publishing market is much more saturated with vampire fiction than three decades ago, the vast majority of popular novels written after 2000 have transplanted vampires to fantasy, young adult and supernatural romance genres, and thus lie outside my scope. The first two novels offer strikingly dissimilar visions of vampiric (and human) families – affirmative and jubilant in Gomez, lonely and perverse in Engstrom – both, however, remain implicated in the culture wars of the late 1980s and early 1990s. When Gomez is examining the second-wave feminist ideal of a boundless love that traverses not only time, but also race and gender boundaries, Engstrom is probing the 1980s New Woman model of independence and the violent backlash following in its wake. Of the three novels, Tem's is the only one in which a seemingly ordinary, white, middle-class family is placed squarely at the centre of the narrative. Still, even this caring unit fails to protect its youngest members from vampiric intrusion. Gomez's novel exposes the limitations of the familial imagery used in contemporary vampire fiction and the ambiguous status of queer theory and queer sensibility readily employed to subvert the cultural and social *status quo*. Her use of abjection centres on the maternal, perverse vampiric

98 • House of Horrors

reproduction and bodily acts which threaten both the social contract and the stability of normative kinship. By contrast, Engstrom and Tem showcase abjection connected with the diseased body and the subjects' failure to enter a community and be accepted into peer groups and their families of choice.

Towards Abjection

Since vampires are primarily associated with blood, the theoretical tool most closely linked to blood is abjection: a complex concept lingering uneasily at the intersection of the material, the psychoanalytic and the anthropological. Julia Kristeva's seminal study *Powers of Horror: an Essay on Abjection* from 1980 (translated into English in 1982)[19] is by far the single most important book on abjection. In it she leans heavily on Lacanian psychoanalysis and Mary Douglas's structuralist research on defilement rituals and the purity/impurity binary. In Kristeva's understanding, the abject is 'the jettisoned object', one that is 'radically excluded' and 'draws [one] toward the place where meaning collapses'.[20] Yet, the abject is neither an object nor a subject; it occupies the badlands of pre-subjectivisation. In order to leave behind the mother's semiotic world and participate in symbolic communication, the child must first refuse and then abject their mother. The moment of shifting from the semiotic to the symbolic (during which the process of abjection takes place) or, more precisely, being at the very threshold of the symbolic is what Kristeva calls a thetic stage. The thetic break occurs when the subject assumes a position in the symbolic. In the vein of Kristeva, Rosemary Jackson links the non-thetic elements (that is, those which have no place in the rational scheme of things) with the fantastic: 'eroticism, violence, madness, laughter, nightmares, dreams, blasphemy, lamentation, uncertainty, female energy, excess'.[21] Thus, the subject repudiates the non-thetic – all that 'is opposed to dominant signifying practice[s]'[22] in order to cross into the symbolic, but what is lost in this movement may be returned through the fantastic in arts. Such a perspective on the fantastic may thus recover not just non-thetic elements but the abject as well.

Kristeva lists three groups of things/objects/events which might be read as abominable, impure and thus might be subject to abjection in Western culture: certain types of food, bodily transformations and death, the female body, and incest.[23] However, Robbie Duschinsky offers a persuasive critique of Kristevan abjection by drawing attention to the rather hazy treatment of such notions as 'purity', 'impurity', 'identity' and 'order' in her writing. He also points out the ambiguity of the term 'abjection' itself, which 'is taken to mean variously: impure, ineffable, disgusting, horrifying, illicitly desirable, outside of logic, rejected by classification, maternal, continuous (as opposed to discrete)'.[24] However, not all liminal objects are impure or abject. One of Duschinsky's most compelling examples is that of blood, which in Kristeva's work resides unambiguously on the side of the impure, but which may still be successfully recontextualised in nationalist narratives or recovered through stories of regeneration and rebirth in the genres of the fantastic.[25] Duschinsky rewrites Kristeva's framework as 'purity and impurity discourses' that can be used to assess how a given phenomenon conforms to or deviates from norms that it is judged against.[26] Such a scheme is arguably better suited to modern-day academic investigations, in that it allows for more nuanced readings of the bodily in horror; not all horror texts posit blood, corpses or semen as inherently abject or non-abject. Rather they often look for moments of rapture/rupture in otherwise homogenous systems or for spaces where affects associated with abjection come to the fore: dread, desire and disgust.

Moving away from psychoanalytically inspired readings, Xavier Aldana Reyes postulates a recovery of abjection as a theoretical tool 'that places corporeal threat at the heart of the experience of Horror'.[27] In his reading, abjection is not gendered, as it relies on universal affects (such as fear and disgust), which are in turn based on images of body vulnerability transmitted and maintained culturally, as well as on more primal responses to the pain and damage suffered by cinematic bodies. While not opposed to gendered readings *per se*, Aldana Reyes argues these should be relegated to the study of themes, not particular images of bleeding or corrupted bodies, which, in his understanding, transcend gender and sex and whose reception sidesteps gendered or sexed selves. A detailed and certainly compelling reformulation of the abjection, Aldana Reyes's analysis works well if bodies are indeed imagined as non-gendered and non-sexed in the affective or emotive sense. Curiously, but perhaps unintentionally, Aldana Reyes keeps referring to examples of typically female/AFAB (assigned female at birth) experiences of embodiment (such as menstruation or motherhood) in his critique of gendered readings, a critical gesture that runs the risk of universalising male/AMAB experiences as non-gendered.

Still, Aldana Reyes's redefinition of abjection as 'fearful disgust' in the wake of universal bodily vulnerability is definitely illuminating in

100 • House of Horrors

that disgust often appears in the wake of abjection and could be read as abjection's primary affect alongside fear and desire.[28] While Kristeva mentions the protective function of vomiting and queasiness, which shields us from the polluted/polluting object, she also acknowledges their failure to hide our fascination for the abject leaving us helpless 'in the middle of treachery'.[29] Kristeva's notion of treachery may be understood as one of the reasons why viewers and readers of horror fictions seek out the thrill of disgust. Pleasure found in disgust might be thus connected with a sense of excitement over border (identity) breakdown: 'Everything seems at risk in the experience of disgust. It is a state of alarm and emergency, an acute crisis of self-preservation in the face of an unassimilable otherness, a convulsive struggle, in which what is in question is, quite literally, whether "to be or not to be".'[30]

Hanjo Berressem reinterprets the abject as that which, in a vampiric manner, drains power from other bodies: 'Abjects drain life out of organic systems. Foul things tend to be abjects, for instance, because in foulness, an abundance of life is rotting from within.'[31] The vampire, by embodying both life and death, represents the ultimate Kristevan abject: the corpse. Vampires' UnDead bodies are unclean and polluting also in the sense of their distorted reproduction and pseudo-cannibalistic desire for blood. Their bodies are not proper, which calls to mind Elizabeth Grosz's description of abjection as 'a sickness at one's own body, at the body beyond that "clean and proper" thing, the body of the subject. Abjection is the result of recognizing that the body is more than, in excess of, the "clean and proper"'.[32] The impropriety of the vampire's existence also hinges on his or her defiance of the boundaries of what remains recognisably human; after all, as Kristeva posits, abjection is a fragile state 'where man strays on the territories of *animal*'.[33]

More generally perhaps, the vampire is abject because it disrupts various forms of social and cultural order. I find Katherine J. Goodnow's discussion of four distinct groups of the abject in cinema useful in thinking about the abject in vampire fiction. The first group, 'the abject without and within the body',[34] is related directly to the two categories discussed by Kristeva: 'excrement and its equivalent (decay, infection, disease, corpse, etc.)'[35] and the bodily fluids and growths, and physical changes that take place mainly on the inside, for instance, pregnancy or cancer. In vampire narratives, this type of the abject is often fused together, as the infected body is both dying and visibly transforming into something new entirely. The second category of the abject, 'the recognizable abject and the abject with a clean, false face', relates to the notion of 'duplicity and disguise in relation to horror'.[36] With reference to vampire fiction, the recognisable abject can be witnessed, on the one hand, in vampires' monstrous embodiment, for instance in Stoker's Dracula. Sheridan Le Fanu's Carmilla, on the other hand, disguises herself as a beautiful aristocrat and hence, her abjection comes with 'a clean, false face'. This doubling of the monstrous and the abject – one is designated as such from the start, and the other's duplicitous abjection is revealed slowly – adds to the overall destabilisation of identity categories. The third group concerns those instances of the abject that remind us of sexual sameness and/or difference. This, of course, could be linked to the Freudian fear of castration and, more generally perhaps, to anxieties over sexual difference, gender non-conformity and loss of patriarchal power. The latter is emphasised via embodied reminders of sexual difference, such as birth, breastfeeding and menstruation. All vampire fictions are deeply concerned with primal scenes, birth scenes and exchange of blood, which blur gender distinctions and capitalise on culturally encoded fears of female embodiment and/or feminisation.

The final group of the abject analysed by Goodnow concerns the maternal. In contrast to the 'merely' feminine threat associated with menstruation (posited as internal wound) and reminder of lack and separation, the mother also signifies authority (which she had yielded before the father) and the power to reproduce. Thus, the sanitised and safe images of birth do not fall into the category of the abject; it is the violent, gory and bloody birth scenes that are posited as abject. The highly sensual but also emphatically secure scene of the Girl becoming a vampire in Gomez's *The Gilda Stories* is a far cry from the blood-spattered scene of Dracula nurturing Mina in a perverse amalgamation of suckling, oral sex and rape.

The final two groups: the abject connected with sexual difference/ sameness and the abject based on the maternal are the ones associated most strongly with familial relations. The critical corpus concerning family in connection with the abject and/or the processes of abjection in the Gothic and horror usually centres on Oedipalisation and nuclear family dynamics, women's attitude towards their mothers and the maternal, and their experiences of the transforming female body. For instance, Susana Araújo states that 'the female gothic appropriation of the female body' shifts the emphasis from a necessarily negative gesture of repudiation to a more positive possibility of re-identification with the maternal. Araújo also points out a certain paradox embedded in feminist rewritings of Gothic fiction: 'the subversion of gender discourses remains possible only through

102 • House of Horrors

the recognition of the inscription of these categories within signification.'[37] I would argue that by rewriting (male-centred) vampire scripts, women writers also rewrite the contours and ramifications of the abject. In a way, just like the abject remains a part and parcel of the phallogocentric system of meaning in which the maternal (and the feminine) must be expelled in the process of subjectification, feminist Gothic and horror reimaginings of the vampire remain firmly within the frameworks already established by male traditions. I agree with Araújo that through a 're-examination of the abject female body' such revisions 'mount pertinent critiques of social constructions of femininity as sustained by male and female Gothic traditions. In doing so, they challenge traditional Gothic roles and parody inherited generic structures and conventions'.[38]

Gilda's Sensual Vampires

First published in 1991, *The Gilda Stories* took Jewelle Gomez ten years to finish. Its ethical complexity, the episodic nature of the narrative, generic ambiguity, and an innovative approach to vampirism have eluded attempts at critical classification for more than three decades. Cedric Gael Bryant places *The Gilda Stories* squarely within the African-American Gothic tradition alongside Toni Morrison's *Beloved* and Richard Wright's *Native Son*.[39] In contrast, Judith E. Johnson contends that Jewelle Gomez's book is not really a horror novel because her rewriting of canonical plots is too extensive and positive identification with the Other transcends the confines of horror or Gothic texts, which makes Gomez' fiction utopian rather than horrific.[40] Jerry Rafiki Jenkins, in 'Race, Freedom, and the Black Vampire', chooses Alexandre Dumas' *Le Vampire* (1851) as *Gilda*'s precursor, thus breaking with the white-only literary tradition.[41] Rather than reiterate the stories of Dracula and his cohorts, Jenkins points to the influence of African, Caribbean and Louisianan vampire mythologies and twentieth-century Black vampires in cinema and literature. Gomez herself situates her work in the tradition of speculative fiction, which to her mind encompasses diverse works of both science fiction and fantasy writers such as H. G. Wells, Anne Rice, Stephen King, Edgar Allan Poe and Ursula Le Guin.[42] In an interview celebrating the twentieth anniversary of the publication of *The Gilda Stories*, Gomez stresses the influence of LGBT and 1980s feminist movements on her work. She adds that *Gilda* could be seen as a direct descendent of Joanna Russ's works, and *The Female Man* (1975)

Blood(y) Ties in Vampire Fictions • 103

in particular stands as a pivotal piece of lesbian, feminist speculative fiction.[43] Gomez also emphasises Gilda's debt to Samuel R. Delany's science fiction novels; not in terms of style, of course, but in that Gilda embodies a queer concept of remaking oneself that has been central to Delany's oeuvre and, more generally, LGBTQ+ speculative fiction of the past four decades. As Jenkins muses in his book-length study of Black vampires, in order 'to claim vampires as her own and to give long-term literary and political significance to the lives of black lesbians', Gomez had to 'de-whiten, de-straighten, de-male, and de-pain the vampire myth'.[44]

Gomez set out to rewrite heteronormative plots, which abject the lesbian by positioning her outside heterosexual kinship structures. In her study of the lesbian Gothic, Paulina Palmer enumerates tactics and techniques employed by women writers to counter the abjection conferred on lesbian characters; she specifically mentions the issue of agency and subjectivity ascribed to lesbian characters (either in the form of first-person narration or a focalised third-person narrative, the latter of which is employed in Gomez's novel). Another tactic would be frustrating stereotypical depictions of lesbians as loners, marginalised outcasts and misfits, and stressing their ties and contributions to the community[45] – this is precisely what Gomez does in *The Gilda Stories*. To quote Palmer again, '[s]trategies of denaturalization and deconstruction, typical of the postmodern, feature prominently in feminist/lesbian culture and literature in relation to institutions such as the family and heterosexuality, along with the reworking of genre and convention'.[46] Wisker also stresses how contemporary women authors rescue the lesbian vampire from her sordid punishment meted out by patriarchal authority for the supposed breach of social decorum and dissolution of familial ties.[47] And just as the lesbian figure is deconstructed via postmodern recuperation of the non-normative, so is the vampire.

The Gilda Stories is a series of chronologically ordered tales beginning in 1850 and ending in 2050. The novel closes on a loop, as the readers follow the life of a Black, lesbian female vampire from her escape from slavery in 1850 to her escape from vampire-hunters in 2050. The unnamed Girl, a fugitive slave, is found by Gilda I (or Miss Gilda), a white woman, who takes her in and, together with her partner and lover, a Lakota woman, Bird, decides to turn her into a vampire with the Girl's joyous consent. Soon after, Gilda I, being tired of all the wars and suffering that she has witnessed, opts for true death (and ends her life permanently) and the hitherto unnamed Girl takes over her name, thus becoming Gilda II (or just Gilda) for the remainder of the novel. We then accompany Gilda over

104 • House of Horrors

the next two centuries as she adopts different identities and social roles: the proprietor of a feminist-inspired nineteenth-century brothel, the owner of a women's beauty salon in the 1950s, a theatre-company producer in the 1970s, a blues singer in the 1980s, and a cyber-romance writer in 2020, among others. In all those roles, she aligns herself with a Black 'womanist' culture and acts as an activist, guardian and artist in relation to other Black women in need of help or inspiration. Through this Gomez tries to bypass what she and Barbara Smith described in their 1990 essay on homophobia in Black communities as the rigidity of Black womanhood stereotypes, inevitably based on heteronormative familial relations: a stately wife and/or a single mother.[48]

The remaking of herself is enabled and fostered through Gilda's relationship with other women, both vampire and human. Reminiscent of Adrienne Rich's lesbian continuum, Gilda's relations with women move smoothly along crisscrossing axes: mother-daughter, friend-lover, sister-stranger. In this respect, her relationships, both in their emotional and material dimensions, echo Deleuzian-Guattarian becomings rather than simple linear movements from A to B. Each time Gilda encounters a new community, she allows herself to be the touched and shaped by new intensities, speeds, flows of desire and embodied experiences, which demarcate not only her romantic and/or platonic relationships with people of different genders but also her feeding encounters with strangers. For instance, Gilda moves between different familial functions such as a daughter and then a lover (to Bird), a sister and then a mother (to Julius). Gilda's coming of age and coming out of her vampiric mothers' embrace frustrate popular assumptions about kinship, heritage and inheritance. As Victoria Amador notes, Gilda's 'lesbian inheritance as well as self-determined demise [of the first Gilda] subverts traditional hetero-patriarchal lineage, law and mentorship'.[49] The absent Gothic mother is supplanted not by one but two mothers, Gilda I and her lover Bird, both of whom bestow knowledge and matrilineal inheritance on the Girl. For Palmer, however, the figure of an absent mother informs all of Gilda's relationship with women,[50] especially those in which she herself adopts a motherly stance towards them and tries to fill both a communal and personal gap in their lives.

Early on, Gilda is schooled by the older vampires in the importance of having a vampire (rather than a short-lived human) family and establishing it very carefully: 'It must be done not simply out of your own need or desire but rather because of a mutual need' (p. 69). Even though the vampire family is, in fact, based on blood ties (just like a conventional heteronormative family), Gomez queers this new familial unit by dismantling 'the male/female dynamic of gendered norms'.[51] The emphasis is placed on the:

> individual's ability to choose and 'create' the 'family' [which] not only bypasses heterosexuality and often negates the male presence as a necessary and powerful 'head' of the family, but also takes agency in the 'act' itself – naming and claiming identity as a family without procreation a necessary component either.[52]

The identity that Gilda develops is not regulated by traditional kinship – that is, by 'joining of race and sex in the reproduction of a pure, unsullied, white, straight bloodline' – rather, her identity emerges as 'the fabrication of nodes of connection via affinities, affections, tastes, distastes, labors, pleasures, technical wirings, attractions, repulsions, and chemical responses'.[53] What is more, the queer family created by Gilda is no longer a place where hierarchical structures are to be recreated in the name of family values or family protection; rather her family of choice serves to provide a safe space for experiencing comfort, intimacy and pleasure.

As already mentioned, Gilda moves from the position of a child to lover or a mother to sister with ease unthinkable within heteronormative kinship frameworks; for instance, after turning Julius – the very first family member she chose on her own – she writes to her friends and says that 'we have delivered a brother for me' (p. 192). Not only does she become Julius's sister, but also shares her parental abilities with her friends by using the plural 'we', even though, strictly speaking, Julius's turning was physically performed by Gilda alone. Similarly, Gomez's concept of vampire family 'carries queer resonances', as Gilda's family repudiates the Law of the Father, and instead structures kinship on 'the direct transmission of blood/sexual pleasure'.[54] This reconstituted queer family 'reflects a genealogy based on the direct exchange of body fluids'.[55] Blood in these exchanges is transformed from an abject, degrading and polluting symbol of a rape-like violation of the victim into a joyous rebirth, an explosion of *jouissance* and a *petit mort*.[56] In Kristeva's original study, *jouissance* is linked to the rejected maternal body and mother-child dyad of the past; however, in *The Gilda Stories* the lost pleasure is recovered by Gilda's successful rewriting of the vampiric blood ritual. In *Lesbian Gothic*, Palmer recalls Creed's study of the monstrous feminine in which Creed links the

106 • House of Horrors

exchange of blood in lesbian vampire fiction with a reversed primal scene of birth, which redefines mother/daughter relationship in terms of pleasure rather than abjection, and which is exactly what Gomez accomplishes in the scene where Gilda I 'births' Gilda II.

Hall underlines how 'the sensual giving and sharing of blood queers the heterosexual dynamics of male penetration and ejaculation into female receptive parts by stressing the mutuality of the acts and the desires'.[57] As Kathy Davis Patterson suggests, 'Gomez deemphasizes the connection between feeding and rape so common in vampire fiction and portrays vampirism itself as no longer an exercise of distinctly masculine power'.[58] Patterson also praises the skilful reappraisal of lesbian vampiric love and female homosexuality as such, which is no longer presented as a repulsive act of draining the victim and destroying her family. In conventional vampire narratives, the female vampire often poses a threat to the patriarchal heterosexual family by targeting helpless brides, daughters and sisters. In this she is positioned as abject because 'she does not respect the dictates of the law which set down the rules of proper sexual conduct'.[59] Gilda, however, is not a narcissist lesbian predator searching for her mirror image – a popular portrayal of lesbian vampires in the 1970s and 1980s.[60] Hall also points out the near-rape scene at the beginning of the novel, which disrupts a non-consensual straight sex act in that it is the Girl who finally penetrates her would-be rapist with a knife likened to her mother's hand earlier in the novel: 'He started to enter her, but before his hand finished pulling her open, while it still tingled with the softness of her insides, she entered him with her heart which was now a wood-handled knife' (p. 11).

Gilda interrupts white male ontologies of desire too, as she refuses to engage in the performance of non-white bodies in pain and/or female bodies in pain, two of the most persistent tropes in postmodern horror fiction. Commenting on the (in)visibility of the Black body, Jenkins points to the ways in which historically Black bodies in pain were staged for white men's consumption across history.[61] Thus, blackness has come to be most visible (and readable) through painful associations and stories of trauma. Gilda, however, never hurts (or kills) people from whom she takes nourishment. More than that, the moment of taking blood, which in classic vampire fictions is heavily laced with patriarchal vocabulary of submission, dominance, hierarchy and sexual violence, is replaced with the concept of a fair exchange. Bird teaches Gilda to leave something good behind in exchange for painlessly drained blood – a feeling, an affect, an idea that would help the human and set them on the right path. Even the stereotypical phallic white fangs are missing; instead, a small vagina-like incision is made for sucking/suckling, which is then healed by the vampire's saliva.

Through these affirmative gestures, Gilda moves away from the double abjection associated both with a lesbian and a vampire. Instead, we can see how Gomez 'reworks, with perverse displacements, the primal scene of birth' and 'by taking a woman as her lover, indirectly embarks on a taboo return to the pleasures of the mother/daughter relationship'.[62] Hall points to the absolute reproductive freedom that Gomez ascribes to Gilda:

> Gomez . . . represent[s] female sexual development and adult sexual relationships that 'queer' traditional familial, male-dominated scripts. Changes that 'normally' happen to 'girls' through time – the transition from original love of the mother to directing desire to the father as love object, to husband, and the trajectory into marriage and motherhood – are notably absent, as are children.[63]

In Halberstam's understanding, queer subjects are those who 'live outside the reproductive and familial time',[64] yet Gilda's queer temporality resides in her decision to look for alternative scripts of reproduction and family formation. It is through the character of Julius, her child-brother-lover, that we can observe a queering of family functions, as his person fuses seemingly conflicting attachments. Commenting on Black vampire fiction (with Gilda being its prime example), Jenkins asserts that queering is an essential feature of contemporary Black vampire fiction; such texts queer not only 'the traditional vampire narrative, [but also] the Black literary imagination, and their guises of universality' and have 'the potential to denormalize our disdain of hybridity, our boundaries of power, and our obsession with utopias'.[65]

Still, although it is tempting to read Gilda as a subversive figure that successfully decentres a number of normative suppositions, the vampires in Gomez's novel do not offer a mere reversal of the margin-to-centre relation or enact a decentring as described by Hollinger.[66] Rather, 'Gomez envisions her protagonist . . . as capable of making choices about how to read and how to (re)locate her/self within the complex politics and aesthetics of (in)visibility and enforced normalcy'.[67] Gilda weaves herself seamlessly into the fabric of American society, joins several different communities (a theatre company, a small town, a Black urban neighbourhood, etc.) and participates quite successfully in the capitalist system. It is only after people begin hunting vampires for their rejuvenating blood that she is forced to leave the United States and go into hiding in South America.

Christopher S. Lewis, in 'Queering Personhood', links heteronormative families with their tacit racialisation of unwelcome others. He writes that:

> The Girl/Gilda's practice of family does not concretize the racialized consumption/"entitlement" of fathers and sons and thereby disrupts the masculinist policies of gender resoluteness that typically define the practice of family. Furthermore, the Girl/Gilda's family exists with racial distinctions that are not hierarchical, but rather, cooperative.[68]

At the end of the novel, in 2050, Gilda's family has finally come together to hide from persecution in South America: all her lovers and friends are there (two Black lesbians, two white gay men, one straight Black man, one Native American lesbian); however, among the various configurations of gender, race and sexuality, a white heterosexual male remains markedly absent.

For Auerbach, Jewelle Gomez's *The Gilda Stories* is yet another illustration of typical 'Reaganesque vampire fiction', in which vampires function as 'a diluted vision of benevolent endangered species'.[69] In her view, queer theorists have rushed to hail the vampires as ideal monsters because they are able to encapsulate the tensions and ambiguities of *queer*, an elusive concept that lurks in the shadows, inherently impermanent, incandescent, frightening and alluring at the same time, spilling out of boundaries and signifying forbidden fruit. Auerbach's ironic distance from queer theory is palpable when she describes *The Gilda Stories* as a work 'meant to be an enlightened response to the sexism inherent in the lesbian vampire tradition, but Gilda's virtue defangs her into another paralyzing stereotype: that of the good woman. Gomez's vampires are inhibited by their self-righteous decade, whose protests dissipate in piety'.[70] Still, it seems that Auerbach does not take into account other late 1980s and early 1990s vampire narratives that do not necessarily follow this Reaganesque defanging, such as Melanie Tem's *Desmodus* (1995) or Elizabeth Engstrom's *Black Ambrosia*, not to mention Poppy Z. Brite's/Billy Martin's early 1990s fiction, which responds very clearly to the changes in the LGBTQ+ communities and new developments in critical theory. One could argue in fact that

Blood(y) Ties in Vampire Fictions • 109

it is Auerbach who does most of the defanging herself in connection to *The Gilda Stories*. Bemoaning the fact that Gomez's fiction lacks the special 'diffuse menace' of a nineteenth-century *Carmilla*, Auerbach remains heavily invested in a plot in which lesbian vampires must challenge patriarchal power and destroy it to be deemed effective and threatening. Gilda's nuanced gender politics and the radical nature of her relationships do not fit the rebellion narrative, which by its very nature must be adversarial and confrontational.[71]

Auerbach also criticises Gomez's vampires for their retreat into 'safe places', thus again valorising an adversarial kind of non-normative action. She insists that both Anne Rice's and Jewelle Gomez's vampire protagonists 'have learned identity politics. They live and love in enclaves of their own, scarcely bothering to infiltrate mortal drawing-rooms or bedrooms or boardrooms. In the Reagensque years, they are so clannish and self-enclosed that they present no threat'.[72] One might ask why should the vampires 'infiltrate' rooms connected with normative family life, reproduction and power, in the first place? Is it vampires' responsibility to be the go-to cultural Other that is always supposed to mount an attack on the centre from its marginalised position? The semantics of 'infiltration' seems troubling too, as it positions vampires as manipulative outsiders who need to 'pass' in order to enact changes in a given community. Gilda proves that change does not have to follow such restrictive and clichéd paradigms.

Escaping the 'Little Wife' in *Black Ambrosia*

While Gomez's vampires were able to find support and protection within their families of choice, Elizabeth Engstrom's 1988 novel *Black Ambrosia* presents a vampire's solitary existence filled with self-doubt and frenzied oscillation between self-abhorrence and self-love.[73] Lisa Kröger and Melanie R. Anderson, authors of *Monster, She Wrote: the Women who Pioneered Horror and Speculative Fiction* (2019), note that Engstrom's writing has been awarded various labels over the past four decades, including speculative fiction and erotica, but then 'she is also a writer of the best kind of horror fiction: stories that present the human condition coming to grips with the aftermath of trauma and grief'.[74] *Black Ambrosia* is structured along a series of escapes: the protagonist, Angelina, manages to escape her lower-middle-class white family and dreary small-town existence, but she can never fully escape her human nature or her vampirism. In contrast to the self-assured vampires from *The Gilda Stories*, Angelina struggles with her vampiric proclivities and experiments with several identities and self-conceptions before finally accepting who (or what) she is. Because Angelina's vampirism is never fully explained (nor confirmed, for that matter), Engstrom is free to investigate different guises of vampiric behaviour and different meanings attached to the vampire. Angelina is alternately presented as a psychologically disturbed person, a member of a separate species, a supernatural creature, a wild animal, a carrier of transmittable disease or a host of a (supernatural) parasite. Interestingly, what links all those identities is the abject nature of vampirism – the killing, bloodletting and blood-drinking, a non-human ferocity, associations with dirt, death and dark maternal eroticism.

The novel begins with Angelina, the protagonist and first-person narrator, admitting that she never intended to become a vampire. This comment marks the first and last self-reflexive moment, where the word 'vampire' is mentioned by her. The book follows a linear narrative in which Angelina describes her life in what we learn at the end is a journal written at a psychiatric hospital. Each entry is followed by a brief note from a chosen supporting character, usually one of the people that she has met on her travels or Boyd, the man who falls for Angelina and then starts hunting her. These short entries, which resemble interview notes or case files, fill in the gaps in Angelina's account, offer a supposedly more objective view on her actions, and slowly reveal Boyd's growing confusion and emotional investment in the hunt. *Black Ambrosia* is to a considerable extent structured as a road novel, as it follows Angelina's journeys across late-1980s America. Her hitchhiking trips are interposed with three longer periods of settling down: in Westwater with Lewis, a man she meets on the road, in Seven Slope living on her own, and finally in her hometown of Wilton, where she is finally apprehended.

Engstrom does not provide definitive answers as to the true nature of Angelina's vampirism. There are clues suggesting that she could be a separate species, a supernatural being with telepathic and hypnotic powers or a mentally disturbed woman suffering from clinical vampirism (porphyria). In fact, during one of her longer periods of blood abstinence, Angelina is sure that she 'must have been insane' and 'seriously mentally ill' to kill four people and drink their blood (pp. 116, 120). Angelina's stepfather admits that he knew something was wrong with her and regrets not killing her the night she left home. Angelina misread his hesitant behaviour that night and thought he was wavering between crying or raping her. One must wonder why her stepfather would want to kill her in the first place and what signs of her future murderous self he might have noticed, sharing a house with her for years.

Angelina is described both in terms of a feral animal and a supernatural being. Her scent is compared to a fox-lair smell, and Lewis thinks of her nocturnal activities as 'reptilian' (p. 101). Another non-human connection is the rats' nest she finds in her Seven Slopes apartment and which she simply embraces. On several occasions she notes the distance between her and other humans; for instance, when she describes how her keen sense of smell allowed her to predict people's emotions and behaviours. At the end of the novel, after having killed a couple of children in her hometown, she can sense the paranoia rising around her: 'witch-hunter, lynch mobs, and angry, outraged gatherings turning monstrous themselves' (p. 296). A young boy who recognises the supernatural nature of her threat knows 'too much lore' and hangs a crucifix above his bed (p. 297), but crosses, garlic and wooden stakes have no effect on Angelina.

Still, even though Angelina snorts at garlic or religious symbols, a few typical vampire tropes are deployed by Engstrom quite effectively. For instance, when Angelina spirals down into a feeding and killing frenzy in Seven Slopes, she decides to build a coffin-like container for herself as a form of protection against her unsavoury desires. She leaves this catafalque in her Bela Lugosi-like cape, which she used to avoid spilling blood on her dresses. Boyd then recalls how her flat 'smelled like a den, or a lair, or a bat cave' (p. 183). When she returns to her hometown and hides in the cellar of her childhood home, she has already mastered the craft of vampiric hypnosis. She chooses children because of their malleability, and she either lures them outside or visits them in their bedrooms, which echoes Lucy Westenra's choice of victims in Stoker's *Dracula*. It seems that the more comfortable she feels in her vampire skin, the more closely she follows traditional vampire scripts. Conversely, when she fails to follow her chosen vampire script, she becomes ill. For instance, when she tries to switch to animal blood, she has an allergic reaction to lamb blood. When she kills Joshua, a war veteran, for no apparent reason and without following the orgasmic feeling that she associates with feeding, she ends up vomiting the blood: 'The sweet, tangy ambrosia that had been mine the night before had turned black and diseased and hateful during the course of the day, during my sleep, bloating my stomach, now to be spewed forth in a raging gush of acid' (p. 177). Wrong blood,

112 • House of Horrors

acquired outside of Angelina's careful ritual, no longer sustains her and transforms into an abjected bodily fluid that she must violently expel.

The novel charts Angelina's second adolescence (that is, the process of becoming a vampire) and her teenage-like symptoms of rebelling against a mysterious female 'Voice' that guides her actions. The novel does not reveal the source of the voice, which could be a sign of Angelina's psychosis, a figment of her imagination (which takes over a maternal function from her dead mother) or a parasitic being schooling her in vampirism. Twice she attempts to drown out the female whisper and consciously re-join humanity. And for a while she does genuinely yearn for 'a life-style of normalcy' and 'yellow kitchen curtains' just like the ones her mother used to own (p. 118). She rents an apartment and gets a job in a call centre, but when winter months come to her sleepy Colorado town, she finds it difficult to resist the call of darkness. She is confused and wishes for a real place in a community:

> The loneliness was suddenly overwhelming. I felt a need to share with someone the terrors of the night, the confusion about my past that strangled my thoughts. I needed someone to talk to, to be with. I needed to learn not just the definition of the word remorse, but to see how other people lived with it. And *remorse* wasn't the only word I didn't understand. Altruism was another. So were compromise, and sacrifice. All those social words. (p. 127, original emphasis)

Paradoxically, her joining the social body is presented precisely in terms of painful sacrifices and compromises. She needs to repudiate those parts of herself that do not fit the social reality and force her vampirism back into the closet. In Kristeva's understanding, abjection is critical not only for delineating the borders of an individual body but of the social body as well. That is why Angelina knows her vampirism cannot be part of her if she wants to settle down in Seven Slopes. No longer feeling 'special' the way she did during her first kills, she now believes a short-term insanity took over her life. The murders and the mutilations were an aberration, a short lapse that she can put behind her quickly and neatly. The fact that she refuses to confront what she did signals her reluctance to see vampirism as part of herself in that she is abjecting her vampiric needs and her vampiric corporeality.

In *Amending the Abject Body* (2004), Deborah C. Covino argues that abjection designates 'those parts of us that we refuse' and that we do not accept in our constitution.[75] The abject then acts as a necessary reminder of the material (not merely maternal). Covino argues that the reigning aesthetics, which deems certain bodies and certain body parts abject, is culturally conditioned and sustained (and thus liable to diachronic transformations), but instead of looking at abjection through the lens of alienation and individuation, she sees abjection as a group project, 'an act of orientation to a welcoming community, populated by clean and proper bodies'.[76] Abjection, then, can be understood as 'a metaphor for the process of maintaining the social body',[77] a body that is accepted in the (real or imagined) community of proper bodies. Such a re-contextualisation of abjection can be extended to both vampire and human communities in *Black Ambrosia*, as in Angelina's case vampirism signifies her inability to connect with others, her psychopathic tendencies, her lack of social skills and scorn for typical human needs linked to communal existence. For a while, as she gets better, she also begins to perform better in social terms: she strikes up friendships with other women at work, and she even begins 'to dress like a young lady' (p. 120). Of course, such descriptions suggest that her belonging to a community depends solely on her acting skills and that she is in fact performing a certain kind of femininity *and* sociality.

Angelina does not want to transgress and become visible in her community. Instead, for a short while she attempts to act like ordinary people – to want the same things they desire and despise the same objects they hate. Of course, she is unable to keep up this façade for long, just as she was unable to play the role of Lewis's companion for long. In fact, her separation from community is also what draws her to Boyd – she is right to sense a similar kind of emptiness and loneliness in him: 'We were in the vast minority . . . Most people were basically the same, showing healthy expressions of their individual differences. They married, had best friends, served on committees, and played bridge' (p. 108). Their connection rests on their shared dissatisfaction with middle-class standards of happiness. Boyd, too, begins to notice his proximity to Angelina and the reasons why he keeps hunting her: 'Because I didn't want school. And I didn't want work. I didn't want the same old friends and the same old place to live, right near my old man and Bill [Boyd's brother] anymore' (pp. 209–10). He no longer wants to follow in his father's footsteps, become a construction worker and remain satisfied with the small life that envelopes him slowly.

Angelina already expresses this anti-materialist sentiment already at the start of the novel. When her mother dies and all her possessions are sold, teenage Angelina is relieved to be unburdened of ownership and is glad to leave her stepfather's house and travel on her own. She spends a year as a transient, moving from place to place, without direction or hurry. When she moves in with Lewis, an amiable albeit boring, man, his house is described as 'a modern nothing', a place entirely foreign to her but where she stays and plays the 'little-wife role' for a while (pp. 36, 43). She remains completely detached from Lewis, feeling neither indebted to nor entrapped by him, but she manages to master at least some semblance of genuine feelings for his sake. However, when her transformation into a night-creature leads to a loss of consciousness during the day, she knows it is time to leave. After all, 'Lewis had standards, requirements. He would want me to be home every night' (p. 96). Angelina does not want to be tied down by conventional long-term relationship expectations such as marriage, sex and parenthood. Leaving Lewis, she wishes 'for rapid appreciation on his home, and a wife and sons to keep his level of respectability right where he felt most comfortable' (p. 103). The sardonic statement unites several tenets of middle-class life: heterosexual romance and marriage, monogamy, financial security, house ownership and, finally, sons rather than daughters to carry the patrilineal family name.

The novel, rather predictably, connects vampiric activity with sexual arousal and sex. Witnessing her mother and stepfather having sex, pre-pubescent Angelina begins to experiment both with masturbating and drinking her own blood. If we were to follow a more logical explanation for her adult vampirism, this episode could serve as an example of an early-age imprint that left Angelina with a blood fetish. Years later, the very first person she kills is a stranger trying to rape her. His friend later recalls that '[t]hat girl was no girl, if you get my drift' (p. 17) – an ambiguous statement pointing both to her non-humanity and potentially disturbing gender non-conformity. Her first kill is shortly followed by her first sexual experience, a cold and detached affair that gives her little pleasure, but which she nonetheless deems necessary in terms of reaching full physical maturity (for a vampire that is). Her first predatory kill is conscious, as she can no longer contain 'an ancient, innate, dormant hunger' that overcomes her thoughts and her body (p. 56). After killing three people, she leaves Westwater and Lewis behind and takes up her road trip again. However, she is now being followed by Boyd, a young man with whom she struck an immediate connection back in Westwater and who soon realised that she is the killer responsible for the deaths in his hometown.

Angelina keeps rationalising her kills in a manner strikingly similar to *The Gilda Stories*. She imagines herself as an angel of death, providing her male victims with pleasure, rest and release rather than excruciating pain and torturous death. She sees herself both as a skilled huntress and a semi-saviour of lost human souls. The voice of her god-like companion tells her to share her 'gift' with her victims (p. 71). Angelina reflects that her 'freedom from responsibility was no mistake . . . Freedom from family tethers, from material assets, from even the basic desires to have these things' meant that she was selected by a higher force for a higher purpose (p. 71). She bucks away from accusations of murder; instead, she insists 'I hadn't murdered the lad at all. I had loved him. I had loved him totally and completely, with my entire body and soul' (p. 85). If anything, she is mad at the townspeople and the police that they are unable to recognise her proficiency, bravery and skill.

Her self-perception as a huntress is another link to Boyd, himself an avid hunter. But while he kills for pure pleasure and release, Angelina genuinely believes she is on a special mission. Yet while he is praised, she is vilified. Even though Boyd is preternaturally linked with her in a soul-mate-like, telepathic manner, he also staunchly refuses to see her as an otherworldly being or a vampire: '[c]ompulsive, obsessive, self-destructive, and homicidal, true, but sick nevertheless. There was nothing supernatural here. It was just Angelina . . . A misdirected, sad, psychopathic case' (p. 322). Boyd's unnatural connection with Angelina is finally proven on the last pages of the novel when readers learn that she carried her 'music' to Boyd when she bit his arm and sucked his blood briefly. It is now Angelina who is becoming the female Voice in Boyd's head, just like an unnamed female voice guided Angelina on her road to becoming a vampire.

After an unsuccessful attempt to keep her darker instincts in check in Seven Slopes, Angelina finally succumbs to them again. This time her feeding is almost indistinguishable from sex. In a scene highly reminiscent of Dracula feeding Mina from a slit in his breast, Angelina grips her male victim's chest and sucks blood out of his breast, 'teasing the nipple of [her] nourishment with [her] teeth' (p. 145). The kind of abjection has as much to do with gender reversal (a woman sucking a man's breast) as with the blurring of boundaries between feeding, suckling and sex. The connotations with feeding are strengthened in that Angelina chooses only the healthiest specimens she can find – non-smoking, non-drinking and athletic single men. Angelina is thus presented as a parasitic succubus, a praying mantis of sorts, who seduces and kills men at the height of sexual

116 • House of Horrors

passion. As Halberstam has noted, this kind of parasitic vampirism 'represents a bad or pathological sexuality, non-productive sexuality, a sexuality that exhausts and wastes and exists prior to and outside of the marriage contract'.[78] Angelina does not refuse a white middle-class ideal of a family life, child-rearing and monogamy, she violently perverts it. The heterosexual act becomes a parasitic rape in reverse and her emphasis on the partners' so-called 'good genetic material' mocks the heterosexual mating process in that she chooses healthy men for strictly dietary, not reproductive, purposes. Because both she and her victims are white, the genetic discourse might be also read in terms of racist anxiety over miscegenation, with vampirism posited as an intimate practice of literal blood-mixing.

The dark eroticism that erupts in *Black Ambrosia* is also linked to the maternal inclinations that Angelina pursues over the course of the novel. On the one hand, Angelina mentions her father only once – he died when she was eight and she has almost no memories of him. Her mother, on the other hand, was a much more important figure for her as evidenced by the capital 'm' that always accompanies the 'Mother'. Soon after her mother dies, Angelina leaves her stepfather and her family house. Her mother seemed to be Angelina's only mooring and without this maternal anchoring she is set adrift. Throughout the rest of the novel Angelina develops and matures through her relations and experiences with women rather than men. After her the very first kill, she begins hearing sensuous music that floods her with pleasure and which she comes to associate with drinking blood – the titular 'black ambrosia'. Embedded in the music she also discerns a voice, which she identifies as belonging to a nameless female presence or 'She' as Angelina calls her. They enter a master-servant relationship, in which Angelina promises to serve Her, satisfy Her and make Her proud of her vampiric accomplishments. Their relationship is also erotically charged, as Angelina finds intense pleasure in Her visits. Usually, she sees her mistress as a mist or as a beautiful mouth near her face. It is suggested that She might be a manifestation of Angelina's dark nature, terrifying and beautiful, but mentally unhinged. She could be 'a she-devil', that is, another vampire who schools Angelina in the dark art of hunting and killing (p. 244). Angelina rebels against her like a teenager and refuses to be 'Her puppet, Her pawn' (p. 164), yet she returns to Her again and again. The bizarre presence is suggestive of an older, more mature and more knowledgeable female, a maternal figure of sorts who educates, sways and seduces the younger woman, feeding into a predatory lesbian stereotype.

Blood(y) Ties in Vampire Fictions • 117

Possibly, both Angelina's vampirism and the female voice are her attempts at dealing with the trauma of being sexually assaulted and having to kill in self-defence. The voice that directs her to kill men and drink their blood may be explained as Angelina creating a protective maternal figure who can assume responsibility for the murders, through which Angelina is re-enacting her sexual assault trauma. The big red mouth that stands for the mysterious female figure can signify vampire's orality, as well as a threat of being swallowed and subsumed by the predatory female presence. In this sense, She might also represent the archaic mother – a figure threatening Angelina's subjectivity and individuation while also tempting her into absolute freedom from selfhood and accountability.

Two other women play important roles in her development: Sarah and Rosemary, both of whom she meets during her travels. Soon after leaving Lewis, she meets Sarah, a single mother of Native American descent. When Sarah finds Angelina, who has been on the road for days and is now suffering from exhaustion and exposure, she takes her in for a couple of days. Soon Angelina comes to see Sarah as her own personal saviour and a paragon of a genuinely happy, well-adjusted, healthy, young woman. For years to come, Angelina thinks of Sarah as a beacon of hope and even makes a conscious effort to be more like Sarah – stable, sane and satisfied with her life. Yet the dark call is too strong; unable to stop herself from killing, she leaves Seven Slopes and seeks Sarah out to find help and support once again. However, the moment she realises that Sarah's strength and happiness have evaporated, and she is now just another exhausted single mother trying to make ends meet, she kills her instead. On discovering that happiness and stability are at best a temporary respite in human life, Angelina's guilt, shame and regret dissipate completely.

Angelina's murder of Sarah is also a result of Angelina's encounter with Rosemary, whom Angelina meets shortly before reconnecting with Sarah. Right after escaping from Seven Slopes, when Angelina is on her way to Sarah, she meets Rosemary, a seemingly harmless elderly lady, who lures her with promises of help, but instead kidnaps Angelina and then rapes and tortures her for two days. Rosemary embodies another maternal figure, one who scars Angelina deeply and abandons her. Once again, the dark and violent maternal eroticism, one that threatens Angelina with total subjugation and disintegration, surfaces, but this time Angelina is no longer its instrument, but a helpless victim. Still, she refuses to acknowledge Rosemary's proclivities in terms of lesbianism. She reserves the highly sensual descriptions of same-sex erotic pleasure only for the Voice: 'She

118 • House of Horrors

was there. She cupped my chin in Her hands, ever so delicately, and Her touch was like velvet. Her love and warmth surrounded my delirious head' (p. 203). Rosemary, in stark contrast, is just a diseased, perverted creature of the night, who nonetheless correctly identifies their shared predilection for dark deeds, their 'baser passions, the ancient ones' (p. 213).

Violated and sick, Angelina attempts to reconnect with Sarah, and when this fails, she returns to Her and recalls how '[s]he welcomed me back with kisses and floods of ecstasy, wave after wave of orgasmic pleasure' (p. 247). What follows is their 'honeymoon': 'I opened myself to Her so completely, so totally, that I felt filleted, exposed, with no secrets, nothing withheld' (p. 249). Such descriptions define their union not only in terms of lesbian desire, but also matrimony and mother-daughter ties. It is only when Angelina insists on seeing Her in full that she finally recognises 'the vileness of Her nature' and the horror of Her existence (p. 251). One could argue that what Angelina sees at that moment is nothing more than her own reflection – her own monstrosity, murderous deeds and the pain she inflicted on others. At first, she is understandably horrified, but then she comes to understand why she cannot escape from Her. From this moment on in the novel, the Voice no longer appears. Angelina notices her new 'lean and statuesque' body, 'a new posture,' which overnight 'changed [her] into a person worthy of worship' (p. 253). Thus, she becomes her own Voice and supplants her previous mistress with herself or, conversely, she finally realises that there never was a She. Angelina ends up assimilating (becoming) her mistress, teacher and a maternal guardian, a process which seems to mock the final separation of an adult child from its overbearing parent.

The novel's ambiguity may thus be interpreted as Angelina's ambivalence towards subjectification. It is only after she sees the full horror of the female presence that the voice disappears, and Angelina's moral and emotional confusion is lifted. It is important to remember that the horrific moment of recognition, which incidentally interrupts the marital bliss of Angelina and her mistress, is yet another image of the archaic mother. Still, instead of repudiation and abjection, Angelina opts for fusion with this threatening figure. In the wake of this process, Angelina announces that 'She and I have become one – or was it always so?' (p. 254). Interestingly, Angelina becomes her cruellest self when her maturation into a fully fledged vampire is completed. If her earlier choice of victims (young and healthy men) might have signified Angelina's desire to work through a traumatic sexual attack, she now chooses the most taboo victim: young, innocent children. She opts for the easiest prey not because she lacks skills but because she enjoys toying with them and wants to instil dread in her old community. She seems to be punishing her hometown in the most macabre way possible; however, Engstrom never explains why Angelina feels the need to do so. The fact that she switches from male victims to children might be construed as a sign of her ambivalence towards reproduction. Back in her hometown, she goes into pure survival mode. Now, as a mature vampire, she feels 'fertile' and knows that 'perpetuating the species' has become of paramount importance (p. 303). On the one hand, she seems to be finally ready for companionship and reproduction; on the other, she kills children, who are the obvious goal of (human) reproduction.

At the end of the novel, as soon as Angelina moves into the cellar of her old family house, she begins to haunt the family that lives there now with disquieting erotic dreams. She selects the mother and her teenage son, Daniel, as her favourite playthings. Even though Daniel was able to resist Angelina's cull (and ultimately assisted Boyd in capturing her), his mother recalls that the pleasure Angelina brought her in her sleep was irresistible. The dreams were perverse and disturbing, but pleasurable, nonetheless. The connection between eroticism and vampirism is sealed through abject imagery of transgressive sex acts. In the mother's case, who maintains her heterosexual orientation, it is lesbian sex, and in Daniel's case it is sex with a minor. One cannot but wonder about Angelina's decision to concentrate her telepathic manipulation on these two family members. The mother, as an adult person, cannot be swayed and controlled as much as Daniel, which is why Angelina stops at teasing the woman through dark and unwanted eroticism. However, with Daniel she adopts a more controlling and demanding stance. For a short while she harbours a hope that the boy could become her apprentice, maybe even a future partner. Paradoxically, while she is trying to persuade Daniel into becoming her protege, she is also actively trying to kill his younger sister, which points to Angelina's ambivalence towards motherhood. Ultimately, Angelina fails to find a suitable apprentice in her hometown and settles for Boyd, who in capturing her becomes preternaturally linked to her.

Since the reliability of Angelina's first-person narration is repeatedly called into question by interceding case notes and interviews, the novel eschews explanations of any kind and refuses to provide any mythological, historical or even physiological background as to the nature of Angelina's vampiric desires. Indeed, her vampirism is also receptive to a more symbolic reading; that is, a parasitic disease of the mind which causes

120 • House of Horrors

increasingly aberrant behaviour in its host. Judging from Angelina's and Boyd's examples, only those people who are already marked as aberrant (i.e., not interested in settling down and meeting social expectations) are prone to this disease. In a particularly reactionary reading, Angelina's monstrosity resides also in her refusal to settle for one man and bear his children. Still longing for a past mother-daughter fusion of identities, she is incapable of making the rational, adult decisions that are expected of her. Instead, she seduces, kills and discards men after deadly one-night stands in a misandrist spectacle of violent female emancipation. And once she transforms into a child-killer, she crosses into the non-human realm. In a more sympathetic reading, Angelina's inability to carve out a space for herself in a society that values only certain types of feminine behaviour and accepts few alternatives regarding relationships and family life (or lack of thereof) means that she is forced to become the very opposite of what is respectable, healthy and welcomed. She transforms into a vampire because in a system based on binary oppositions, she must choose a side, and since she is not interested in the 'proper' middle-class existence, she opts for its very antithesis. Because Angelina's lust for blood is posited as being at odds with her delicate girly looks and her feminine gender (as noted often by herself and other characters), the 'troubling ontology' of her vampirism also points to her conflicted inner self.[79] As Milly Williamson explains, the conflict between the beautiful façade and monstrous internal desires in a vampire corresponds to the difficulty of experiencing one's self when one does not enjoy a normative identity[80] – an identity that, in Angelina's case, would mean being someone's happy 'little wife'.

Prodigal Children (Not) Coming Home

The winner of the Bram Stoker Award for the best debut novel in 1991 (tied with Koja's *The Cipher*), Melanie Tem's *Prodigal* might seem an odd choice for analysis in this chapter for a number of reasons: it does not concentrate on the vampire but rather on his victim; it focuses on spiritual/emotional vampirism; and it does away with blood as well as other traditional vampiric paraphernalia. *Prodigal* is also the only novel of the three that manages to sidestep Anne Rice's and Bram Stoker's hefty influence altogether. Mary Wilkins Freeman's 'Luella Miller' (1902) seems a more suitable literary predecessor for *Prodigal*, as both stories feature life-draining psychic vampires. Tem's novel also focuses on human-vampire friendships as seen

Blood(y) Ties in Vampire Fictions • 121

through the human protagonist's eyes, a narrative feature that harks back to Le Fanu's *Carmilla* and John Polidori's *The Vampyre*; although in contrast to those nineteenth-century classics, it is now a young child's focalisation that structures the whole plot.

Similarly to Engstrom's *Black Ambrosia*, Tem's *Prodigal* has been accorded virtually no academic scrutiny, with the sole exception being Gina Wisker's works. In *Horror Fiction*, she briefly describes a couple of Tem's stories and underlines how in her fiction 'family relationships are a prime location for horror, an expose of hypocrisy and simple repressive binary oppositions, taboos, and rituals, which prioritise some behaviours and exclude, demonise, and punish others'.[81] Although she focuses only on Tem's short stories, her comment on the centrality of family relationships in Tem's fiction can be extended to *Prodigal* as well:

> Melanie Tem undercuts conventional horror's neat reinforcing of the status quo in its closure, its packing away and staking of that which is terrifying because Other, abject, threatening to the status quo. Her work exposes and refuses the demonizing of our animal nature, our other selves, and the easy maintenance of taboos as ritual spells against any bit of questioning of this neat set of behaviors and beliefs.[82]

In another article, Wisker mentions Melanie Tem, alongside Katherine Forrest and Jewelle Gomez, as examples of women writers 'speaking the unspeakable' and 'counteract[ing] the marginalization and silencing of conventional, oppressive texts'.[83]

The title suggests a welcome return of the prodigal (son), but the son who returns is abjected through associations with physical decay, death and disease. The second site of the abject is located within psychic vampirism - an addiction-like disturbance that is linked to the eroticism of early adolescence, menarche and menstrual blood, birth/re-birth and Freudian primal scene. Risking the obvious, the title places the family at the centre of the narrative: the biblical story of a wayward son who turns away from his parents but is then forgiven and re-integrated into the family forms the main plot, which traces first the escapes and then the returns of its teenage protagonists. Because the novel's focaliser, Lucy, moves along the axis of childhood-adolescence, we can witness her changing perspectives on her older siblings' desertion, her parents' failures and her own budding teenage angst and sexuality.

122 • House of Horrors

We meet Lucy as she is struggling with her older brother's ghostly presence. Ethan, who escaped from a court-mandated children's home almost two years earlier, is now haunting Lucy and her mother. Interestingly, the hauntings began before his actual death, and they continue after it. The second oldest child, Rae, soon follows in her brother's footsteps and graduates from general teenage malaise to shoplifting, taking drugs and running away. Rae, just like her brother, then begins to haunt her parents and tries to warn Lucy that she might be next. A social worker, Jerry, who used to take special interest in Ethan and then Rae, invites Lucy to his group sessions – soon he is revealed to be a vampiric monster draining life from troubled kids.[84] Although the word 'vampire' is never used, the narrative leaves little doubt as to Jerry's supernatural status and the scenes of his feeding are always accompanied by suckling, slurping and biting sounds.

The narrative charts Lucy's progress from a precocious but innocent eleven-year-old to a moody and enraged twelve-year-old self. Ironically, when Lucy still firmly identifies as a child rather than a teen or a pre-teen, she can sense that there is something wrong with Jerry. Yet, the moment she hits puberty, she begins to navigate towards Jerry and yields easily to his charm. Tem brilliantly weaves together all the potential signs of trouble and the grooming tactics employed by Jerry. Lucy's conflicted and confused feelings and drastic mood swings, while typical for children her age, are precisely what draws Jerry to her in the first place.

The Brill family consists of eight people – the parents, Ethan (the son who is the first to disappear and die) and Rae (the oldest daughter who disappears soon after Ethan's death) and four younger children, but the narrator focuses on Lucy's relationships with her parents, especially the mother, and her two missing siblings. Because the narrative concentrates on the older children exclusively, Tem is free to portray the sheer predictability and repetitiveness of teenage angst. Each teenager in the Brill household goes through the same motions and falls into the same trap, and in each case the parents and younger siblings are unable to counter Jerry's influence.

Even though the title suggests a long-awaited return of an errant child, both Ethan's and Rae's attempts at returning are positioned as abject, meaning they are both caught in a limbo between living and non-living, and are neither subjects with agency (teenagers coming home) nor objects to be discovered (hidden corpses). It is the sweet and sour smell of decomposition that usually alerts Lucy to their presence. After one of Rae's visits, Lucy can still smell in her room 'a kind of sickening [smell],

Blood(y) Ties in Vampire Fictions • 123

like something half-dead or really really dirty' (p. 107). Ethan manifests himself similarly: 'She tasted coldness; her mouth puckered and her teeth hurt. She smelled Ethan, sour, as if he hadn't taken a shower in a long time, as if he were sick' (p. 36). Although Ethan needs her help, he cannot speak: 'His mouth was hanging open, crooked, as if hurt. It looked full of dirt or blood; Lucy felt sick' (p. 36). She also recalls that even before his disappearance Ethan had trouble communicating and was reduced to saying 'ugly things to everybody, obscenities and accusations and lies' (p. 37). However, after disappearing, he completely 'lost the power of speech' and was reduced to physical violence as his only means of communication. Manifesting as a wraithlike presence, he attacks Lucy and his mother and tries to strangle them on several occasions. The novel never explicitly states whether Ethan's ghostly violence towards his mother and sister is a sign of his resentment or a cry for help. In fact, the novel is also unclear as to whether these are genuine ghosts, psychic residues of the two teens' anger or figments of Lucy's imagination. Although Ethan visits his family both before and after his actual physical death, Rae does not die and her 'ghost' appears while she is still locked in Jerry's cellar.

Ethan reveals himself primarily to his mother, whereas Rae chooses her father, a fact that baffles Lucy. The father suggests to Lucy that this gendered pattern might be connected to 'teenagers' ambivalence toward the parent of the opposite sex' (p. 88). This pop-psychological reference to the Oedipal complex is complemented by scenes underscoring familial tensions arising from parent-child gender dynamics. For instance, when Lucy witnesses one of Rae's attacks on their father, she initially misinterprets it as a loving embrace. Lucy realises the truth only after a few moments: '[Rae's] arms were around his neck not because she loved him, but because she hated him. She wasn't kissing him, she was biting and sucking. She was trying to hurt him' (p. 120).

The kind of abjection occasioned by the convergence of taboo intimacies features prominently in *Prodigal*. Lucy's growing interest in sex makes her think about her parents and their bedroom activities. The one time she suspects that her parents are having sex, she is mortified to discover that the two naked, moaning people in bed are in fact her mother and Ethan's spectre. The horror of this realisation is such that she cannot process what she is witnessing – the shock resides both in the incestuous desire made manifest and the blurring of boundaries between giving and taking life. Twice the narrator has to repeat what Lucy is seeing: 'Ethan was in bed with Mom' (p. 62). Lucy, however, does not understand what is happening: 'There was

124 • House of Horrors

something awful about this; Lucy wasn't clear, couldn't have put words to it, but her skin crawled' (p. 62). The sickly sour-sweet smell that accompanies ghostly Ethan now reminds her of her infant brother, thus conceptually linking death and birth. And even though she is unable to relay what she is witnessing, it slowly dawns on her that she is actually watching her mother 'having a baby, only backward, because nothing's coming out, Ethan's going back in' (p. 63, original emphasis). Lucy is understandably horrified, but she is also envious of Ethan's absolute closeness with their mother. She yearns to take his place at their mother's side but is nonetheless repulsed by such a fantasy. The scene reads not only like a reverse birth, but also a reverse process of subjectification. Ethan, first robbed of language and then of his life, is making 'sounds that came before words, gurgling, hiccupping, mewling' and his and his mother's bodies are so intertwined that it is impossible to distinguish their contours (p. 62).[85] Carolyn Korsmeyer, reading Kristeva on the abject, delineates 'a profound and transgressive magnetism [which] lingers in desire that is tantalized though never satisfied in images that return the self to its undifferentiated state'.[86] The longing for being returned to the former self and for being reunited with the maternal, though enticing and thrilling, constitutes a serious threat to one's subjectivity, but it is also precisely what Ethan attempts. While Ethan is sucking and biting his mother's breast, he becomes smaller and smaller until he disappears completely, at which his mother 'groan[s] and arche[s] her back and spread[s] her knees' (p. 63). Lucy interprets her mother's arching body as a body in childbirth, but the same description could apply to an orgasmic climax. Later, Lucy imagines feeling her brother inside her mother's belly 'kicking and feeding and curling tighter and tighter around himself' (p. 86).

Of course, one could easily read Lucy as an unreliable focaliser; she is just a child. At one point, her mother points out that sometimes small children fantasise that their parents are in their dreams or imagine them in various scenarios, thus suggesting that Lucy might be imagining things. And before Rae disappears, Lucy sees Rae giving her father a back rub in a rare scene of domestic bliss. However, Lucy first misreads this tableau as Rae's violent attack. Then she moves immediately to a sexually charged description of both 'her father and her sister breathing rhythmically together' (p. 68). When she cannot stand the tension any longer, she escapes to the bathroom. One might ask if what Lucy witnessed was truly inappropriate, or whether it was Rae who orchestrated the scene for Lucy's dis/ease and dis/pleasure, or whether Lucy, lacking relevant language, leaped to disturbing conclusions. Once again, as with Ethan and their mother laying in the

Blood(y) Ties in Vampire Fictions • 125

same bed, Lucy reads physical contact between a parent and their teenage daughter/son in terms of violence and/or eroticism.

Unsurprisingly then, when Jerry finally kidnaps Lucy, the vampiric draining and feeding is intermingled with images of death and rebirth, with love and rape:

> He needed her . . . She pushed between the seats, between the gear-shift and Jerry's thigh; Jerry's thigh gave, as if it were making itself hollow to take her in.
>
> He put his arms around her and she relaxed into him. Then he pushed her down across the seat and wedged one massive leg over her. She struggled to free herself but couldn't; he wasn't very heavy, but he was bigger, stronger, and he needed her to stay where she was.
>
> 'It's okay, Lucy, it's okay.'
>
> He was murmuring against her ear, against her temple. She felt her own pulse there, and his tongue and teeth against it.
>
> 'You feel rage. It's good to feel rage. Rage is nourishing. Feel it, my love. Feel it as big and as full as you can, and then give it to me.' . . .
>
> Rage hot and cold, red and flashing silver and every color, burst-ing out of her ears and mouth and vagina. She was screaming. She was moaning. Jerry pressed his open mouth over hers and sucked.
>
> 'That's good, that's good, oh, you're so good, you're so beautiful. Give it to me, Lucy, give it to me.'
>
> Then his huge, heavy, growing body stiffened and shook on top of her. He groaned into her open mouth, and she knew she was dying or being born again or turning into something she'd never been before. (pp. 176–7)

In the very last feeding scene, which follows the one quoted above, Lucy lies naked in Jerry's secret basement, while other young people, including her sister, are holding her down and channelling her pain towards Jerry in a group ritual. Again, the scene combines incest taboo imagery (as her sister's breath and her tears fall on Lucy's pelvis and between her legs) and the ultimate abject of the dead and/or diseased body (as the people hold-ing her down resemble the living dead, zombies). Rae and Lucy are able to combine their forces and destroy Jerry at his most vulnerable moment – when he begins feeding on their mother, who followed them to Jerry's secret hideout. Rae and Lucy have what other kidnapped teenagers lack – a family connection capable of breaking Jerry's magnetic pull.

126 • House of Horrors

Pain, anger and sexual arousal are mixed even earlier, as Lucy visits Jerry at home. When he pulls her to his lap, she can feel his erection and becomes excited herself. But all the places that he touches on her body become loci of pain. Jerry then asks Lucy to imagine her pain as a red substance that he then proceeds to consume. Immediately after this intense 'session', Lucy experiences menarche. Thus, this imagined red essence of pain stands for both Lucy's menstrual blood and emotional 'blood' drained by psychic vampires. The abject nature of menstrual blood resurfaces also in connection to Rae, who on the night of her disappearance leaves behind a ruined bed and sheets soaked with (menstrual) blood. Associations with death and dying are immediate, but the fact that the blood turns out to be menstrual suggests a birth scene rather than a death scene. In both scenarios, however, the flowing blood marks the liminal zone, where the erotic mingles with the horrific, as in scenes of vampiric feeding. Kristeva underscores the importance of blood and sees it as 'the propitious place for abjection, where *death* and *femininity*, *murder* and *procreation*, *cessation of life* and *vitality* all come together'.[87] As Creed notes, since vampire myths are linked closely to menarche and defloration,[88] menstrual and hymenal flows are posited as abject and even dangerous substances in horror narratives.

Initially, Jerry offers friendly support and understanding to the wayward and lonely teenagers. In this, he approximates the pre-Dracula vampires who 'were dangerously close friends' and offered intimacy that threatened not only class distinctions but also paternal authority.[89] Yet, with time, especially in the second half of the book (after Rae's disappearance), the interactions between Lucy and Jerry no longer resemble a forbidden friendship and become evocative of paedophiliac grooming. He goes through all the recognisable motions: he establishes a false sense of trust; he shares with Lucy little secrets that make her feel special; he kisses her and uses endearing pet names. When the therapy sessions move to Jerry's house and he 'works' on Lucy's anger, the scenes are clearly reminiscent of sexual abuse: Lucy continues to tell Jerry that what he is doing to her hurts too much and that he is actually making her pain even worse, but during the group sessions he continues to drain her anger and frustration into him, often with the help of other confused kids who hold her in place.

When Lucy skips school and comes to his place on her own, Jerry appears similarly abjected as her brother and sister: 'He was panting, and she could see his tongue, coated with some kind of white stuff . . . his breath smelled awful' (p. 141). Accordingly, vampirism is presented as a disease that affects (albeit differently) both the carrier and their victim. The reigning metaphor for vampirism in *Prodigal* is, however, addiction. It is Jerry himself who half-jokingly warns Lucy and her friend that he does not want to overdose on their pain. Later, even Lucy's parents finally begin to discern Jerry's obsessive behaviour in terms of a desperate addiction (p. 171). Following Auerbach's suggestion that each epoch instils onto vampires particular cultural and social fears, *Prodigal* could be read as a cautionary tale expounding on the dangers of drug addiction among children and teenagers, a typically Reaganesque concern manifested most (in)famously in the iconic 'Just Say No' campaign. Teenagers from apparently rock-solid middle-class suburban households, whose whiteness and social status were supposed to protect them from deeply racialised urban decay, are made abject in that their healthy young bodies become diseased, corpse-like and ghost-like, a fact underlined by Tem a number of times.

'[A]ll intuition and – metaphysics' is what Lucy's father provides as an explanation for his growing mistrust of Jerry (p. 172). Interestingly, the word 'metaphysics' is the closest any of the characters comes to describing the vampire's supernatural nature. During the final confrontation between Jerry and the two sisters and their mother, he finally admits that he was always drawn to the pain of others. But as he grew older, he needed to drain more and more suffering. He became a social worker only to use the power, authority and a certain social invisibility to manipulate troubled kids, give shape to their teenage angst and intensify their pain, and then drain them dead. All Jerry's victims have been affected by his addiction: those who are found in the secret basement are emaciated, dull-eyed and completely dependent on their master. Teenagers are an easy target, Tem's novel suggests, because no matter how stable and secure their home situation is, by virtue of being young and misunderstood, they are susceptible to external manipulation. Jerry could thus be read as a cult leader who selects only troubled teenagers, grooms and seduces them, and offers them an alternative family, a new home, all in order to satisfy his urges.

Despite Lucy's growing infatuation with Jerry, she remains aware of the threat he represents and, to an extent, tries to fight off the infection that he carries. Her desire to be with him is also partly driven by the fact that she has caught glimpses of Rae in his house and knows there are secret, locked rooms at his place that she would like to explore. Thus, Lucy's fascination with Jerry, which constitutes both a repetition and continuation of Rae's experience, is linked to the sisters' relationship. Rae and Lucy share a strong, if a bit frayed, bond. It is Rae who initiates Lucy into feminine

128 • House of Horrors

rituals, such as shaving legs or deciding when to wear a bra. And when Rae begins flirting with Jerry, Lucy feels both 'a grudging admiration for her older sister' and 'a strong desire to be like her' (p. 55). As Rae's younger and more cautious self, Lucy is able to critically look at Jerry and see him as 'a fairy-tale tree. With homes inside the trunk and branches for tiny, scared creatures with made-up names' (p. 18). It 'bothers' Lucy to think about him and to recall the family sessions when Ethan was still with them (p. 23). At first, she associates Jerry's big stature with a threatening force that disrupts her family life, and she is glad when she is able to avoid him: 'She didn't like this big thick man . . . He was the last one to see her brother alive. He was the first one to see him dead' (pp. 44–5). Subconsciously, she can discern the danger he poses to her and her family. Yet seeing Rae falling in love with Jerry makes Lucy reconsider her negative opinion of the clumsy social worker. Somehow her older sister's crush makes him more desirable in Lucy's eyes. He becomes 'cute' and his beige eyes seem pretty, even beautiful.

The very first sexual stirrings that she experiences in connection to Jerry's body quickly turn from 'a funny feeling in Lucy's groin' to nausea (p. 56), which underlines the abject nature of paedophiliac sexuality, as well the diseased vampiric abjection that Jerry epitomises. The nausea that she experiences acts as a protective foil produced by her body against the horrifying abjection she encounters. In this, Lucy's nausea and disgust resemble Kristeva's description of bodily reactions that protect the subject from potentially polluting elements, especially the corpse. Of course, Lucy is also fascinated by Jerry's body: its ability to transform, to fill in and deflate, to switch between weightlessness and heaviness. The fact that his body alternates between impossible states – he is large but feels empty, he is strong but lacks substance – also points to his ambiguous, liminal status. Neither a subject nor an object, he floats between categories and frustrates them, and in doing so elicits repulsion and attraction simultaneously.

The presence of a psychic vampire, Jerry, brings into focus the maddeningly bleak realisation that an average nuclear family – not dysfunctional or pathological in any sense – is fundamentally flawed and radically open to external intrusions and manipulations. It is the Oedipal triangle that is the most exposed entry point for potential abuse, both physical and psychological. Jerry knows which buttons to press in young people, and readers can assume that he is able to repeat the same process precisely because child-parent tensions are so common and pervasive. The intense physical bond that Jerry establishes between himself and Lucy answers not

Blood(y) Ties in Vampire Fictions • 129

only Lucy's desire for attention (which her parents must divide between their six children) but also her yearning for a complete union with a parental figure, something that she glimpses in the erotically charged reverse birth-scene between her mother and Ethan's spectre.

It is also possible to read Tem's novel as a conservative take on the familial politics of the early 1990s – a book that exploits popular panic scares that set innocent teens against ruthless drug dealers and abusive sectarians. The danger came from the outside, the somewhat naïve parents were not really to blame, and no one really stood a chance against such a wicked predator who weaselled his way into the Brills' suburban household. Still, by underscoring the bleak repetitiveness of Jerry's actions, *Prodigal* also implies that the very structures, concerns and beliefs of a conventional middle-class kinship are what enables the vampire to lock onto its members. The Brills are helpless not because the predator is a supernatural creature with fangs, but because he can insinuate himself so easily into their ranks. The painful truth that Lucy is forced to accept is that the family can protect her only from certain dangers, but '[s]ome things nobody can protect [her] from' (p. 105). Still, the fact that Jerry was defeated because familial bonds proved to be stronger than he anticipated offers a glimmer of hope in this otherwise bleak story.

Conclusion

While for Kristeva the abject as such remains unrepresentable, for many feminist theorists who have engaged with *Powers of Horror*, the abject is an identifiable site of culturally coded repulsion and fascination centred on female corporeality; and, 'abject criticism' offers a way to 'expos[e], disrup[t] and/or transcod[e] the historical and cultural associations between women's bodies, reproduction and the abject'.[90] Although it can be persuasively argued that the cultural practices of reading, unveiling and decoding the abject have little to offer when faced with real-life matricide and violence against women, the abject remains a valuable critical tool in analysing the narratives of reproduction, body horror and vampirism. Importantly, the abject encounter is unwelcome in terms of bodily affects it triggers (nausea, shudder, disgust), but it may also erupt in a burst of *jouissance*, an ego-shattering leap into the taboo realm of sexuality, reproduction and intimacy. In the three novels analysed in this chapter, close and personal encounters with abject substances, beings and practices trigger not only

130 • House of Horrors

disparate body affects (disgust and delight) but also ambivalence towards individuation, reproduction and sexuality.

In *The Gilda Stories*, Gomez concentrates on the ways in which one's sexuality is inseparable from race and the historicity of one's life. The vampire becomes a vehicle for the investigation of the abject usually associated with the maternal, the feminine and the bodily. By emphasising the sensual and pleasurable aspects of intimate maternal bonds, the abjection associated with the break with the mother is to an extent neutralised. Gilda's growth as a Black female vampire is not predicated on a violent repudiation of her maternal figures, but rests on an affirmative embrace of their physical love and support. Abjection in Gomez is also revealed 'as inherently mobile, and as descriptive of a mechanism by which various others are stipulated as excluded, in particular, raced, classed and sexually deviant others.'[91] Gomez skilfully rewrites the Gothic narratives of lesbian desire by showing how the excess, which Gilda signifies for the symbolic order, has 'a destabilizing effect on heterosexual institutions such as the family and society in general'.[92] The abjection used by Gomez is employed affirmatively and successfully to show alternative configurations of desire and kinship. Still, the bleak ending and the cyclical nature of historical injustice and violence towards non-normative bodies and alternative kinship suggest that the scope of repair work done by Gilda and her family is woefully restricted.

In Elizabeth Engstrom's *Black Ambrosia*, a white, heteronormative, middle-class family lifestyle is violently rejected along with all the communal responsibilities that go hand in hand with settling down, starting a family and buying a house. The novel shows Angelina struggling to accept her abject condition, her status as an outsider who threatens the community and who cannot coexist with others for long. Because Angelina is portrayed as a failed experiment in radical female empowerment, first exacting revenge on her would-be rapist and then killing men while seducing them with promises of sexual release, she could be read as an ironic commentary on the supposed links between femininity and monstrosity. She is frightening in her 'unwomanly' emotional detachment, supposedly unfeminine killing skills and the ease with which she kills children. At the same time, her inability to withstand prolonged loneliness and her budding desire to perpetuate her species suggest Angelina's longing for love and companionship. Engstrom thus investigates the multiple abject positions accorded to Angelina: a murderess, a non-human subject, a madwoman, a predatory vampire and a woman who refuses to follow

Blood(y) Ties in Vampire Fictions • 131

conventional heteronormative scripts. In the end, the eruption of the abject is augmented not only because Angelina is a vampire (who represents our fascination with blood, corpses and the erotics of death), but also because she is a woman whose very corporeality is already positioned as a potential site of the abject. What is more, because her vampiric development is defined by and through her relationships with women, especially maternal figures, Angelina experiences first-hand both the orgasmic pleasure of being reunited with the maternal as well as the horror of being faced with the archaic mother figures who threaten to engulf her subjectivity.

In a similar way to the other two novels, Melanie Tem's *Prodigal* examines the questions of growing up, separating from one's parents and/ or parental figures and finding one's voice and place in the world. Even though the vampirism described by Tem is psychic and thus bloodless, she places heavy emphasis on the images of blood and violence, menstruation and the physicality of puberty, monstrous births and death, taboo sexualities and dark eroticism. What makes *Prodigal* unique is the way that it handles middle-class anxieties over drug abuse, teen angst and teenage sexuality, threats associated with cults and sects, and sexual abuse. In Tem's fiction, the nuclear family is not a site of empowerment, emotional support and physical safety; rather, it is a liminal space, with children unsure of their identification and parents insecure about their authority, where conflicting urges and feelings erupt in intense bursts of the abject, often centred around the maternal body, the teenage body and (sexual) intimacy. The Brill family seem a rather weak and ineffective unit, one that can be easily infiltrated and manipulated by someone who understands their inner workings, tensions, desires and (mis)identifications. The sheer repetitiveness of *Prodigal*'s plot suggests that every middle-class suburban family is susceptible to such intrusions and abuse. What is even more disturbing, the very institutions that are supposed to support families (that is social services) are not free from corruption.

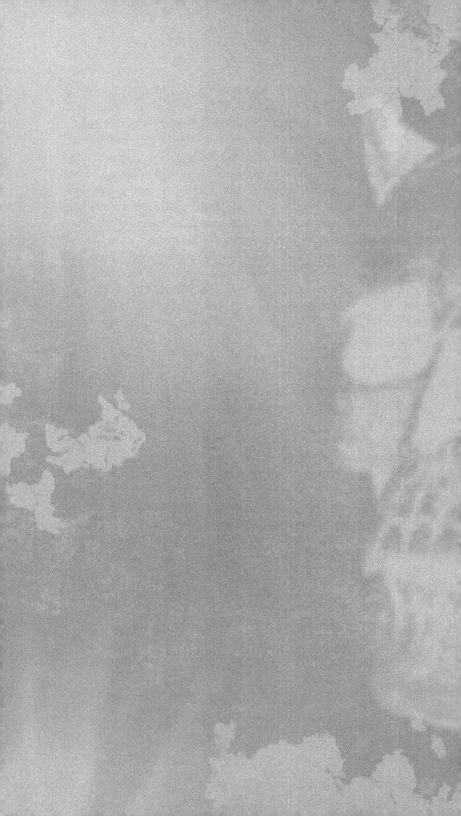

4

Spectral Kinship and Ghostly Selves

Introduction

ALTHOUGH I ADDRESSED haunted house narratives in the first chapter, I intentionally avoided discussing ghost stories. Ghosts and spectral visitors in general exceed the haunted house trope and appear in a surprisingly versatile corpus, in which the focus is often the process of haunting rather than the setting. Although haunted houses are conventionally associated with the appearance of spectral visitors, in ghost stories it is the people that are subjected to haunting, the building being a secondary or even tertiary concern in the ensuing drama.

The spectral motif can be traced back to antiquity, but contemporary ghost stories owe much of their character to folk and medieval threads within Romanticism and the Gothic, as well as the fantastic genres developed over the two centuries since the Enlightenment. Contrary to assurances in the Age of Reason, the supernatural was not banished from the collective and individual imagination. As Terry Castle has persuasively argued in *The Female Thermometer*, ghosts were simply redefined to fit a new paradigm: they were transformed from external beings into internal components of the human psyche. The resulting spectralisation of the mind has made it increasingly difficult to distinguish between genuine ghostly hauntings and psychological figments of the haunted self.[1] Castle noted how the materiality of other people 'became strangely insubstantial and indistinct: what mattered was the mental picture, the ghost, the

134 • House of Horrors

haunting image'.[2] Thus, the eighteenth century witnessed 'the internalization of the spectral – the gradual reinterpretation of ghosts and apparitions as hallucinations, or projections of the mind',[3] a process culminating in the advent of psychoanalysis in the late nineteenth century. In a sense, Freud inherited the 'crypto-supernatural language' of Enlightenment rationalists, as well as 'their sense of the psyche as a vulnerable domain subject to frightening spectral intrusions'.[4]

As the 'material, psychic, and supernatural' aspects of life became increasingly imbrued in spiritualism, clinical psychology and religious revivals, and scientific and technological developments continued to breach the gap between the tangible and the intangible, ghosts, never completely rejected or repressed, came to occupy the centre stage of popular imagination in the late nineteenth century.[5] The metaphorical potential of ghosts – readily employed in analyses of 'disturbing forms of otherness', the alienation underpinning capitalist structures and the uncanniness of new inventions and scientific discoveries – was tightly connected to the notion that spectral visitors could be objects of study, as evidenced by a plethora of groups and societies dedicated to ghost-hunting, clairvoyance and paranormal research in all its guises.[6] However, a gradual withering of belief in actual ghosts and spirits took place in the early twentieth century. In his 1919 essay, Freud forcefully rejected the supernatural as the true source of the uncanny, in favour of repressed infant anxieties and remnants of an animistic past. In other words, 'the uncanny ha[d] to be exorcised – cleansed of ghosts – precisely because, to maintain its status as a normal, even privileged experience, it [could not], at least not exclusively, be associated with the (non-repressed) primitive' conception of the world.[7]

In twentieth-century cultural and literary criticism, ghosts, spectres and phantoms have most often resurfaced in psychoanalytic discourse, certain strands of continental philosophy, and deconstruction. By 2002, when Roger Luckhurst coined the phrase 'the spectral turn',[8] the most important and innovative works within the burgeoning spectrality studies had already been published: the English translation of Jacques Derrida's *Specters of Marx* (1994),[9] Avery Gordon's *Ghostly Matters* (1997)[10] and Peter Buse and Andrew Stott's *Ghosts: Deconstruction, Psychoanalysis, History* (1999),[11] to name but a few. This 'spectral turn' coincided with a renaissance in Gothic studies and the flourishing of cultural and literary criticism of the supernatural, the haunted and the monstrous during the late 1990s and early 2000s. Two seminal collections edited by Maria del Pilar Blanco and Esther Peeren – *Popular Ghosts: the Haunted Spaces of*

Everyday Culture (2010)[12] and *The Spectralities Reader: Ghosts and Haunting in Contemporary Cultural Theory* (2013)[13] – helped consolidate various strands of spectrality studies and underline the interdisciplinary and intersectional nature of ghost(ly) research.[14] In their introduction to *The Spectralities Reader*, del Pilar Blanco and Peeren drew attention to how ghosts and haunting had moved from the realm of everyday clichés, Gothic plot devices and objects of study for ghost-hunters and parapsychology enthusiasts, to become 'influential conceptual metaphors', which, in contrast to other more mundane figures of speech, perform actual theory and can be deployed as analytical tools.[15]

Many spectrality studies engage with Derrida's *Specters of Marx*, whether to embrace its foundational status or question its canonicity. Primarily a discussion of Marxism in a post-Soviet world, *Specters of Marx* also functions as a compelling 'account of spectrality, ghosts and spirits'.[16] Derrida associates the figure of a spectre with 'absolute alterity, notions of inheritance, hospitality, and the messianic',[17] concepts that have arguably gained new import since 9/11. Spectrality and hauntology have proven useful springboards for interdisciplinary research dealing with otherness, strangers and trauma, but also necrotic capitalism, ecological collapse and migrant crises. Del Pilar Blanco and Peeren note that Derrida 'uses the figure of the ghost to pursue . . . that which haunts *like a ghost* and, by way of this haunting, demands justice, or at least a response'.[18] Through this, Derrida examines the ethical dimension of a ghostly encounter, echoing the Levinasian Other, 'whose otherness we are responsible for preserving',[19] and anticipating a larger discussion of recognition, otherness and the politics of mourning and grievability found in, for instance, Judith Butler's *Frames of War: When is Life Grievable?* and *Precarious Life: the Powers of Mourning and Justice.*[20]

In her book-length study of the uncanny, Masschelein reads Derrida's hauntology as a 'philosophy of haunting, of the return of the repressed, in which the spectral takes precedent over being, existence'.[21] She argues that Derrida links Heidegger's *Unheimlichkeit* (a phenomenological experience of not-being-at-home, a homesickness that defines a human subject) and Freud's uncanny to create his own version of the uncanny. For Masschelein, this 'Heidegger-Freud-Derrida connection in "hauntology" leads to a new domain of the uncanny', which, in turn, is used in various research disciplines that focus on spectrality and hauntings.[22] Although I disagree with Masschelein's insistence that the uncanny constitutes the core of Derridean spectrality, I believe she is right that the greatest weakness of

136 • House of Horrors

hauntology is its 'fundamental distrust of technology, of contemporary bio-power and globalized capitalist systems, and nostalgia'.[23] Derrida's hauntology, if envisioned as a critical project, appears too expansive, while his call to install haunting at the core of other concepts is at the very least unrealistic. Derrida's dehistoricising approach posits the ghost and haunting as universal concepts; yet these are typically Western concepts, heavily laced with Judeo-Christian definitions of life and the afterlife, body and soul, reality and imaginary realms. As postcolonial theory and necropolitical and spectropolitical scholarship remind us, ghosts do not haunt all subjects in the same way and the Western definition of spectrality is one among many. Gayatri Chakravorty Spivak, a vocal critic of Derrida's spectrality, rebukes him for including a 'universalizing *danse macabre*', through which a haunting is rewritten as 'a masculine economy', blind to its own hegemonic practices of excluding women and minorities.[24] In his seminal work, *Slavery and Social Death* (1982),[25] Orlando Patterson has elaborated the concept of 'social death': a lack of connection with one's ancestral past, cultural heritage, language, religion and kinship to which enslaved subjects were subjected.

A different strand in spectrality studies returns to psychoanalytic discourse, the original repository of hauntings and unwanted emotional possessions. Here, Colin Davis notes Derrida's unacknowledged debt to the work of French-Hungarian psychoanalysts, Nicholas Abraham and Maria Torok, the dissemination and popularisation of which Derrida actively advanced. Davis takes great pains to maintain a clear distinction between Derridean spectres and Abraham and Torok's phantoms, which appear in their examination of unintended transgenerational trauma. The phantom signifies 'the presence of a dead ancestor in the living Ego, still intent on preventing its traumatic and usually shameful secrets from coming to light'.[26] The phantom does not provide revelation; instead, it works hard to deceive the haunted subject and prevent hidden knowledge being brought to light. By contrast, Derrida's ghosts are not carriers of knowledge and one does not speak with them in the hope of unearthing secrets; '[r]ather, [the encounter] may open us to the experience of secrecy as such: an essential unknowing which underlies and may undermine what we think we know'.[27] While the psychoanalytic tradition emphasises the interpretative practice of close reading of particular texts, deconstructive analysis is more open to speculation and somewhat sweeping, yet often productive, generalisations. For Derrida, a ghost should remain hidden to enable a meaningful encounter with the Other, but in the earlier psychoanalytic view, the ghost functions as a manipulator and intruder that must be identified and expelled. It is little wonder then that Derrida's logic of hauntology holds such appeal for deconstructionists, who perceive a link between the tropes of haunting and ghosts, and 'the processes of literature and textuality'.[28]

It is the function and/or purpose of a ghost that most clearly structures ghostly narratives. A great many ghost stories subscribe to the restorative model, in which ghosts have a curative rather than destructive role and can be appeased only once they have achieved recognition or restitution. Still, a neat division between curative and lying ghosts can take us only so far. Many contemporary ghost stories do not invoke healing and reparative functions, as evidenced by the novels analysed in this chapter. Some ghosts are bent on exacting vengeance and their intense hatred over past wrongs cannot be remedied in the present; others are simply non-human agents, whose agenda eludes the narrow human understanding of good and evil. The spectral disturbances in all three novels selected for this chapter – Sara Gran's *Come Closer* (2004), Tananarive Due's *The Between* (1995) and Ania Ahlborn's *Within These Walls* (2015) – defy clear-cut distinction into order and disorder, restoration and destruction, absence and presence. These writers share an impulse to complicate the spectral figure, to present a ghost as a character of its own, rather than a mere instrument of vengeance or knowledge distribution.

The Ghostly Other in Horror Fiction

During the heyday of American and British ghost stories in the late nineteenth and early twentieth centuries, some of the most popular ghost-story writers were women, including Mary Wilkins Freeman, Sarah Orne Jewett and Edith Wharton. Although ghosts continued to appear as plot devices and clichéd tropes in American Gothic and the genres that it directly influenced, such as urban fantasy, weird fiction, Southern Gothic and modern horror, it was not until the late 1960s and 1970s that supernatural horror once more came into vogue. The first bestselling books and wildly popular horror movies were tales of demonic possession and supernatural visitation, such as *Rosemary's Baby* (1968), *The Exorcist* (1973) and *The Omen* (1976). Following the success of both mainstream and independent horror cinema in the 1970s, coupled with the legitimisation of literary horror and Stephen King's bestselling status, a wide variety of horror stories were published throughout the 1980s and

138 • House of Horrors

later, including stories of ghosts, hauntings, haunted/possessed objects, haunted places and supernatural possessions.

The renewed interest in the spectral during the late twentieth century is also reflected in literary and cultural studies. The first fully fledged work on ghosts in literature, Julia Briggs's *Night Visitors*,[29] was published in 1977. For Briggs, a 'ghost story' denotes all tales of the supernatural, including such disparate beings as demons, possessed individuals, werewolves, vampires and ghouls. Briggs's broad approach may relate to the persistent omnipresence of ghosts in Western literature: as Srdjan Smajic has noted, they 'evidently belong everywhere in literature – and consequently, one might say, nowhere in particular'.[30] As ghostly figures appear timeless and ahistorical, they are often approached from a psychoanalytical perspective, which does not necessarily engage with a ghost's spatial or temporal specificity. Fortuitously, renewed interest in the notion of spectrality and the 'spectral turn' have provided the spectral with new life in literary and cultural studies. Alongside the diverse examples of literary and cultural criticism collected in del Pisar Blanco and Peeren's two anthologies, one should also mention, among others, Brian Norman's *Dead Women Talking* (2012),[31] Kathleen Brogan's *Cultural Haunting* (1998),[32] Jeffrey Andrew Weinstock's (ed.) *Spectral America* (2004)[33] and Julian Wolfrey's *Victorian Hauntings* (2001).[34]

A recent growing interest in the spectral can also be linked to calls to tackle the effects of cultural erasure, historical trauma, ethnic, racial and gender-related violence, and the continuing repercussions of slavery and the colonisation of Indigenous territories in North America. In *Cultural Haunting*, Kathleen Brogan links the resurgence of ghost narratives to American ethnic literature, which not only frequently includes non-Western ghosts and spectrality but often employs ghosts as metaphors to unravel the entanglements of past events, work through mourning, and deal with racialised and gendered violence. An increased interest in collective as well as individual history, national identities and social fragmentation has inspired *Spectral America*, a collection of essays edited by Jeffrey Andrew Weinstock. In his introduction, Weinstock draws attention to the communal aspect of Derrida's spectre, which, by virtue of being 'no more one' and 'more than one', points to both individual and collective subjectivity.[35] He links the early twenty-first-century fascination with ghosts to a post-structuralist awareness of the fragmentation and disintegration of history, in which a collection of narratives, private and public, minor and major, minoritian and majoritarian, compete. Weinstock compellingly

Spectral Kinship and Ghostly Selves • 139

argues that the spectral turn in American culture signifies a 'millennial anxiety' surrounding the return of repressed knowledge, which threatens the future by destabilising accepted versions of the nation's past.[36]

Being both alive and dead, spectral visitors frustrate dyadic thinking and effectively interrupt the boundaries between self and Other, as well as the one and the many, and form useful conceptual tools to deal with private and public traumas, familial secrets and the role of kinship on an individual and group level. As Abraham has underlined, 'what haunts us are not the dead, but the gaps left within us by the secrets of others'.[37] With its focus on transgenerational haunting, Abraham's psychoanalytic cryptonomy is 'an especially fitting mode of Gothic investigation' that places family drama at its centre.[38] Such enquiry into the spectral fits perfectly in postmodern and post-structuralist texts with their 'interrogation of the nuclear family unit, narrative lacunae and fractured narrative subject'.[39] This is precisely how the ghost and the ghostly come into play in the three novels that I analyse here.

In contrast to earlier chapters, the lines between a thematic horror/ Gothic feature and a matching conceptual tool are purposefully muddled. The haunting, understood as a theme of spectral visitation common to horror and Gothic literature, functions as a critical tool in spectrality studies to alert us to a loss of bodily autonomy, selfhood and agency, to racialised trauma, to the ethics of hospitality (and hostility) and the myriad disappointments of normative family life and failed intimacies. In Sara Gran's *Come Closer* (2004), Tananarive Due's *The Between* (1995) and Ania Ahlborn's *Within These Walls* (2015), family life is tested by the intrusion of spectral Otherness, which encompasses a potential demonic possession in *Come Closer*, spectral visitors and doubles in *The Between*, and a ghostly haunting and subsequent possession in *Within These Walls*. Both Gran and Ahlborn tackle the restrictive norms of white femininity and an underlying yearning for an all-encompassing companionship that appears to offer release from social conventions. Where Gran supplements her narrative with a biting satire on white, middle-class professionals and the empty comforts of consumption, Ahlborn examines the inner workings of a cult and the way that younger members are manipulated into violent intimacies. In *The Between*, the protagonist struggles with both a transgenerational trauma that has shaped his entire life and the heavy social and personal expectations placed on middle-class Black men. As the spectral Others in all these narratives are imperceptible, their influence is not felt or recognised immediately, making their motivations unclear.

140 • House of Horrors

As ontologically unstable entities, spectral visitors act as catalysts for that which has been left unmentioned, unarticulated and unanswered: ghostly dis/possession can signal the return of repressed material that is not necessarily linked to the uncanny; the process of 'ghosting' may imply the erasure of improper or improperly integrated elements; spectres can act as harbingers of past trauma and carriers of transgenerational hauntings; spectral visitors can function as the protagonists' dangerous doubles; and, finally, ghosts may illuminate conspicuous absences and gaps in history, identity or kinship.

Dangerous Dis/possessions in *Come Closer*

Sara Gran's *Come Closer* (2004) is a short novel in which the narrator, Amanda, pragmatically and methodologically describes her life spiralling out of control after becoming possessed by a demon. Although Amanda's dead-pan descriptions of her white, yuppie lifestyle, her successful career as an architect, her husband Ed and their post-industrial loft shift the overall mood from the horrific to the satiric, the trail of gore and destruction left in the demon's wake leaves no doubt as to the novel's generic loyalties. The novel never clarifies whether Amanda is actually possessed, suffering from a late onset of schizophrenia or psychotic break, or evading responsibility for her actions by projecting blame onto a non-existent entity. The demonic possession becomes a narrative device, an extended metaphor that allows Gran to combine a number of topics: an ironic commentary on the yuppie lifestyle, the violent return of a repudiated femininity and corporeality, and a deep-seated hunger among women for meaningful relationships. Crucially, the possession/madness that Amanda experiences exposes serious cracks in her seemingly perfect marriage. The ideal heterosexual romance that she and her husband have woven together is revealed to be a commodity; a clever marketing ploy targeted at hip urbanites. The haunting, as envisioned by Gran, is founded on the idea of an evil double, whose impropriety, misconduct and criminal activities both fascinate and repel the heroine.

As a Freudian 'harbinger of death',[40] Amanda's demonic doppelganger highlights the frailty of her life, marriage and even her personality. Possession doubles as *dispossession*, as Amanda loses everything in a physical frenzy of lust and violence. The desires she once successfully 'ghosted' return and insinuate themselves back in her life; in an ironic

Spectral Kinship and Ghostly Selves • 141

twist, it takes a spiritual possession for Amanda to re-engage with her corporeality and re-discover what her body actually wants. Amanda's failed attempts to secure help posit her as a hysterical female, an unstable hypochondriac in need of containment. However, no patriarchal figures come to her rescue: her husband slowly withdraws, medical professionals are all sympathy but wholly ineffectual, and spiritual advisers are New Age charlatans.

Elaine Showalter has noted that madness is often the only legitimate form of self-expression for women in literature.[41] Yet, female madness always runs the risk of being re-cast as succubus-like sexual aggression, rather than the strictly brutal and non-eroticised madness afforded to men.[42] *Come Closer* mocks this typecasting by presenting madness/possession in terms of both demonic hypersexuality and extreme misandrist violence. The textual madness in *Come Closer* remains veiled by Amanda's correct grammar and sophisticated literary language, emerging only in lapses of memory, ironic self-distancing and wilful dis-remembering. What Kristeva has identified as 'the speech of non-being', a feminine writing of 'silence, and the unspoken, riddled with repetition',[43] provides an interesting clue to Amanda's first-person narration. Amanda's refusal to reveal herself and the extent of her possession/madness is due not only to her fear of facing the facts but also to the fact that language cannot contain the haunting and appropriately express her insanity. Like Charlotte Perkins Gilman's classic 'Yellow Wallpaper' (1892), *Come Closer* can be read as both a supernatural haunting and a tale of madness, and as in Gilman's story, the indecipherability of the heroine's plight highlights the fact that a woman's tale of madness/possession exceeds the cultural markers and signifiers attributed to it in phallogocentric language. By refusing to follow through with a single explanation, Amanda cannot be fully classified as either a possessed woman or a madwoman, both of whom would require restraint and/or cure by patriarchal authorities.

The novel unhurriedly opens with a sequence of odd events, such as strange messages at work and seemingly innocent pranks. Mysterious tapping noises are then heard in Amanda and Ed's apartment whenever she is present. After the tapping – a rather playful nod to the famous Gothic messenger in Poe's poem – Amanda and Ed find themselves constantly at odds. Thus, the possession progresses in line with the slow disintegration of Amanda's marriage. In the months to come, Amanda graduates from picking fights with Ed to modest instances of anti-social behaviour, such as stealing lipstick. Again, notwithstanding the real or imagined supernatural

142 • House of Horrors

presence, these acts are not entirely alien to Amanda's character. Even though Amanda does not or chooses not to remember the actual moment of stealing the lipstick, she does recall a pre-teen make-up shoplifting spree when her grandmother forbade her from using make-up. What is more, even though the brick-red lipstick is far from Amanda's colour of choice, not only does she continue wearing it all summer, she returns to the shop and steals more when it runs out.

Sitting at home one evening, Amanda burns Ed with her cigarette. She attempts to rationalise her behaviour as normal curiosity, something everyone wonders from time to time: how it would feel to give someone a cigarette burn. Amanda believes her hand moved without her volition. She also starts to lose time. The first 'time lapse' takes place after an angry exchange with the owner of a magazine stand, who is murdered later that day. A couple of months later, unsurprisingly, Amanda realises she had killed him. She begins to drink excessively and hooks up with the type of men that she preferred in her early twenties before settling down with Ed: bad boys with tattoos. Her description of the first time she cheats on Ed is from the perspective of a helpless bystander rather than a willing participant: '[i]t was like looking at a photograph, seeing the room but not really being in it' (p. 88). Feeling remorse, Amanda decides to cook Ed his favourite dinner, but the 'demon slither[s] back into [her] thoughts' as she shops, making her angry at Ed's lack of interest. Instead, she goes to buy shoes, thus choosing instant gratification over hard and somewhat pointless emotional work.

After a failed depossession ritual, Amanda increasingly assumes the role of bystander, describing what 'she,' a female demon called Naamah, does when in control of Amanda's body: 'What she wanted most of all, even more than shopping or cigarettes, was men . . . Of course, I only saw them afterwards, when Naamah would leave and I would sink back into consciousness, naked and shivering, in bed with a man I had never seen before' (pp. 117–18). Amanda becomes violent towards her male lovers, eventually seducing and killing a male work rival. Soon after this she stops going to work and begins to introduce herself as Naamah. The narrative becomes increasingly confused as Amanda has fewer and fewer lucid moments; the novel ends with Naamah murdering Edward and Amanda being locked in an asylum.

Throughout the months leading to Amanda's transformation into Naamah, readers learn about the life Amanda is deconstructing. She and Ed live in a heavily gentrified urban area in a post-industrial loft that she

Spectral Kinship and Ghostly Selves • 143

has carefully refurbished and redesigned. The white décor, smooth surfaces and sparse furniture reflect Amanda and Ed's existence: spotless, neat, bland and blatantly white. Although now an up-and-coming architect, Amanda had initially majored in art. It was her father's death and the ensuing financial difficulties that prompted her to choose an easier and safer direction in life. Architects 'dressed a hell of a lot better than the art professors', had better cars and were more likely to find partners and lead secure lives (p. 54), exactly what Amanda wanted, or at least thought she did. In a way, Amanda has not only become a professional architect and interior designer, but also the architect of her own lifestyle. She refers to 'the old Amanda', the one before Naamah appeared, as 'the one [she] had chosen for [her]self and cultivated for years' (p. 86).

In Amanda's model life, Ed represents stability, dependability and reason. He is the person who introduced a much-needed order into her happy-go-lucky twenties, when she ate ice-cream for lunch and kept her tax records in a shopping bag. Ed, in contrast, is the perfect companion and a thoroughly normal guy, someone 'who could finish any crossword puzzle, open any bottle, reach the top shelf at the grocery store' (p. 12). For Amanda, Ed is another ticked box: '[o]n the whole, Ed and I were happy – with each other, with the loft, with our careers' (p. 23). She pragmatically points to their financial and professional security before describing Ed as a man who can be trusted and 'a big-boned healthy blond' (p. 23). Although Amanda hates her husband's obsessive neatness and cleanliness, and his neurotic yearning for order and regularity in all spheres of life, she never allows herself to feel disappointed, angry or hurt. Instead, she opts for 'a certain amount of irritation' as her constant marital companion (p. 25). From this perspective, Amanda's gradual estrangement from her husband, the fights she initiates, and the pain she inflicts on him are not surprising. When Ed visits her towards the end of the novel, Amanda wants to tell him everything: 'I love you and I miss you and I don't know why this happened. To us, out of everyone in the world' (p. 158). She reminisces about their shared past, their first dates and 'Sundays at the flea market' (p. 158). She recalls plans they once made to travel the world, buy a new car and get a new dishwasher. In a rare moment of lucidity following Ed's murder, Amanda thinks back to their life: 'the good times . . . his blond hair falling over his eyes . . . And our home, our great big beautiful loft' (p. 165). Her sadness over losing Edward notably intermingles with sadness about losing their beautiful flat, furniture and appliances.

144 • House of Horrors

As previously mentioned, *Come Closer* can easily be read as a satire on the twenty-first-century yuppie lifestyle. Amanda's need for material comfort and her appreciation of the finer things in life are thus transformed into a shopping frenzy under Naamah's tutelage. Seeking satisfaction through ownership, Amanda spends until her credit card is maxed out. As a family unit, she and Ed had rejected reproductive futurity from the beginning, opting instead to increase their own wealth and comfort. Seen in this light, Amanda and Ed are actually caricatures of the stereotypical, upper-middle-class professionals who are routinely chastised for postponing having children and being selfish, hypermaterialistic and immature. Naamah's insatiable hunger for new objects and thrills mocks the idea of identity-formation through consumption under late capitalism, and Amanda's demonic *possession* is twisted into a pun on earthly possessions and their almost supernatural hold on Amanda and Ed. As Brogan has argued, possession in American literature is often presented as 'a malignant pregnancy', an act of giving birth to a returning past, but can also be 'conveyed through metaphors of consumption' and cannibalism, both of which inform the exchanges between Amanda and Naamah.[44]

As Amanda only accepts certain features of idealised heterosexual romance, such as monogamy and marriage, and rejects such aspects as procreation, she appears more open to other types of non-normative life disruption. Halberstam has noted that many people in the postmodern Western world 'will and do opt to live outside of reproductive and familial time as well as on the edges of logics of labor and production' and '[b]y doing so, they also often live outside the logic of capital accumulation'.[45] Halberstam suggests these 'queer subjects' do 'live (deliberately, accidentally, or of necessity) during the hours when others sleep and in the spaces (physical, metaphysical, and economic) that others have abandoned, and in terms of the ways they might work in the domains that other people assign to privacy and family'.[46] Amanda's increasingly 'improper' behaviour – stealing, sleeping with random men, and spending money she is no longer earning – plus her refusal to take part in what is considered a 'normal', healthy and productive routine by sleeping late, drinking alcohol and smoking cigarettes, place her somewhat closer to the 'queer' end of Halberstam's spectrum. At the same time, this rather generous understanding of queerness is bolstered by intense homoerotic desire for Naamah.

In one of Amanda's dreams, Naamah licks her face and tells her she belongs to her; in another, Naamah asks Amanda to stop fighting her and tells her she deliberately chose Amanda and will never abandon her: 'She put her arms around me and pulled me tight against her. Our ribs crushed together, and our hipbones slammed and she pulled me tighter until I couldn't breathe, I was choking, and my spine met hers, vertebrae against vertebrae' (p. 36). Such imagery not only implies sexual activity but also complete physical merger, which, together with the fact that Amanda is beginning to physically resemble Naamah, suggests that she is being devoured or replaced. In another scene, heavily imbued with both homo-eroticism and sexual violence, Naamah pushes Amanda onto a concrete pavement. Amanda cries, moans and gasps for air.

Predictably, Amanda is entirely debilitated by her 'bad girl' persona. Any initial satisfaction vanishes as she is reduced to a silent and helpless witness to Naamah's increasingly anti-social antics. It also becomes clear that Amanda uses satire and irony to distance herself from the perverse pleasures that Naamah has to offer, suggesting a fear of her own corpore-ality. The temporal gaps in Amanda's narrative and her self-positioning as a witness rather than willing participant also indicate a deeply conflicted relationship with her needs and sexuality. Possession allows Amanda to access her taboo desires, a standard trope in possession horror. Popular possession horror movies such as *The Exorcist* (1973), *The Possession* (2012) and *The Exorcism of Emily Rose* (2005), to name but a few, often cen-tre on young teenage girls and their budding sexuality.[47] The monstrous performance of an uncontrollable, ecstatic and often eroticised female body is thrilling but also troubling for the audience. Hence, at the end of these movies, an unruly woman must be exorcised and subdued by a male authority figure: a priest, father, husband or paranormal investigator.

Rather than a young girl on the verge of womanhood, Amanda is a seemingly happily married and professionally successful adult.[48] Perhaps her socialisation into responsible adulthood prevented earlier hauntings, but her errant sexuality and thirst for the improper have finally materi-alised when she can no longer maintain the pretence of happiness. Gran openly suggests that Amanda has met Naamah before: at the age of five she had an imaginary childhood friend, Pansy. This combination of an older, knowledgeable friend, sister and 'mother substitute' (p. 19) appeared a few years after Amanda's own mother had died. By the age of nine, Amanda understood Pansy was merely a figment of her imagination, yet vividly remembers meeting this pink-skinned woman with a mane of black hair. As Amanda's nine-year-old self knew this could not have happened as Pansy was not real, she buried the memory deep inside and repressed all knowledge of her childhood friend.

146 • House of Horrors

When describing her childhood, Amanda suddenly skips forward to her college years. Remembering Pansy makes Amanda think about the deaths of her father and stepmother. This intrusion into her description of Pansy suggests Amanda is subconsciously searching for a connection between the black-haired woman with 'bisque' skin and the fatal scuba-diving accident on a Jamaican coral reef. Amanda's emphasis on pink makes the connection apparent, although Pansy's motives for the killing remain ambiguous. Bearing in mind that Naamah will later act as an agent of her deepest desires, it could be argued that Amanda unconsciously wanted to punish her father for remarrying. As an unreliable narrator, Amanda does not directly address her taboo desires, but it is made clear that she deeply resented her stepmother and was angry with her father for allowing his new wife to squander the family money. It was this extravagance that forced Amanda to seek financial security in architecture and become the person she is.

Amanda learns from the Kabala that Naamah – whose name means 'charming' and 'pleasant' in Aramaic – was Adam's second wife. To ensure Naamah met Adam's requirements, God created her from scratch in front of her future husband. Unfortunately, Adam was so disgusted with the visceral process of creation that he cast her out. After killing Ed, Naamah speaks for the first time in the novel, explaining her actions by describing Adam's reaction: 'He had imagined a person as sleek and neat on the inside as outside. He couldn't stand the mess, the chaos, the blood. I wasn't needed. I wasn't wanted' (p. 162). Gran suggests that by refusing to accept Amanda in all her complexity and corporeal chaos, Ed has repeated the offence.

In a recurring dream, Amanda meets Naamah by a red sea of blood. Naamah's reddish skin and red lipstick further strengthen an association with blood, entrails and bodily functions. Rejected for her own corporeality, Naamah offers Amanda all that is culturally rejected and abjected: that is, the pleasures of carnality and the female body. Deep within Amanda is a desire to return to the earlier, rougher and less proper version of herself, making it impossible for her to continue resisting, as Naamah recalls:

> Of course she [Amanda] fought at first. They all do. And then they see the possibilities and they're happy to go along. She could have gone on forever, in her small lonely life. But sometimes the door to a bigger life opens, and it isn't so easy to say No. You can't spend your whole life saying No. Sometimes you have to say Yes, and see where it takes you. (p. 166)

Although Amanda is institutionalised for killing Ed, Naamah continues to wreak havoc in the asylum, attacking inmates and sleeping with male staff members. The demon is not punished for her transgressions, no one saves Amanda, and there are no powerful male authority figures to expel Naamah. Instead, possession is ironically belittled as merely another millennial anxiety or 'first world problem'. When Amanda orders a book on design she receives a self-help guide to demon possession, which she picks up one evening out of boredom and completes a test to determine whether she may require an exorcism. The first time she scores four out of ten and immediately forgets the issue. However, when she later scores seven out of ten, Amanda decides to visit a spiritual adviser listed in the guidebook: Sister Maria, the owner of a New Age shop crammed with beads, crystals and tacky Madonnas. Sister Maria declares there is a demon sitting next to Amanda and gives her a bottle of special body wash called NUMBER #5: DEMON FIGHTING, which fails to have the desired effect. When Ed later suggests a therapist, Amanda is initially relieved: 'I wasn't possessed – I was insane!' (p. 101). The psychiatrist assures Amanda that she is simply experiencing the growing pains of becoming an assertive independent woman and should not resist.[49] Unsatisfied, Amanda visits another spiritual adviser, Dr Ray Thomas, director and CEO of the Ray of Hope Fellowship. As he and his followers do not use the 'e-word' he offers her 'depossession'. Having signed a release form stating that whatever Amanda agrees to undergo is for 'entertainment purposes' alone, she is subjected to a mix of visualisation, meditation, hypnosis and psychobabble. The demon takes full possession of Amanda and happily writes Thomas a cheque for $250.

Possession stories frequently start with a pseudo-invitation, often presented as curiosity or an apparent openness to spectral visitation coded as a transgression of social norms: Regan is not baptised by her single mother in *The Exorcist* (1973); Em buys a weird wooden box at a garage sale in *The Possession* (2012); and Deborah digs where she should not in *The Taking of Deborah Logan* (2014). These examples complicate the relationship between the possessor and the possessed and emphasise the ambivalence of the visitation, unwelcome and terrifying in most respects, thrilling and exuberant in others. Writing about the relationship between hosts and guests, Derrida has described two subtypes of hospitality: conditional and unconditional.[50] Conditional hospitability remains bound by language and the normative rules of communication and social exchange, such as issuing or accepting an invitation, or

148 • House of Horrors

revealing one's name to the host, thereby easing anxiety surrounding the essential unknowability of the Other. In contrast, unconditional hospitality is not limited by language and works *with* rather than *against* difference. As Andrzej Marzec has noted in his book-length study of hauntology, it is precisely this lack of knowledge about the foreigner/guest/visitor that constitutes absolute hospitability.[51] Not knowing who we have accepted into our home, we willingly and anxiously agree not to pursue our guest's identity and their secrets. Such an understanding of hospitability puts the host in an emotionally fraught situation, as a stable, fixed and unified self needs to maintain absolute power over their familial space in Western understanding. In this sense, the unwelcome visitor, the haunting entity, the ghostly Other, invades the familial space and violates the power structure and implicit hierarchy of the host's home.

When Amanda's house is invaded by absolute Otherness under Naamah's guise, her carefully structured selfhood collapses. The absolute hospitability she has inadvertently offered by not questioning her 'guest' and asking her to leave threatens Amanda's integrity, which gradually disintegrates over the course of her narrative. This is not an entirely unwelcome process, as Amanda's rigid and integrated self is, at best, 'a nostalgic vision of subjectivity'[52] and, at worst, a delusionary misconception. The novel subtly implies that the coherent 'self' that Amanda constructed for herself in her early twenties was, due to its underlying presumption of wholeness and finitude, not only false but facile. Another concept, that of *hostipitality*, a pun on hostility and hospitality coined by Derrida in *Of Hospitality*, points to the inherent ambiguity of hospitability, which can never wholly separate itself from a potential for violence.[53] As Amanda's guest/ghost violates house rules and breaks the tacit agreement that Amanda is the one in control, the ensuing violence may be unavoidable. Gradually, Amanda is transformed from a curious host accommodating a strange guest to the horrified host of a parasitic entity, ultimately taken hostage in her own corporeal space.

Amanda may have invited Naamah in due to an accumulation of marital disappointments. The night following a Valentine's Day fiasco, Amanda dreams of a beautiful, pink-skinned, dark-eyed and black-haired woman playing in a 'red ocean . . . rimmed with a shore of darker crimson sand' (p. 17). When Naamah asks Amanda to stay with her, she readily agrees. Lying next to Naamah on the red beach, Amanda wants this perfect and constant companion, friend, sister and lover to stay

Spectral Kinship and Ghostly Selves • 149

forever. Spurred on by Naamah, Amanda starts to smoke again, a habit she relinquished for Ed but missed 'like an old friend moving out of town' (p. 26). Thus, Amanda returns to her old self, perhaps her primary self, the one she was as a child and a teenager, with no social restrains or dreams and ambitions that were not her own.[54] Naamah appears to be helping Amanda reclaim this older self: a girl majoring in the arts who is a bit wild, reckless with her health and finances, and prefers bad boys to bland bores.

The female solidarity and intense friendship that fills the gap left by an absent mother are the cornerstones of Amanda and Naamah's relationship. Amanda has no close female friends or role models: as mentioned, her stepmother was a gold-digger who squandered the family money, and her grandmother is mentioned in passing as someone who restricted her budding femininity. Still, Naamah's promise of female solidarity proves to be rather unsubstantial when she fails to protect Amanda from the consequences of her (their?) actions. During dinner with the couple's friends, Alex and Sophia, Amanda realises she is not the only one to be possessed. Sophia, who appears to have accepted her demon, tells Amanda to relax and enjoy the power she will soon acquire. Amanda begins to notice other strong, stunning and self-assured women and men who are either possessed or demons themselves. Yet there is no sense of solidarity, only a tacit understanding of the secret demonic power they now share. Ultimately, Amanda wants Naamah to leave her, but as Naamah explains, 'I never made you do anything. I only let you do what you wanted. I told you, Amanda, I can't have fun without you' (p. 142). Amanda admits she got what she wanted all along: someone to love her completely and never leave, no matter what. Thus, Amanda's relationship with Naamah is far more meaningful and solid than her marriage to Ed.

Carla Freccero has claimed that ghosts frustrate easy definitions of ownership and belonging, as '[t]here is no "propriety," no "proprietariness" in ghostliness'.[55] Naamah's wish to possess Amanda is thus complicated by the fact that Amanda wants to be/be with Naamah and, at least subconsciously, welcomes this arrangement. Naamah embodies every improper aspect of Amanda's personality, everything she has striven to hide, mask or mould into something socially acceptable. Again, many of the transgressions Amanda perpetrates feel *proper* to her in the sense that she gains satisfaction from rebelling against that which is widely considered appropriate, and her impulses become understandable when contrasted with the whitewashed lifestyle she secretly abhors.

150 • House of Horrors

The 'Wandering Subject' in *The Between*

Tananarive Due's novels are often described as supernatural or speculative fiction, a scholarly gesture that links Due's output to the critical embrace of Afrofuturism during the 1990s, 'a decade of counterhegemonic multiculturalism'.[56] This critical reluctance to locate Due's works within the horror genre has slowly dissipated over the past decade, as evidenced by references to and analyses of Due's fiction in Kinitra D. Brooks's *Searching for Sycorax*, Jess Nevins' *Horror Fiction in the Twentieth Century*, Venetria K. Patton's *The Grasp that Reaches Beyond the Grave: the Ancestral Call in Black Women's Texts*,[57] Gina Wisker's *Contemporary Women's Gothic Fiction*, and Lisa Kröger and Melanie R. Anderson's *Monster, She Wrote*. Her semi-autobiographical novel, *The Between* (1995), can be read as 'a combination of horror novel, detective story, and suspense/thriller',[58] although, to my eyes, the emphasis on spectral visitation resolutely marks it as horror fiction.[59]

Due's novel taps into a rich tradition of African-American Gothic, which primarily deals with what Kathleen Brogan has termed cultural hauntings rather than ghostly visitations or possessions.[60] Brogan has detailed how contemporary African-American writers have added to the classic Gothic tradition, in which ghosts have largely served as a plot device 'to illuminate the more shadowy or repressed aspects of characters'; the ghosts in African-American Gothic 'signal an attempt to recover and make social use of a poorly documented, partially erased cultural history'[61] and enable authors 'to re-create ethnic identity through an imaginative recuperation of the past and to press this new version of the past into the service of the present'.[62] The communal aspects of a cultural haunting are heavily underlined; thus, the ghost functions as more than an externalisation of the haunted self, interacting with a larger community from which an individual cannot easily disentangle themselves. The ghost links both individual memory and group history, and 'ghostly "kinship" replaces biological descent as the basis for ethnic affiliation'.[63]

On the one hand, this novel yields easily to a psychoanalytic reading, in which Abraham and Torok's concept of transgenerational haunting takes centre stage: the protagonist, Hilton James, cannot cope with a traumatic secret that he unknowingly inherited from his grandmother. Alternatively, the splintered temporality of the narration is reminiscent of the disruption produced by Derrida's spectre, the *revenant/arrivant*, who disregards linear progression and clear-cut causality. Crucially, this lack of

Spectral Kinship and Ghostly Selves • 151

narrative linearity and embrace of cyclicity release *The Between* from Western narrative restrictions and allow the novel to be read in terms of *sankofarration*, a term first coined by John Jennings and productively adapted by Kinitra D. Brooks, Alexis McGee and Stephanie Schoellman in their study of Black literary horror.[64] Combining a Twi word from the Akan Tribe of Ghana, *Sankofa*, to refer to the retrieval and reuse of the past in the present, with *narration*, a progress-orientated conceptualisation of stories used in the West, sankofarration proclaims the non-linearity and cyclical nature of time. By deploying sankofarration as their critical framework, Brooks, McGee and Schoellman are able to dislocate 'the trauma of enslavement' as the quintessential source of Black horror fiction and open their analysis to the rich folkloric and artistic African and African-American traditions that permeate contemporary Black horror writing.[65] In their words, 'speculative sankofarration actively claims literary hauntings as interstices of resistance',[66] and reading *The Between* as an exercise in sankofarration rather than a conventional Western ghost story reveals the complexity of Hilton's spectral status.[67]

Hilton has inherited his grandmother's ability to flee the spirits of death. This is both a gift and a curse, enabling Hilton to save his family but almost driving him mad in the process. As a child, he witnesses the miraculous resurrection of his grandmother Nana, but represses this harrowing memory in the wake of his own near-death experience. It is suggested that his grandmother cheated death in order to save young Hilton from drowning the following year. In a similar manner, when a husband and father, Hilton saves his family from death at the hands of a neo-Nazi bomber. Unhinged by hate mail and racist threats, Hilton almost drives into a hearse, which, as he had forgotten to fasten his seat belt, would have been fatal. For a split second he smells salty air, an olfactory reminder of his brush with death in 1964, as well as charred rubber, a signal from the timeline in which he dies in this car accident. Immediately before this near-death experience, Hilton had seen a ghostly figure inside the hearse asking how many more times he will cheat death. And, just as Nana became restless and irritable after her first death, Hilton is plagued by horrific nightmares and hallucinations as his mental health swiftly deteriorates. Yet, unlike his grandmother, Hilton is not aware of his gift, at least not consciously, and attempts to ignore everything that indicates he is a half-ghost haunted by a horde of embittered death spirits.

It is only when rational explanations become untenable that Hilton finally asks his adoptive parents about the swimming accident. They

152 • House of Horrors

confirm that his heart stopped beating and he was officially dead for a couple of minutes. Through hypnosis he discovers there are mysterious 'others' who are angry with his ability to move to and stay 'in the between', the limbo state between life and death (p. 218). He has managed to appropriate thirty birthdays from these 'others', death spirits who manifest as Hilton's alternative selves from other timelines. The hypnosis session reveals that on some level Hilton understands what is happening to him and to Nana three decades earlier, but his conscious self refuses to process the information. Each time he falls asleep, Hilton's spirit escapes to a different timeline, explaining why many of his memories appear impossible.

Desperate to find a rational explanation for his nightmares, distortions in time perception, mis-remembered facts and hallucinations, Hilton finally contacts a friend's brother, Andres, who has experience of investigating near-death experiences. From Andres, Hilton learns about Marguerite, a woman who went through a strikingly similar ordeal. A Vodou priest declared Marguerite to be 'walking dead', someone who should have died but had come back to life and now 'walked between life, death, and the gods' (p. 241). In a word, she found herself 'in-between'. Andres tells Hilton that doorways lead to different spirits and different realities. On her death, Margarite's spirit escaped to a different reality, one in which she did not die. Entering a different doorway each time she fell asleep, Margarite found herself in a slightly different version of reality when she awoke. It is suggested that she decided to stay alive longer to save her young cousins from a house fire. Rather predictably, Hilton still rejects the walking dead hypothesis, preferring to find consolation in the rational diagnosis of late-onset schizophrenia.

This ability to escape death is explained through Vodou in Marguerite's case, suggesting a wider mesh of spiritual connections and associations, all non-Western in origin. An even stronger connection emerges in a conversation about Ghanaian spirituality. Hilton learns that his native Ghanaian mother-in-law, Kessie, insisted on changing her granddaughter's name from Imani, a Kiswahili name meaning 'faith' chosen by his wife, Dede, to the Ghanaian name, Kaya. As a cousin of Dede explains, this symbolic 'born-to-die name', which translates as 'stay and don't go back', was intended to trick the death spirits that inhabited the child. When Hilton presses Kessie, she relates a story from her childhood in a village near Accra. Her mother had witnessed a death spirit above the head of her newborn brother an hour before he stopped breathing and died. Though unwilling to accept such superstition, Kessie believes she saw a similar

Spectral Kinship and Ghostly Selves • 153

spirit above Kaya's crib, prompting her to demand Dede changed her baby's name.

Kessie also tells Hilton that her grandchildren, Kaya and Jamil, initially seemed insubstantial, each baby seemingly 'less than a corpse . . . nothing' (p. 153). This refers to the fact that, like Hilton, they were not meant to be born. It was Nana who interfered with the timeline by refusing to die, then staying alive long enough to save Hilton from drowning. Yet the idea of a 'proper' timeline destroyed by Nana and then Hilton is repeatedly challenged. In a dream, Kaya is visited by the ghost of Antoinette, a girl her age who died of AIDS and was a patient of Hilton's at the drug-rehab centre. Antoinette comes to Kaya to warn her about the neo-Nazi harassing her family, but also inadvertently sheds light on Hilton's predicament. Antoinette's ghost explains that she had trouble finding the right doorway because Kaya James did not exist in some places. As Nana explains to Hilton in a dream, his children are living on borrowed time: 'they have no time that belongs to them. They came to be from what you stole' (p. 224). Although Antoinette tells Kaya she was not supposed to be born, she also assures her she will grow up to be a great scientist, instrumental in the fight against HIV.

Rather than a nightmare, Kaya's dream feels melancholic and almost mundane. Through the effortless intermingling of the dead and the living, Due challenges the typically Western separation of the two realms. Due uses the anglicised term, 'born-to-die', for the child-spirits known in traditional West African stories as *ogbanje* or *abiki*. According to the Yoruba and the Igbo, *ogbanje* and *abiki* describe a child that is born many times but, as it remains chained to the spirit world, dies young. Hilton, who is caught between being a human and a 'born-to-die' *ogbanje*, cannot be exorcised or re-buried by others; neither can he function as a speaker for the past or as a victim demanding retribution. Nana, her body taken by the sea and her grave remaining empty, could be viewed as a more traditional ghost figure. However, returning to haunt Hilton's dreams thirty years later, Nana's ghost does not follow the Western ghost-story tradition and demand a proper burial, but intends to help Hilton rectify his and her own errors and pass over. Nana's agenda changes once she gets to know Dede and her grandchildren: she decides to help Hilton save his family.

Hilton's 'in-between' status is also akin to the concept of a 'wandering subject', theorised by Achille Mbembe in his analysis of the Nigerian author, Amos Tutuola, and his fiction based on Yoruba folktales. The 'wandering subject' continues to:

154 • House of Horrors

produce himself in the unknown, by means of a chain of effects that have been calculated beforehand, but never materialize exactly in the terms foreseen. It is thus in the unexpected and radical instability that he creates and invents himself. There is thus no sovereignty of the subject or life as such.[68]

In contrast to Western spectrality, there is no exorcism here and rather than a 'counterweight or corrective' to a stable sense of unified self, the ghost acts as a reminder that permanence and unity are in and of themselves illusory at best. [69] Mbembe sets out to demonstrate how invested Western ontology is in the ideal of a rational, self-governing subject, which, in its post-Enlightenment formulation, attempts to suppress passion, imagination and the spiritual, as well as deny or mistrust '[t]he world of instincts and animality'.[70]

As a 'wandering subject', Hilton frustrates the stability of self, time and truth. There is no clear genealogy in *The Between*, and no obvious continuity between the past, present and future. Intended to drown at the age of seven, Hilton has children who should not have been born: he is '[a] dead tree dropping seedlings' (p. 126). Although Venetria K. Patton has stated that as an *ogbanje*, Hilton was never meant to become an ancestor,[71] she also observes that in some beliefs, *ogbanjes* can be persuaded to stay and start families. In a way, starting a family is a way of repaying Nana's sacrifice.[72] When he finally dies, Hilton swims to his grandmother, waiting for him on the shore.[73] He is a child again, repeating his first near-death experience, and holding a medical pin that he was given by Kaya: he can no longer recall its meaning, but knows it was from someone he loved, 'a very great woman, a famous healer he knew once, long ago' (p. 287).[74] Thus the various timelines and phases of his life collapse in the afterlife: his past as Kaya's father recedes as he returns to his seven-year-old self, the original self that was lost when his grandmother prevented his death. His 'famous healer' daughter belongs to a future Hilton has not lived to see. As sankofarration, Due's novel is indebted to neither 'the linear progressive narratives of modernity' nor 'the embrace of its antithesis in fragmentary postmodernity'; instead, it welcomes 'a cosmos of imaginative returns that open the way for the retrieval, and reinvention, of lost futures'.[75] In all this generative chaos, what binds Hilton's realities together is his unwavering commitment to his family and their future(s).

The fractured temporality of Hilton's own existence as half-human, half-*ogbanje* is superimposed on two significant periods in

African-American history: the promise of the 1960s and the failure of the 1990s. As Patton has noted, the 1990s, marked by the Los Angeles riots of 1992, increasingly resentful and racist debates about affirmative action and multiculturalism, and the steady growth of carceral capitalism, witnessed the end of many gains achieved by the Civil Rights Movement.[76] Consequently, Due's decision to cast a white supremacist as the villain points to the enduring importance of race politics, despite the novel's lack of engagement with America's racial past and the legacy of slavery to the same extent as, for instance, Toni Morrison's *Beloved*. A comparison with this Gothic neo-slave narrative is warranted: Beloved can be read as a death spirit whose motivation cannot simply be subsumed under a quest for retribution or proper burial, but rather speaks to 'the social and spiritual unease' the characters experience in their everyday life.[77]

Racism remains the most prevalent form of 'social and spiritual unease' reverberating through Due's novel. In fact, it is the death spirits who select Charles Ray as their agent of Hilton's demise and instruct him through dreams. Death is thus presented as a mastermind who can 'dispatch all kinds of agents, inanimate and animate including, in this case, the ocean, roads, motor vehicles, racism, a neo-Nazi, and a letter bomb'.[78] The novel emphasises that of all these dangers, their constant companion, racism, is the one most likely to succeed in destroying Hilton's family.[79] In fact, as racism is so deeply ingrained in their lives, Charles Ray's hate mail is initially ignored by Dede's office. As Okonkwo points out, Charles Ray not only targets Dede because of her ethnic background, but also her gender and the power and authority that accompany her class mobility.

Romantic relationships, as presented through Hilton's focalisation, reveal his investment in racially coded stereotypes of Black femininity and masculinity, as well as heterosexual romance. It could be argued that the ghostliness constructed by Due to mark Hilton's ontologically indefinite status, his children's precarious existence, and his uneasy relationship with the past, brings not only the weight of racism into focus but also that of normative masculinity. Hilton admits he went to grad school to secure two things: a master's degree and a wife. Originating from a working-class (Nana) and lower-middle-class (his adoptive parents) background, Hilton perceives working-class and lower-middle-class women as only good enough for dancing and sex. At college, he sought someone more sophisticated: a woman from a middle-class professional background who would, in turn, elevate his social status. Some college friends suggested that he should date educated white women with their 'imaginations fixated on

156 • House of Horrors

the Congo' (p. 19). Scoffing at this idea, Hilton chooses Dede, a fierce and independent woman with a Ghanaian mother and well-respected pastor for a father. 'After a year's worth of Earth, Wind & Fire concerts, poetry readings, and black student meetings', they were engaged (p. 20). Yet, from the very beginning, and dangerously close to the 'angry Black woman' stereotype that saturates the American mainstream media, Dede is cast in the role of jealous nagging wife, prone to verbal outbursts and unmanageable fury. Hilton's work among predominantly female social workers and many young, female rehab clients does nothing to assuage his wife's obsessive doubts about his fidelity. The fights increase in intensity over the years, with Dede consistently presented as the irrational instigator. It is suggested her jealousy is a family legacy: her father spent his final years facing rumours that he had installed a female lover in a town apartment. The way that Hilton explains Dede's behaviour further ensures his role as a blameless victim of his wife's paranoid hysteria, and yet in one of the realities to which Hilton escapes he sleeps with a client called Danira. Although he hastily leaves this reality and moves in and out of realities without the 'Danira incident' for the remainder of the novel, he has cheated on his wife, suggesting that Dede's fears were not unfounded.

When Kaya is seven and Jamil a toddler, Dede and Hilton reach an impasse that requires marriage counselling. Thanks to therapy, Hilton realises his obsession with giving back to the community is a way of repaying the grandmother who died to save him and can confront his unacknowledged childhood guilt: despite disobeying his grandmother by swimming out too far and causing her death, Hilton was rewarded with indulgent adoptive parents. Having confronted this guilt Hilton can move on, and the nightmares stop, only to return following Hilton's brush with death in a car accident. This suggests a clear correlation between family crises and Hilton's ambiguous half-ghost status. Each time his family life comes close to collapse, reality starts to crumble and Hilton becomes unmoored and unable to hold on to one timeline, set of memories and stable identity.

Hilton also struggles with the high demands placed on Black masculinity. On the one hand, he becomes increasingly irritable and paranoid due to fatigue, lack of sleep and exhausting switches between realities; while on the other hand, his paranoia, anger and violence could also be read as a reaction to his decreasing authority in his own household as well as his powerlessness as a Black man in American society. Having accidentally hurt his son in a panic attack, Hilton calls Dede an 'ungrateful bitch' in the ensuing fight, and in an ineffectual attempt to reassert his masculinity, tells her that if it were not for him, his children would not have been born (p. 210). Hilton, feeling slighted and unappreciated, cannot contain his anger. On some basic level, he expects co-operation and gratitude for buying a guard dog and a gun and keeping guard over the family through the night. However, on a deeper level, his anger derives from the knowledge that he has overstayed his welcome in this world. Hilton is staying for a family who cannot comprehend the scope of his suffering and sacrifice. Dede tells Hilton that he has changed to 'a man who lives here, you walk with that gun, you're watching over us all the time like some sort of guardian angel. But other than that, I don't know you' (p. 129). All elements, personas and components of his identity unrelated to protecting his family's future are obliterated through Hilton's constant flights between realities. In a cruel twist, he is reduced to the caricature of a family man, a ghostly presence obsessed with a family that barely know him.

It is in his dreams that Hilton is most mercilessly haunted by the death spirits. The dreamscape is posited as a liminal space between life and death in which he can talk to Nana and his other selves. Hilton comes to see this as his own personal hell, filled with nightmares, hallucinations, lucid dreams and, finally, Charles Ray. Lines of identical houses appear in his dreams, each containing a different would-have-been or should-have-been reality. Rather than seeing his own reflection in the mirrors that appear in his dreams, Hilton sees hundreds of men covered in blood and 'with glowering eyes full of hate', all asking him to stop running (p. 42). Having evaded death and opened so many doors, Hilton is an abomination to the spirits. 'I left you a curse, not a blessing' (p. 134) states Nana in one dream; she accepts she was wrong to save Hilton and admonishes him gently, 'Child, you done swum out too far' (p. 90).[80]

Although Nana's ghost indicates the past as the source of Hilton's current predicament, the novel's conclusion, in which he reverts to his seven-year-old self with no memory of an adult life, suggests a temporality not bound by past wrongs and future renewals. Due underlines the importance of ancestral protection that Nana extends over Hilton, thus joining the past, the present and the future literally into one sankofarration and uniting the familiar and the familial in death. Hilton is haunted by the empty spaces left by his grandmother in both his past and his selfhood, upholding Abraham's assertion that it is not the dead that haunt us but rather the gaps 'produced in us by the concealment of some part of a love object's life'.[81] Nana functions as a phantom in Abraham and Torok's sense

158 • House of Horrors

in that she protects secret knowledge from surfacing and masquerades in Hilton's mind as a distant yet pleasant memory, rather than a true connection to his past and his troubling gift of flight. It takes therapy and hypnosis for Hilton to recover true memories of his early childhood in order to deal with the repercussions of his own escape from death.

Okonkwo points to the *ogbanje*'s 'ideological entanglement in questions of borders and border crossings, displacement, exile, belonging, double vision, and identity-formation'.[82] Hilton's entire life could be seen as a series of crossings and journeys between different realms and states: he moves between families, identities, social classes and alternative realities. Hounded by death spirits, but also positioned as a half-spirit himself, Hilton cannot escape the sacrifices accompanying his journeys. Each passage revolves around the issue of belonging to *a* family, either the one he lost as a child or the one he is trying to save as an adult. As a half-ghost stuck in the titular between, Hilton struggles to hold on to the aspects of his identity that most clearly define him: a grandson, a husband and a father.

Familial Disintegration in *Within These Walls*

Tom Gunning suggests that '[a] ghost puts the nature of the human senses, vision especially, in crisis'[83] – that is, a ghost signifies an epistemological impossibility that demands recognition and swift rectification. Seen in this light, the protagonists' refusal to acknowledge the ghosts populating Ania Ahlborn's *Within These Walls* (2015) signals their unwillingness to accept the rifts threatening their family life and the emptiness of pseudo-familial substitutes. In contrast to Due's novel, *Within These Walls* draws heavily from conventional ghost stories, in which the ghost signifies an aberration and a dangerous intrusion into everyday life. While some of the ghosts that Ahlborn introduces urge the living not to repeat their own tragic pasts, others manipulate and lie to further their own selfish ambitions. As Avery Gordon has eloquently stated, ghost stories are ultimately stories about '*permissions and prohibitions, presence and absence, about apparitions and hysterical blindness*'.[84] *Within These Walls* lends itself easily to this reading, as the Gothicised family drama revolves around patriarchal control and neglect, broken lines of communication, hubris and a stubborn refusal to face reality. On a literal level this is the story of a young girl haunted and manipulated by spectral visitors, but this haunting also challenges us

Spectral Kinship and Ghostly Selves • 159

to reconsider the ways in which patriarchal power is distributed, certain subjects are driven into a spectral void, and many stories are haunted by silences and misrecognitions long before the arrival of actual ghosts.

In *Within These Walls*, Ahlborn, the Polish-born author now living in Portland weaves together two narratives: the first follows the present-day story of Lucas Graham, a failed writer attempting to resuscitate his career with a true-crime book on Jeff C. Halcomb, a cult leader responsible for a gruesome massacre three decades earlier; the second narrative charts the events leading up to the deaths of eight young people in Halcomb's commune during the early 1980s. The story begins with death row inmate Halcomb contacting Lucas with a promise of exclusive access to himself on the condition that Lucas moves into his old house: 'You want my story, you live in my house' (The Letter).[85] Lucas, who has been struggling to repeat his initial success for over a decade, is too thrilled by this opportunity to question Halcomb's unusual request. With his marriage failing, Lucas persuades his soon-to-be ex-wife to grant him a few months with their pre-teen daughter, Jeanie. In the second storyline, readers are introduced to Audra, a soft-spoken, fragile girl who has been abandoned by her upper-class parents. Living alone in a beautiful summer house, Audra is gradually being manipulated into joining Halcomb's commune and allowing them to move in.

At first glance the two narratives do not appear particularly original: Lucas is yet another self-absorbed father ignoring his prepubescent daughter's mood swings and teenage angst until it is too late to save her, and Audra is just another lonely young girl consumed by a misogynist cult through a skilful combination of psychobabble, hippie spirituality and false promises of emotional support. Yet, as Ahlborn places the narrative focus on characterisation and relationships rather than the supernatural, *Within These Walls* primarily presents a bleak tale of protagonists haunted by familial disintegration and dysfunction. The sense of inevitability permeating the novel is heightened through particular narrative choices, the most important being how the hauntings are structured. The strange occurrences that begin the very night Lucas and Jeanie move into the Montlake Road house fall into two main categories: temporal disturbances that echo the events from the early 1980s related in the second storyline; and encounters with the ghosts of Halcomb and his followers, most intensely experienced by Jeanie. An important theme that Ahlborn also explores is the question of identity formation within familial structures, specifically the ritual acts of naming and renaming oneself or others.

160 • House of Horrors

The present-day plot alternates between the perspectives of Lucas and Jeanie. Lucas is presented as a man haunted by his past success and failed marriage. It is desperation that prevents him from not only questioning Halcomb's proposal but also leaving the increasingly dangerous Montlake Road house. Lucas becomes aware that '[t]his was a mistake. A bad idea. The house wasn't meant to be lived in by anyone, not after the things that had happened within these walls' (Chapter 12). Yet knowing that Caroline will probably win sole custody and Jeanie will be left with the memory of 'a washed-up loser of a dad' (Chapter 19) compels Lucas to stay. Unsurprisingly, Halcomb refuses to see Lucas once they have settled into Audra's house and commits suicide soon after. Lucas, lured into staying by his neighbour, Echo, fails to notice his daughter's increasing estrangement and her unhealthy involvement with Echo and Halcomb's ghost. In a tense finale, Halcomb's ghost returns to complete the ritual he and his followers had begun with Audra's infant baby in 1983. Using Jeanie as a surrogate for Audra, Halcomb kills her and takes over Lucas's body.

Lucas believes he is 'trying to fix things, not just for himself, but for the three of them as a whole. As a family. As something they used to be. Something he hoped they could be again' (Chapter 1). His and Caroline's past as young Goths remains a significant reference point for Lucas, who bemoans the fact that his wife is no longer the black-haired girl he fell in love with, but a 'proper' and naturally blonde businesswoman. Rather than being proud of his wife for financially supporting the family, her success makes Lucas miserable. His feeling of emasculation is compounded by the knowledge that Caroline is having an affair and the fact that he is unable to confront her. Despite viewing her as 'a liar. An adulteress. A provocateur' (Chapter 1), Lucas allows himself to be humiliated by Caroline's angry outbursts, perhaps in an unconscious acceptance of his own inadequacy.

Lucas's unyielding refusal to confront reality manifests in various ways. Afraid of what could happen if Jeanie learns too much about his failed marriage and career, he disregards all opportunities to communicate with his daughter. He prefers to read Jeanie's black kohl and sulkiness as signs she is following in his footsteps rather than admit he knows virtually nothing about his daughter. Similarly, Jeanie withdraws into her own world, ignoring the rare possibilities of mutual understanding between her and Lucas. These missed opportunities are thematically re-enacted towards the end of the novel. Jeanie misinterprets her dad's actions, believing that he is chasing ghosts rather than searching for her. During their final hours at the house, a delirious Lucas realises that Halcomb had always planned

Spectral Kinship and Ghostly Selves • 161

to kill him and his daughter. Jeanie also realises that the ghosts are there to kill, not to help. The father and daughter are now locked in the same physical space but in two separate timelines: Lucas in the present day, his daughter in 1983. When the two temporal planes collide, only Halcomb, in Lucas's body, survives.

Jeanie is manipulated by Echo and the ghosts of Halcomb's followers into falling for Jeff. This would not have happened, Ahlborn suggests, had she had the support of her parents. Jeanie, who had been quite happy until her tenth birthday when her parents started fighting, is smart enough to recognise the power game being played out between them, and the fact that Lucas is attempting to use his Goth scene insight to win over his daughter and annoy Caroline. Also aware of her mother's affair, Jeanie is disgusted by her father's silence. Despite such awareness, Jeanie is too young to be able to distance herself from her parents' problems and believes their divorce is somehow her fault. She also knows that rather than being cruel to her father she could simply tell him how much she loves him and understands his passion for writing. Her inability to do so results in guilt and self-loathing: '*It's like there's something wrong with you. You're broken, Vee* [her own nickname]. *He'll be happier without you, too*' (Chapter 28).[86] Like Audra three decades earlier, Jeanie is prone to self-doubt: '*You're a coward, that's all. A spineless kid who wants to be tough, but when it gets even a little bit scary, you wuss out* . . . She was terrified of everything. Ghosts. Boys. Divorce' (Chapter 21). Over time, however, Jeanie shifts the blame to her father for abandoning her in favour of his work and begins to feel stronger. This, too, parallels Audra's journey from self-reproach to condemnation of her parents.

Having learnt the history of the Montlake Road house, Jeanie is slowly drawn into the world of Jeff Halcomb, who, in her dreams, resembles 'Jack White and Johnny Depp, kind of vampiric with his pale skin and black hair, sexy in a quiet yet dangerous sort of way' (Chapter 21). As the ghosts promise not to harm her, Jeanie decides against telling her father about her budding romance and supernatural encounters. After receiving a cryptic sign from the ghosts, Jeanie relaxes, believing that Halcomb will take care of her: '[i]t was his [Halcomb's] eyes. They promised to dissolve Vee's fears. All that anxiety about her parents, about fitting in, about what was lurking in the dark . . . he'd make it go away, if only she believed' (Chapter 21). Despite Jeff's intention to kill rather than sexually abuse Jeanie, the grooming she is subjected to is clearly modelled on paedophiliac behaviour.

162 • House of Horrors

Jeanie's full name is Virginia, but, in defiance of her parents' nickname 'Jeanie', she refers to herself as 'Vee'. Thus, in contrast to Audra, who is presented with a new name by Jeff, Jeanie starts out with a degree of agency. Yet, like Audra, she remains exceptionally vulnerable and does not recognise Echo's attempts to divide her and Lucas. It is Echo who provides Jeanie with a new nickname 'Vivi', and encourages her reliance on Jeff:

> I knew you were the one from the first moment I saw you, Vivi . . . You're just like them, you know. Lost, wanting more than what you have, deserving of more than what you're being given. Kids like you – that's who Jeffrey loved the most. That's why they turned to him, Vivi. He knew what they needed, and Jeff gave them everything he promised. (Chapter 38)

When Echo gives Jeanie a photo of Jeff with a signed note reading 'Dearest Vivi, See you soon. – J.', she is confirming her as Audra's replacement. Three decades earlier it had been Audra hailed as 'the one'.

This emotional mirroring of Audra and Jeanie is emphasised a number of times, despite the two girls apparently having little in common. Jeanie conveys the impression of being a rather mature twelve-year-old, able to see through her parents' deceptions and not afraid to take risks when making new friends. In contrast, the incredibly frail and anxious Audra relies on acceptance and attention from other people for her self-esteem. However, both girls feel abandoned and unloved by their parents. In the penultimate chapter of Audra's timeline, we learn that one of the names she had chosen for her unborn child was 'Vivi', and in her final moments, Jeanie, now wan and sickly looking, becomes a stand-in for Audra.

Three decades earlier, Audra is abandoned by her politician father and socialite mother in the small seaside town of Pier Pointe. Her only friend is Marguerite 'Maggie' James, who lives less than a mile from her house and has a small daughter named Eloise, later known as Echo. When Audra attempts suicide at the age of twelve, her mother is more concerned with saving a bathmat from the resulting blood than her daughter dying.[87] To combat such self-destructive behaviour, Audra is on anti-depressants, paid for by her father. Used 'to feeling inconsequential' (Chapter 2), Audra's life changes when she meets a group of drifters camping on the beach near her house. Initially mistrustful of Halcomb's commune, she quickly bonds with Deacon, a handsome boy from a similar background of rich

Spectral Kinship and Ghostly Selves • 163

but disinterested parents, who offers Audra a tempting mix of self-reliance and emotional independence from her parents, in exchange for dependence on a new form of kinship: 'Whoever made up that crap about blood being thicker than water didn't have a clue, and that's where we come in. You can't pick your blood family, but you can pick your spiritual one' (Chapter 3). To her delight, Deacon addresses her as their 'new sister' the second time they meet.

Jeff's commune adopts the typical cult framework: a charismatic male leader, communal living, free love and countercultural antimaterialism, religious references to rebirth and eternal life, anti-establishment politics and, most importantly, the formation of a new family to replace the old. Research into the role of the family in cult involvement and new religious movements (NRMs) has been ongoing since the 1970s. As Sebastian Murken and Sussan Namini have noted, NRMs are often accused of being 'anti-self', 'anti-society' and, finally, 'anti-family',[88] demonstrating the centrality of social and familial issues in public debate about the phenomena. In pop-cultural representations, sects and cults are consistently presented through familial tropes: a new and improved family is established, misunderstood by the outside world; an escape is made from abusive or uncaring relations to a more supportive family; an attempt is made to protect a new family by escaping from an abusive cult; and brainwashing results in hatred towards the 'natural' family. Research confirms that early family experiences have a substantial bearing on an adult's decision to join an NRM, and suggest membership can provide 'some kind of compensation for individuals with problematic family backgrounds' and absent parents.[89] Audra is looking for a compensatory family and, with both her parents absent, paternal and maternal figures. Paradoxically, as she invites Jeff's commune into her house and provides them with food, shelter, her material and emotional resources and, finally, her own body, Audra finds the maternal figure in herself. For a while, before she is reduced to a vessel for Jeff's sacrificial child, she even harbours the hope of becoming Jeff's wife and 'mother' to the whole group.

Each person's entry into this new family is marked by a quasi-baptism, in which they are given a new name by Jeff. Thus, Georgia became Gypsy, and Shelly was welcomed as Sunnie. When Jeff meets Audra he calls her 'Avis', meaning 'bird, perfect for a girl who's ready to learn how to fly' (Chapter 9). On an impulse, Audra invites Jeff's commune to stay at her house and slowly adapts to her new friends, music, the smell of incense, even her new name. This convention of renaming feels appropriate for

164 • House of Horrors

Audra: 'It was a way to purge the soul of its past life and welcome it into its newfound family. Somehow, "Avis" felt right, like the name she should have had all along. As though, maybe, the fact that she had been born mislabeled has somehow contributed to a less-than-happy life' (Chapter 11). Only later do readers learn that Audra was accepted into Halcomb's family as a replacement for Sandra, a woman who refused to carry Jeff's baby and managed to escape.

Unsurprisingly, despite its communal and non-heteronormative aspects, the cult is organised in a highly hierarchical manner with Jeff at the top, his male followers below and women at the very bottom. This gendered hierarchy is particularly evident during meals, when the women prepare food but are allowed to eat only once the men have finished. Audra's belongings are shared by all. The same soon applies to her body, as Jeff's concept of free love amounts to the constant sexual availability of women. All the cult members are dedicated to 'loving one person': Jeff Halcomb (Chapter 20). Audra is aware that Jeff demands blind faith: 'A red flag waved wildly in the back of her mind, assuring her that only the insane would agree to such allegiance . . . Every aspect of such devotion went against what she knew about free will' (Chapter 11). However, being part of the group still feels preferable to 'battling inner demons' alone. Audra finds solace in being led, given strong convictions and substance: 'Believing in the group was, in essence, believing in herself' (Chapter 11). She is ready to exchange her individuality and loneliness for 'a new name and a constant companionship' (Chapter 11): in one week she goes from 'Audra Snow to Avis Collective. Avis Togetherness. Avis One-For-All' (Chapter 20). Dominated by her father and emotionally crippled by her mother, Audra is an easy target for Jeff. He convinces her that while her parents bribe her with occasional promises of 'false love', they are simply bad people exploiting her traumatic past to keep her emotionally chained to the family. Ironically, these are the very same methods employed by Jeff, and Audra has merely replaced an authoritarian father with an emotionally and physically abusive tyrant.

That Jeff is not the benevolent spiritual leader that he claims to be is made clear during Audra's first sexual encounter with him, described in terms that strongly suggest rape. Although she believes Jeff is 'finally rewarding her for her faith', Audra cannot help crying as he undoes his trousers and forces her onto the mattress: 'She wept, and she told herself it was joy' (Chapter 20). Later, when it becomes clear Audra's faith is not as strong as that of the other members, Jeff declares her place in the Halcomb family to be in jeopardy. As punishment for her weakness, she is subjected to a group rape by all the men in this so-called family: 'Four pairs of hands groped at her flesh. Teeth dragged across her skin . . . She sobbed as they pulled at her bra and underwear, tearing at them like aggressors, like animals, like nobody she'd have ever called her family at all' (Chapter 42). By now she is pregnant and too scared to leave the commune. The breaking point, however, takes place sometime later, when Audra is forced to kill a homeowner during a burglary. Her reluctance prompts the group to keep Audra under constant surveillance until the day of the ritual, when all eight followers poison themselves with arsenic, and Jeff cuts Audra open and kills her newborn child.

Police officers arrive on the scene before Halcomb can offer Audra's baby to supernatural forces. Ahlborn provides little information about Jeff's motivations: he may be a Satanist or a psychic, or have been chosen by a mysterious deity for an unknown purpose. Although his 'philosophy' is never explicitly described, sacrificing his followers and Audra's baby was intended to grant Jeff eternal life. He tells Audra 'I'm on this earth to usher a select few to a perfect world – a world of kindness, happiness . . . of unconditional love. And you're here to help me achieve that' (Chapter 42): this implies that his control over others was so profound and long-lasting that it felt practically supernatural.[90]

Clearly, the Halcomb's faithful are not only Jeff's co-conspirators but also his victims. Rather than malevolent spirits hell-bent on revenge, these are souls trapped in time through an unfinished ritual who, fooled by Halcomb, believe they too will be resurrected through Jeanie's blood. Their naïve belief in the pseudo-religious nonsense that Jeff proclaimed in the early 1980s makes them his obedient servants, even in the afterlife. These guardians protecting Jeff's terrible secrets remain ironically oblivious to the truth about the failed ritual in 1983. Audra's ghost, witnessed by Jeanie on her first day in the house, is the only one that attempts to warn her, but Jeanie misinterprets this as a cry for help. All those who died for Jeff are trapped in the afterlife as he, now calling himself Lou Graham, writes a fictionalised version of the events leading to the deaths of Jeanie and Echo that espouses his spiritualist philosophy. He then embarks on creating a new commune. On the final pages of the novel, readers meet 'Lou' at a book signing, already on the lookout for alienated teenage girls. As a shy young girl approaches him for an autograph it is made clear that the cycle of abuse will continue, and damaged young women starved of protection and love will always be in danger.

166 • House of Horrors

The ghosts of Halcomb's faithful manifest themselves differently to father and daughter. With Lucas, they mostly rearrange furniture and hang photos upside down, something they used to do when breaking into houses. Lucas hears laughter and glimpses strange shapes in the dark corners of the house, but doggedly rationalises these incidents. In contrast, Jeanie's haunting is immediately far more substantial and serves a completely different purpose. While the antics of these spectral beings is only intended to disorientate Lucas and goad him into staying at the Montlake Road house, Jeanie must be groomed for their leader.

Jeanie is in the orchard when she sees her first ghost, a wide-eyed boy who was part of Halcomb's original group. This incident also marks the first temporal disturbance: the boy she sees and the screams and laughter she hears are a ghostly echo of Audra being chased through the orchard by Halcomb's followers in 1982. Later, Jeanie sees Audra's reflection in her bathroom mirror instead of her own. Audra is silently screaming as blood pools on her sweater: 'Vee mimicked the girl's expression, unable to fight against the thudding of her pulse. Was she imitating the girl because they *were* the same person? What if, by some trick, the girl took her place while Vee got stuck in the mirror somehow?' (Chapter 10, original emphasis). While her father insists on reason and logic, Jeanie leaps to the most naïve and dangerous explanation: the ghosts, '[t]he people living within the walls. Jeff's brood', simply need her help (Chapter 48). Both Lucas and Jeanie are aware of the haunted house atmosphere at the Montlake Road residence but consider themselves above horror-movie clichés.[91] Lucas's wilful rejection of the supernatural is to an extent a conscious decision: he is no more ready to see the ghosts than he is to admit his own responsibility in the disintegration of his family. Meanwhile, Jeanie has always believed her fascination with the paranormal, dark and creepy would make her immune to fear.

Jeanie comes to believe a spectral door has been opened in the house that cannot be closed without her help. She even wonders if she could help the 'stuck' girl (Audra's ghost) cross to the other side and thus become a hero in her own ghost story. In a way, this makes Ahlborn's novel a neo-Gothic text: Jeanie acts as a female proto-detective, unable and unwilling to leave the haunted house. Like typical Gothic heroines, she is drawn to the dark mysterious Halcomb and rebels against her well-meaning, but increasingly non-communicative father; her mother is on a business trip to Europe with her new lover.

Jeanie convinces herself there is 'something broken here. Something that didn't quite fit in with the rest of the world. It was as though there had

Spectral Kinship and Ghostly Selves • 167

been a shift that had never quite managed to reset itself . . . Either Jeff's family was stuck in a constant state of travel or the house had somehow been stripped of the boundary between here and nowhere' (Chapter 48). When she falls in love with Halcomb, Jeanie completely forgets her friends and teenage crush, Tim. She no longer cares for either of her parents and wants to join a new, larger family, one 'that understood, that actually *cared*' (Chapter 48, original emphasis). Even death no longer scares Jeanie as she will be united with Jeff. When Halcomb's ghost finally appears at the Montlake Road house following his suicide, he promises Jeanie everything she ever wanted: eternal love and happiness and a place in a new, preferable family: '[Your parents] don't deserve you, Vivi. We'll run away together, just you and me and my friends. You'll have a new family, and we'll be *happy*' (Chapter 54, original emphasis). Still, a part of Jeanie resists: she knows that running away from her parents would leave them broken and herself an empty shell. As a result, she finally sees through the youthful veneer of Halcomb's ghost and discerns 'an old man's hard stare. Angry, impatient, a look that told her she was thinking too much, hesitating for far too long' (Chapter 54).

Like Melanie Tem's *Prodigal*, Ahlborn's *Within These Walls* delves into the slow disintegration of a middle-class nuclear family, facilitated by a charismatic, albeit highly dangerous outsider. In contrast to Tem's novel, however, here it is the parents who lead to this downfall, by failing to communicate and thus leaving Audra and Jeanie vulnerable to Halcomb's cunning. His victims were 'runaways', 'disenchanted youth' and '[u]nap- preciated victims of parents that not only misunderstood their children but also didn't seem to care' (Chapter 24). In her study of gender and the nuclear family in twenty-first-century American horror cinema, Kimberly Jackson, has described a bleak post-patriarchal reality, in which fathers are either absent or helpless husks of their former selves, their patriarchal power an empty promise of protection.[92] Ahlborn's novel follows this algo- rithm in that Lucas, frustrated by a bourgeois masculine ideal he is unable to reach, cannot save his marriage, Jeanie or even himself. However, this failure by a weak father translates into success for a monstrous tyrannical father, proving that patriarchal power is not finished, merely relocated and disguised.

In Ahlborn's novel, haunting is mistaken for a tool to uncover and rectify the past, the meaning most often attached to ghosts in the Western imaginarium. This is why Jeanie cannot read Audra's message as anything but a cry for help and invitation to discover more about Jeff's cult. Lucas

168 • House of Horrors

similarly decides to stay at the house to unravel Halcomb's mystery and, if necessary, wrest it from the ghosts. But these spectral beings function only as agents of misdirection and cult recruiters. Gordon has described haunting as the instance in which 'abusive systems of power make themselves known', especially in matters supposedly finished and safely sequestered in the past.[93] The abuse to which Audra is subjected in Halcomb's cult reverberates through the years in the Montlake Road house, but its new inhabitants, Jeanie and Lucas, refuse to acknowledge her trauma and its repetitive nature. It is telling that rather than Lucas, a nameless narrator supplies Audra's story. Lucas views Audra as just another name on the long list of Jeffrey's victims. He also sees the house, first and foremost, as Halcomb's place, just as he sees what he is writing as the story of Halcomb, not his victims. In the end, *Within These Walls* becomes a story of 'exclusions and invisibilities,' of wilful misrecognitions and a form of hysterical, and historical blindness: in short, a true ghost story.[94]

Conclusion

The figure of the ghost remains ambiguous and unruly. As a conceptual metaphor it points to the epistemological instability of perception and an (over)reliance on vision in the formation of knowledge, as it 'specifically invokes what is placed outside [knowledge], excluded from perception and, consequently, from both the archive as the depository of the sanctioned, acknowledged past and politics as the (re)imagined present and future'.[95] The ghost brings to mind 'connotations of invisibility and fluctuations in visibility' and can function 'as an image for liminality and border-crossing'.[96] As the ghost is associated with the return of the dead and unresolved trauma, it may also trigger associations with uncanny doubles, repetition and cyclicity.

The three novels analysed in this chapter demonstrate the malleability and flexibility of the conceptual work the ghost can perform in cultural texts. All these ghosts signify a violent disruption of temporal linearity as, despite originating in the past, their task is orientated towards the future and/or present. Interestingly, most of the spectral visits described by these three writers do not neatly subscribe to the traditional restorative ghost-story model. These spectral presences have their own agenda and thus frustrate the conventional hierarchy in which ghosts exist only in relation to the living.

Spectral Kinship and Ghostly Selves • 169

It is the intrusion and disruption associated with the spectral that impacts directly on the protagonists' family life in typical ghost narratives. In the works selected for this chapter, family conflict is at the forefront and familial relationships endure the worst of unwelcome disturbances. In contrast to the previous chapters, which examined alternative kinship formations, families of choice and queer families, this chapter has featured works that problematise the traditional heterosexual family in its various late twentieth and early twenty-first-century iterations: a couple of stereotypical white yuppies, a middle-class Black family buckling under a racist threat, and a disintegrating white nuclear family with a volatile pre-teen daughter. In all these cases, hauntings are used to probe the limits of a Gothicised family drama in its most basic and conventional understanding: the affluent heterosexual family. That is not to say there are no ghost stories with queer characters or queer families. Shirley Jackson's classic *Haunting of Hill House* (1959), as well as more recent publications such as Molleen Zanger's *Gardenias Where There Are None* (1994) and Sarah Waters's *Affinity* (1999), attest to the popularity of haunting, possession and supernatural visitation as potent vehicles for the discussion of non-normative desires, homosexual passing and the price of non/conformity, and cultural or social ghosting. These subjects have been discussed at length by Terry Castle (1993), Phyllis M. Betz (2011)[97] and Paulina Palmer (1999, 2012).

Ghosts can appear as uncanny doubles that bring improper desires and abjected materiality to the surface. Gran's *Come Closer* is a highly effective example of using the evil doppelganger figure to reveal the price paid for repressing one's corporeality and choosing false security over freedom. Naamah's origin story clearly shows it is women and girls who are subjected to the most scrutiny and harshest restrictions concerning their bodies and physical needs. Being haunted by Naamah turns into an experience of 'transformative recognition'[98] for Amanda, who is forced to confront the frailty of the identity and lifestyle that she has chosen for her adult self. The theme of uncanny doubles also reverberates through *The Between* as Hilton struggles with dangerous death spirits from alternative realities. In *Within These Walls*, Jeanie misinterprets her spectral double's actions as a cry for help, rather than a warning of the impending tragedy.

A refusal to accept painful truth is tackled in all three novels, although in *The Between*, this truth concerns reality itself rather than, as in *Come Closer*, one's corporeal self, or the ghosts' intentions, as in *Within These Walls*. Presenting a traditional domestic setting that Hilton wants to protect at all costs, *The Between* is perhaps the most conservative novel of the

170 • House of Horrors

three. What differentiates Due's novel from the others is the disruption of the Western division between the realms of the living and the dead. Half-human and half-spirit, Hilton moves between different realities, and it is his own spectral nature that disrupts family life more than the racist threats to which they are subjected. As Rosemary Jackson has emphatically stated, this is what ghosts do: they '[d]isrupt the crucial defining line which separates "real" life from the "unreality" of death, subverting those discrete units by which unitary meaning or "reality" is constituted'.[99]

All three novels also illustrate the damage a lack of communication can wreak on families. In *Within These Walls*, Audra, Lucas and Jeanie fall prey to their own phantasmatic conceptions of what family life should be and refuse to see the people – and ghosts – around them for what they really are. Consequently, the ghosts that populate Ahlborn's novel bring about an acute epistemological crisis that the characters refuse to acknowledge. The novel could also be read in terms of a ghostly conflict between Audra and Jeff as they vie for narrative focus. Audra's tragic story haunts the readers, but not the characters, who are far more interested in the ever-elusive cult leader, Jeff Halcomb, and his story, which, ironically, no one ever receives. Halcomb's malicious presence haunts the characters and warps their cognitive abilities to such an extent they are no longer able to leave the house of their own volition; a process that mirrors the recruitment of Audra into Halcomb's cult decades earlier.

Afterword

ACCORDING TO Fred Botting, there is nothing natural about the horror genre: one must learn how it is to be experienced and recognised. In his reading, horror marks a violent rejection of that which is perceived as natural: 'Horror thus originates in a cultural differentiation of human from animal, a process in which taboos are created in order to police the limits that preserve a definition of humanity.'[1] Horror is thus constructed as an abrupt disruption of the normative dichotomies around which the very concept of humanity is structured: human/animal, rational/irrational, natural/artificial. Of course, that which is deemed natural is socially constructed and time-specific, and in Western arts and philosophy, the burden of the natural has been historically assigned to women and the feminine. Grosz drives this point home in *Volatile Bodies*:

> the female body has been constructed . . . as a leaking, uncontrollable, seeping liquid; as formless flow; as viscosity, entrapping, secreting; as lacking not so much or simply the phallus but self-containment – not cracked or porous vessel, like a leaking ship, but a formlessness that engulfs all form, a disorder that threatens all order.[2]

Grosz's description, though deeply resonating, strikes me as disturbing in that it moves ever so swiftly between two poles of Western attitudes

174 • House of Horrors

towards female embodiment, femininity and womanhood. At one end of the spectrum, woman is a monstrous aberration, a seepage that threatens the rational, self-enclosed (male) subject with contamination; at the other, however, she is an irresistible object of enquiry, a truly stunning spectacle to behold.

Recognition of horror is thus linked to the recognition of female corporeality, feminised forms of reproductive work and women's symbolic association with the intensely private and privatised space of the idealised family home. In the twelve novels analysed here it is often this familial space, conventionally associated with intimacy, safety and the maternal, that is transformed into an uncanny, even hostile territory by external or internal disturbances. Crucially, horror experienced within intimate relations, while fuelled by phallogocentric anxieties, emerges out of a dense matrix of variously deployed power, social exclusions and hierarchies, chief among these a rigidly constructed gender binary, universalised whiteness and unfeasible middle-class goals. In some of these novels the protagonists' bodies, as both carriers and receivers of patriarchal, racist and classist power relations, have been severely traumatised (*Drawing Blood, The Gilda Stories, Prodigal*); in others, their bodies are repudiated and constrained (*Come Closer, The Between, The Cipher*). Some protagonists mistrust their bodies and find them unreliable (*Within These Walls, The Drowning Girl, Dead in the Water*); others grapple with their bodies' real or perceived monstrosity (*Black Ambrosia, The Rust Maidens, Sineater*).

Literary horror is an intrinsically physical genre, one centred on the violation of bodily integrity, corporeal and affective sensations of fear, dread, terror, disgust and unease, and the sheer physicality of life, death, sickness and procreation. I have chosen to look at corporeality through the lens of relationality, as in kinship, family and personal bonds. This has enabled me to use 'intimacy' as a meta-tool to analyse horror fiction from a much-needed new perspective. Employing intimacy to map relationships, I focus on the formation of kinship structures, body and corporeality, sex and sexuality, gender roles and identities. In each chapter, my analysis oscillates between the bodily and the familial, all the while underscoring the potential risks of intimacy, openness to the o/ Other and the vulnerability underpinning human relationships. Several narratives chart attempts to found non-heteronormative families, understood as both LGBTQ+ families (*Drawing Blood, The Gilda Stories, The Drowning Girl*) and families of choice consisting of strangers (*Dead in the Water*) or friends (*The Rust Maidens*). Protagonists are faced with the collapse or near-collapse of their romantic relationships (*The Cipher*, *Come Closer*) and their straight families (*Within These Walls*, *Sineater*, *Prodigal*, *The Between*), they are uncertain whether they are willing or even able to commit to relationships (*Black Ambrosia*, *The Cipher*, *The Drowning Girl*), or insist on entering relationships that prove disastrous (*Come Closer*, *Within These Walls*). Contrary to homophobic stereotypes, straight families are not a source of safety and comfort (*Prodigal*, *Within These Walls*, *Sineater*), and queer relationships, perhaps banally, run the entire gamut, from supportive (*Drawing Blood*, *The Gilda Stories*) to deeply toxic (*The Drowning Girl*).

These twelve novels provide a fascinating cross-section of subgenres and literary traditions that have hitherto been overlooked or underrepresented in horror fiction scholarship. Although these twelve writers selected typical subject matter for horror fiction, their emphasis on intimacy and personal relationships often places them in marginal positions in relation to more 'canonical' horror fiction writers. However, rather than form a uniform counter-canon of 'women's horror', these novels demonstrate the rich generic and thematic diversity of horror fiction. This richness is evidenced by women writers over the last decade who have assailed the generic borders between horror, science fiction, dark fantasy, literary fiction, adventure fiction, young adult and the New Weird. Honourable mention goes to, among others, Gemma Files, Lisa Mannetti, Kelly Link, Margo Lanagan, Rena Mason, Livia Llewellyn, Helen Marshall, Nicole Cushing, Silvia Moreno-Garcia, Caitlin Starling, Alma Katsu, Zoje Stage, Mira Grant, Nisi Shawl, T. Kingfisher, Sonora Taylor, Kristi DeMeester, Molly Tanzer, Wendy N. Wagner and Ruthanna Emrys. Similarly, non-binary, trans and/or queer authors such as Kacen Callender, Rivers Solomon, Daniel M. Lavery, K. M. Szpara, Aiden Thomas and Sarah Gailey, are successfully experimenting with the genres of the fantastic.

Having read more than a hundred novels by women and non-binary writers, deciding on a mere twelve was hardly an impartial affair, and the choices I have made speak to the tenuousness of such concepts as literary excellence, taste or originality, just as they reveal volumes about my reading habits and personal predilections. I am also acutely aware that my critical choices and attachments are informed as much by my academic education in Poland as by serendipity and personal inclinations, and as such constitute just one way of reading these horror novels.

I look forward to reading future articles and books that investigate contemporary horror fiction from within disability studies and crip theory, whiteness studies and masculinity studies, feminist new materialisms and speculative realism, to name a few fields of cultural and literary criticism, increasingly visible in Horror Studies. I do hope, however, that this study presents a starting point for discussions on contemporary horror production, gendered structure and sexual politics of horror, the uses and abuses of popular horror themes and devices, the continuing presence of the Gothic, and feminist engagement with corporeality and sexuality in horror fiction.

Notes

Introduction

1. Lisa Morton, 'Women Destroy Horror! Roundtable Interview: Linda Addison, Kate Jonez, Helen Marshall, and Rena Mason', *Nightmare Magazine: Women Destroy Horror Special Issue*, 25 (2014), 182.
2. Morton, 'Women Destroy Horror! Roundtable Interview', 188.
3. See, for instance, Nancy Fraser and Axel Honneth, *Redistribution or Recognition? A Political-Philosophical Exchange* (London and New York: Verso Books, 2003).
4. For more on 'minor literatures', see Gilles Deleuze and Félix Guattari, *Kafka: Towards a Minor Literature*, trans. by Dana Polan, foreword by Réda Bensmaïa (Minneapolis MN: University of Minnesota Press, 1986 [1975]).
5. I refer to Billy Martin's horror novels using both his real name and the name under which the books were originally published, 'Poppy Z. Brite', which now functions as his literary nom de plume. I use male pronouns, as Martin identifies as a trans-man and gay writer. I include Billy Martin in my analysis as his early novels formed an important and critically acknowledged part of women's horror writing of the early 1990s. Including his work in my analysis reflects the reception of his work in the 1990s, but also leaves other potential avenues open, such as reading his work as part of gay horror fiction, or as fiction interrogating (trans-)masculinity or queer desires. After publishing three horror novels and two short-story collections in the 1990s, he shifted to dark humour fiction centred on the New Orleans restaurant scene. Having

178 • House of Horrors

given up writing in 2010, he returned from retirement in 2018 and started a non-fiction book on the work of Stephen King. See also, Martin's LiveJournal entry 'I'm Basically Retired (For Now)', 9 June 2010 *http://docbrite.livejournal.com/2010/06/09/* (last accessed 17 February 2023) and his Patreon profile *www.patreon.com/docbrite* (last accessed 17 February 2023).

6. Throughout this book I refer to 'genre' as a generative rather than descriptive concept. My usage of 'genre' echoes John Frow's approach: '[F]ar from being merely "stylistic" devices, genres create effects of reality and truth, authority and plausibility, which are central to the different ways the world is understood in the writing of history or of philosophy or of science, or in painting, or in everyday talk. These effects are not, however, fixed and stable, since texts – even the simplest and most formulaic – do not "belong' to genres but are, rather, uses of them; they refer not to "a" genre but to a field or economy of genres, and their complexity derives from the complexity of that relation.' See John Frow, *Genre* (London: Routledge, 2005), p. 2.

7. Concerning the 'how' question, one should mention, for instance, thought-provoking works emerging from affect studies: Xavier Aldana Reyes, *Horror Film and Affect: Towards a Corporeal Model of Viewership* (London: Routledge, 2016); from film phenomenology: Julian Hanich, *Cinematic Emotion in Horror Films and Thrillers: the Aesthetic Paradox of Pleasurable Fear* (London and New York: Routledge, 2011); and even from the evolutionary social sciences: Mathias F. Clasen, *Why Horror Seduces* (New York: Oxford University Press, 2017). These stimulating studies provide an escape from restrictive academic boundaries and analytical clichés. However, perhaps because of their macro ambitions, they tend to ignore, gloss over and even devalue the ways in which one's ability to experience and process the world is already gendered, sexed, racialised and naturalised, to name just a few 'coarse axes of categorisation' involved in meaning-making processes. See also Eve Kosofsky Sedgwick, *The Coherence of Gothic Conventions* (New York: Arno Press, 1980), p. 22.

8. Joseph Grixti, *Terrors of Uncertainty: The Cultural Contexts of Horror Fiction* (London: Routledge, 1989).

9. Jack Halberstam, *Skin Shows: Gothic Horror and the Technology of Monsters* (Durham NC and London: Duke University Press, 1995); and Jeffrey Jerome Cohen, 'Monster Culture (Seven Theses)', in J. J. Cohen (ed.), *Monster Theory: Reading Culture*, NED-New edition (London and Minneapolis MN: University of Minnesota Press, 1996), pp. 3–25.

10. Robin Wood, 'The American Nightmare: Horror in the 70s', in M. Jancovich (ed.), *Horror: The Film Reader* (London: Routledge, 2002), pp. 25–32.

Notes • 179

11. Barbara Creed, *The Monstrous-Feminine: Film, Feminism, Psychoanalysis* (London and New York: Routledge, 1993). A reader may wonder why there are so many references to critical works on horror cinema in a study devoted to horror literature. It is worth remembering the strong reciprocity and mutual attraction between American horror literature and cinema, which explain the ease with which concepts from literary theory travel into film studies and vice versa. Interestingly, despite horror fiction attracting less critical scrutiny than horror cinema, a great many horror works are addressed in Gothic studies, which often treats horror as a subtype or outgrowth of the Gothic. See also Michael J. Collins, 'Culture in the Hall of Mirrors: Film and Fiction and Fiction and Film', in T. Magistrale and M. A. Morrison (eds), *A Dark Night's Dreaming: Contemporary American Horror Fiction* (Columbia SC: University of South Carolina Press, 1996), pp. 110–22.

12. See, for instance, Linda Williams, 'Film Bodies: Gender, Genre, and Excess', *Film Quarterly*, 44/4 (1991), 2–13; Tony Williams, *Hearths of Darkness: The Family in the American Horror Film, Updated Edition* (Jackson MS: University Press of Mississippi, 2014 [1996]); and Carol J. Clover, *Men, Women, and Chain Saws: Gender in the Modern Horror Film – Updated Edition* (Princeton NJ and Oxford: Princeton University Press, 2015 [1992]).

13. Wood, 'The American Nightmare', pp. 25–32; Franco Moretti, 'The Dialectic of Fear', *New Left Review*, 136 (1982), 67–85.

14. John Clute, *The Darkening Garden: a Short Lexicon of Horror* (Cauheegan: Payseur & Schmidt, 2006); Rosemary Jackson, *Fantasy: the Literature of Subversion* (London: Routledge, 2003 [1981]); and Tzvetan Todorov, *The Fantastic: a Structural Approach to a Literary Genre*, translated from the French by Richard Howard, with a foreword by Robert Scholes (Ithaca NY: Cornell University Press, 1975).

15. See, for instance, S. T. Joshi, *The Evolution of the Weird Tale* (New York: Hippocampus Press, 2004); S. T. Joshi, *The Modern Weird Tale* (Jefferson NC: McFarland & Company, 2001).

16. Gina Wisker, *Horror Fiction: an Introduction* (London: A&C Black, 2006); Fred Botting, *Limits of Horror: Technology, Bodies, Gothic* (Manchester: Manchester University Press, 2008); and David Punter, *The Literature of Terror: a History of Gothic Fictions from 1765 to the Present Day*, vol. 2 (New York: Routledge, 2013 [1996]).

17. Isabel Cristina Pinedo, *Recreational Terror: Women and the Pleasures of Horror Film Viewing* (Albany NY: SUNY Press, 1997).

18. Terry Castle, *The Female Thermometer: Eighteenth-Century Culture and the Invention of the Uncanny* (Oxford: Oxford University Press, 1995).

180 • House of Horrors

19. Noël Carroll, *The Philosophy of Horror: or, Paradoxes of the Heart* (New York and London: Routledge, 1990).

20. See also Jane Tompkins, *Sensational Designs: the Cultural Work of American Fiction, 1790–1860* (New York: Oxford University Press, 1985).

21. Linda Badley, *Writing Horror and the Body: the Fiction of Stephen King, Clive Barker, and Anne Rice* (Westport CT: Greenwood Publishing Group, 1996), pp. xiii, 15. See, for instance, Linda J. Holland-Tell, *As American as Mom, Baseball, and Apple Pie: Constructing Community in Contemporary American Horror Fiction* (Bowling Green OH: Bowling Green State University Popular Press, 2001), p. 1, pp. 9–11.

22. Holland-Tell, *As American as Mom*, p. 1.

23. Holland-Tell, *As American as Mom*, p. 15.

24. Stephen King, *Danse Macabre* (New York: Simon and Schuster, 2011 [c. 1981]), p. 421.

25. Clive Bloom, 'Horror Fiction: In Search of a Definition', in D. Punter (ed.), *A New Companion to the Gothic* (Maldon MA: John Wiley, 2012), p. 222 (original emphasis).

26. Clive Barker quoted in Bloom, 'Horror Fiction', p. 222.

27. Mark Jancovich, *Horror* (London: Batsford, 1992), p. 9.

28. Darryl Jones, *Sleeping with the Lights On: the Unsettling History of Horror* (Oxford University Press, 2018), p. 12.

29. Rosi Braidotti, *The Posthuman* (Cambridge: Polity Press, 2013), p. 15.

30. The prominent American horror editor, Ellen Datlow, has stated that, for her, horror is 'a genre of unease'. Of course, in practice this can be generated within any genre ('Interview: Ellen Datlow'). See also E. C. Myers, 'Interview: Ellen Datlow', *Nightmare Magazine*, 4 (2013), *www.nightmare-magazine. com/nonfiction/interview-ellen-datlow/* (last accessed 19 October 2021).

31. Williams, 'Film Bodies'; Jennifer Cooke, 'Making a Scene: Towards an Anatomy of Contemporary Literary Intimacies', in J. Cooke (ed.), *Scenes of Intimacy: Reading, Writing and Theorizing Contemporary Literature* (London and New York: Bloomsbury Academic, 2013), p. 3.

32. In *Horror Fiction: an Introduction* (2006), Gina Wisker characterises horror as 'a branch of Gothic writing' that is more prone to graphic representations of 'violence, terror, and bodily harm' (p. 8). In *Limits of Horror*, Botting moves seamlessly between horror and the Gothic, describing how the two concepts become, if not interchangeable, then tightly interwoven, especially in the late twentieth century and early twenty-first century, when the transgressive features of the Gothic are heightened by new technologies of the body and reproduction, as well as the expanding technobureacracy of late

capitalism. Botting argues that '[t]he new horror demands a broader Gothic frame: fiction and film cross into everyday life, displaying the permeable, shifting boundaries between reality and fantasy and enveloping every social positions' (p. 6). Still, he also suggests that the Gothic, as an intrinsically hybrid formation, has perhaps been so profusely dispersed over the past two centuries that it has become 'meaningless and redundant, a diffusion of significance and affect in the fantasies and anxieties of culture' (p. 162).

33. Catherine Spooner, 'Crime and the Gothic', in Charles J. Rzepka and L. Horsley (eds), *A Companion to Crime Fiction* (Chichester: Wiley-Blackwell, 2010), p. 246.

34. Maurizio Ascari, *A Counter-History of Crime Fiction: Supernatural, Gothic, Sensational* (Basingstoke: Palgrave Macmillan, 2007), p. 58.

35. 'A "definition" of "Gothic" thus outlines a large, irregularly shaped figure, an irregularity that implies the limitations of language – appropriate for the category containing this unspeakable "other." Although I began with the term "genre," so many refinements and ramifications must be added to the usual sense of that term that it becomes unsatisfactory, for "Gothic" is a "something" that goes beyond the merely literary. Similarly, it is more than a "mode" or a tradition, or a set of conventions.' Anne Williams, *The Art of Darkness: a Poetics of Gothic* (Chicago IL: University of Chicago Press, 1995), p. 23.

36. Charles Crow, *American Gothic* (Cardiff: University of Wales Press, 2009), p. 15.

37. See also Ellen Moers, *Literary Women* (Garden City NY: Doubleday, 1976).

38. Steffen Hantke, 'The Decline of the Literary Horror Market in the 1990s and Dell's Abyss Series', *The Journal of Popular Culture*, 41/1 (2008), 59.

39. See also interviews with Cavelos: Paula Guran, 'Interview. Jeanne Cavalos: Abyss, Odyssey & Beyond', *DarkEcho*, 1996, *https://web.archive.org/web/20170720153344/, http://www.darkecho.com/darkecho/archives/cavelos.html* (last accessed 21 November 2020); Paula Guran, 'Interview. Jeanne Cavalos: Scientist, Editor, Writer, Teacher . . .', *DarkEcho*, 1998, *www.darkecho.com/darkecho/archives/cavelos2.html* (last accessed 5 October 2013).

40. Hantke, 'The Decline of the Literary Horror Market', p. 62.

41. Hantke, 'The Decline of the Literary Horror Market', pp. 65–6.

42. Steffen Hantke, 'The Rise of Popular Horror Fiction', in X. Aldana Reyes (ed.), *Horror: a Literary History* (London: British Library, 2016), p. 182.

43. Kathryn Ptacek (ed.), *Women of Darkness* (New York: Tom Doherty Associates, 1989).

44. Kathryn Ptacek (ed.), *Women of Darkness II: More Original Horror and Dark Fantasy by Contemporary Women Writers* (New York: Tom Doherty Associates, 1990).

182 • House of Horrors

45. Lisa Tuttle (ed.), *Skin of the Soul: New Horror Stories by Women* (London: Women's Press, 1990).

46. Poppy Z. Brite/Billy Martin (ed.), *Love in Vein: Twenty Original Tales of Vampiric Erotica* (New York: HarperPrism, 1994); Poppy Z. Brite/Billy Martin (ed.), *Love in Vein: Eighteen More Tales of Vampiric Erotica* (New York: HarperPrism, 1994).

47. Pam Keesey (ed.), *Daughters of Darkness: Lesbian Vampire Stories* (Pittsburgh PA: Cleis Press, 1998).

48. Since the early 1990s, anthologies of the 'best of' type have filled the space left by specialty presses that folded or were eclipsed by the aggressive attempts of publishing industry moguls to further consolidate the market. One should mention the now discontinued Karl Wagner's *The Year's Best Horror Stories* (1980–94) and Ellen Datlow and Terri Windling's *The Year's Best Fantasy and Horror* (1987–2008). Still extant are Datlow's *The Best Horror of the Year* (2009–) and a number of online magazines such as *Nightmare Magazine* (2012–), *Uncanny Magazine* (2014–), *Weird Fiction Review* (on hiatus), and *Cemetery Dance* (1988–).

49. Gina Wisker, *Contemporary Women's Gothic Fiction: Carnival, Hauntings and Vampire Kisses* (London: Palgrave Macmillan, 2018).

50. Paulina Palmer, *Lesbian Gothic: Transgressive Fictions* (London: Cassell, 1999).

51. Benjamin A. Brabon and Stéphanie Genz (eds), *Postfeminist Gothic: Critical Interventions in Contemporary Culture* (Houndmills: Palgrave Macmillan, 2007).

52. Sarah E. Whitney, *Splattered Ink: Postfeminist Gothic Fiction and Gendered Violence* (Urbana IL: University of Illinois Press, 2016).

53. Diana Wallace and Andrew Smith (eds), *The Female Gothic: New Directions* (Basingstoke: Palgrave Macmillan, 2009).

54. Andrew Hock Ng Soon, *Women and Domestic Space in Contemporary Gothic Narratives: The House as Subject* (Basingstoke: Palgrave Macmillan, 2015).

55. Avril Horner and Sue Zlosnik (eds), *Women and the Gothic: an Edinburgh Companion* (Edinburgh: Edinburgh University Press, 2016).

56. Helene Meyers, *Femicidal Fears: Narratives of Female Gothic Experience* (New York: State of New York University Press, 2001).

57. Lisa Kröger and Melanie R. Anderson, *Monster, She Wrote: The Women Who Pioneered Horror and Speculative Fiction* (Philadelphia PA: Quirk Books, 2019).

58. In her 'Historical Overview of Classic Horror Novels', American horror, fantasy and science fiction writer Lucy S. Snyder cites statistics published

in *Strange Horizons* and *VIDA: Women in Literary Arts* to emphasise the gap between male and female authors in terms of the number of reviews and the amount of attention bestowed upon specific works. See Lucy A. Snyder, 'An Historical Overview of Classic Horror Novels', *Nightmare Magazine: Women Destroy Horror Special Issue*, 25 (2014), 169–73.

59. A case in point is the prestigious anthology on literary horror edited by Xavier Aldana Reyes and published by the British Library in 2016. In the penultimate chapter, on popular horror (1971–2000), Steffen Hantke includes an overview of Kathe Koja's fiction, with shorter paragraphs devoted to Anne Rice and Lucy Taylor, alongside the work of arguably more recognisable male writers. In the last chapter, on post-2000 horror, Xavier Aldana Reyes refers to a few women writers but does not discuss their work, focusing instead on a familiar list of male writers: Stephen King, Clive Barker, Ramsey Campbell, Joe Hill, John Ajvide Lindqvist, Laird Barron, Jeff VanderMeer and Max Brooks. See also Xavier Aldana Reyes (ed.), *Horror: a Literary History* (London: British Library, 2016).

60. However, it should be mentioned that both Kathe Koja and Poppy Z. Brite/Billy Martin left the horror literary scene during the 1990s, and Caitlín R. Kiernan, recognised for the short stories that revisit the Cthulhu Mythos rather than their stand-alone novels, is often described as a New Weird writer and a feminist successor/challenger to Lovecraft.

61. Jess Nevins, *Horror Fiction in the 20th Century: Exploring Literature's Most Chilling Genre* (Santa Barbara: Praeger, 2020).

62. Grady Hendrix, *Paperbacks from Hell: The Twisted History of '70s and '80s Horror Fiction*, with Will Errickson (Philadelphia PA: Quirk Books, 2017).

63. See, for instance, Clover, *Men, Women, and Chain Saws*; Creed, *The Monstrous-Feminine*; Williams, *Hearths of Darkness*; Kimberly Jackson, *Gender and the Nuclear Family in the Twenty-First Century Horror* (New York: Palgrave Macmillan, 2016); Erin Harrington, *Women, Monstrosity and Horror Film: Gynaehorror* (New York: Routledge, 2017).

64. See, for instance, Sabine Bussing, *Aliens in the Home: the Child in Horror Fiction* (Westport CT: Greenwood Press, 1987); Karen J. Renner (ed.), *The Evil Child in Literature, Film and Popular Culture* (London and New York: Routledge, 2013); Karen J. Renner, *Evil Children in the Popular Imagination* (New York: Palgrave Macmillan, 2016); Andrew Scahill, *The Revolting Child in Horror Cinema: Youth Rebellion and Queer Spectatorship* (New York: Palgrave Macmillan, 2015).

65. See also, Rebecca Janicker, *The Literary Haunted House: Lovecraft, Matheson, King and the Horror in Between* (Jefferson NC: McFarland & Company,

2015); Dave Bailey, *American Nightmares: the Haunted House Formula in American Popular Fiction* (Bowling Green OH: Bowling Green State University Popular Press, 1999).

66. For more on splatterpunk, see Xavier Aldana Reyes, *Body Gothic: Corporeal Transgression in Contemporary Literature and Horror Film* (Cardiff: University of Wales Press, 2014); Aalya Ahmad, 'Transgressive Horror and Politics: The Splatterpunks and Extreme Horror', in K. Corstorphine and L. R. Kremmel (eds), *The Palgrave Handbook to Horror Literature* (New York: Palgrave Macmillan, 2018), pp. 365–76. While neither author discusses women writers at length, Ahmad does point out that a '"splatter-feminism," which deserves a much fuller discussion, can be discerned in the nineties-era work of writers, such as Kathe Koja, Christa Faust, Caitlín R. Kiernan, and Billy Martin (formerly Poppy Z. Brite), to name a few. Splatterpunk feminism foregrounds gender transgressions, subcultural styles, deviant sexualities, and strong, sometimes terrifying, women/genderqueer characters' (376).

67. On feminist film phenomenology, see Vivian Sobchack, *Carnal Thoughts: Embodiment and Moving Image Culture* (Berkeley CA and Los Angeles CA: University of California Press, 2004); Laura U. Marks, *The Skin of the Film: Intercultural Cinema, Embodiment, and the Senses* (Durham NC and London: Duke University Press, 2000); Angela Ndalianis, *The Horror Sensorium: Media and the Senses* (Jefferson NC: McFarland & Company, 2012).

68. Cooke, 'Making a Scene', p. 3.

69. As Jacqui Gabb has argued, intimacy 'now denotes an emergent intellectual framework around the detraditionalisation of interpersonal exchanges and kin formation'. Jacqui Gabb, *Researching Intimacy in Families* (Basingstoke: Palgrave Macmillan, 2008), p. 2.

70. Lauren Berlant, 'Intimacy: a Special Issue', *Critical Inquiry*, 24/2 (1998), 281.

71. See, for instance, Lauren Berlant, *The Female Complaint: the Unfinished Business of Sentimentality in American Culture* (Durham NC: Duke University Press, 2008); Lauren Berlant and Michael Warner, 'Sex in Public', *Critical Inquiry*, 24 (1998), 547–60; Leo Bersani and Adam Phillips, *Intimacies* (Chicago IL: University of Chicago Press, 2008); Leo Edelman, *No Future: Queer Theory and the Death Drive* (Durham NC: Duke University Press, 2004); José Esteban Muñoz, *Cruising Utopia: the Then and There of Queer Futurity* (New York: NYU Press, 2009); Anthony Giddens, *The Transformations of Intimacy: Sexuality, Love and Eroticism in Modern Societies* (Stanford CA: Stanford University Press, 1992); Jack Halberstam, *The Queer Art of Failure* (Durham NC and London: Duke University Press, 2011).

Notes • 185

72. Maile Arvin, Eve Tuck and Angie Morrill, 'Decolonizing feminism: Challenging connections between settler colonialism and heteropatriarchy', *Feminist Formations*, 25/1 (2013), 8–34; Scott Lauria Morgensen, *Spaces Between Us: Queer Settler Colonialism and Indigenous Decolonization* (Minneapolis MN: University of Minnesota Press, 2011); Mark Rifkin, *When Did Indians Become Straight? Kinship, the History of Sexuality, and Native Sovereignty* (Oxford: Oxford University Press, 2011); Kim Tallbear, 'Making Love and Relations Beyond Settler Sex and Family', in A. Clarke and D. Haraway (eds), *Making Kin Not Population* (Chicago IL: Prickly Paradigm Press, 2018), pp. 145–63; Ben-zvi Yael, *Native Land Talk: Indigenous and Arrivant Rights Theories* (Hanover NH: Dartmouth University Press, 2018).

73. Berlant, 'Intimacy', 285.

74. Berlant, 'Intimacy', 285.

75. Anna Muraco, 'Intentional Families: Fictive Kin Ties Between Cross-Gender, Different Sexual Orientation Friends', *Journal of Marriage and Family*, 68 (2006), 1313.

76. Cristyn Davies and Kerry H. Robinson, 'Reconceptualising Family: Negotiating Sexuality in a Governmental Climate of Neoliberalism', *Contemporary Issues in Early Childhood*, 14/1 (2013), 39–40.

77. Gabb, *Researching Intimacy in Families*, pp. 70–1.

78. Davies and Robinson, 'Reconceptualising Family', 42.

79. Davies and Robinson, 'Reconceptualising Family', 42.

80. Judith Butler, *Undoing Gender* (New York: Psychology Press, 2004), pp. 102–3.

81. Kath Weston, *Families We Choose: Lesbians, Gays, Kinship* (New York: Columbia University Press, 2013 [1991]).

82. Nancy E. Levine, 'Alternative Kinship, Marriage, and Reproduction', *Annual Review of Anthropology*, 37 (2008), 379.

83. Muraco, 'Intentional Families', 1320.

84. Colleen L. Johnson, 'Perspectives on American Kinship in the Later 1990s', *Journal of Marriage and Family*, 62/3 (2000), 624.

1.   Uncanny in the House of Fear

1. Andrew Hock Ng Soon, *Women and Domestic Space in Contemporary Gothic Narratives: the House as Subject* (Basingstoke: Palgrave Macmillan, 2015), p. 2.

2. Andrew Hock Soon Ng, 'Conceptualizing Varieties of Space in Horror Fiction', in K. Corstorphine and L. R. Kremmel (eds), *The Palgrave Handbook to Horror Literature* (New York: Palgrave Macmillan, 2018), p. 442.

186 • House of Horrors

3. Ng, *Women and Domestic Space*, p. 7, original emphasis.

4. Tyson Lewis and Daniel Cho, 'Home Is Where the Neurosis Is: a Topography of the Spatial Unconscious', *Cultural Critique*, 64 (2006), 69.

5. 'On the one hand, Gothic represented a mythical medieval Britain, where chivalry held sway, social order prevailed, and religious belief was unchallenged. On the other, it represented a time of barbarity and feudalism before the blessed arrival of the Enlightenment and the benefits of science and reason that it bestowed. These two separate urges were politicized: reactionary and progressive, Tory and Whig, nostalgic and proto-modernist. They resulted in two very different forms of art: on the one hand, the Gothic Revivalism of eighteenth- and nineteenth-century architecture and painting; on the other, the sensational narratives of the Gothic novel. These two strands are sometimes (understandably) confused, because of their shared name and fascination with the Middle Ages.' Catherine Spooner, *Contemporary Gothic* (London: Reaktion Books, 2006), p. 14.

6. Susanne Becker, *Gothic Forms of Feminine Fictions* (Manchester: Manchester University Press, 1999), p. 66.

7. Roberta Rubenstein, 'House Mothers and Haunted Daughters: Shirley Jackson and Female Gothic', *Tulsa Studies in Women's Literature*, 15/2 (1996), 320.

8. Ruth Bienstock Anolik, 'The Missing Mother: the Meanings of Maternal Absence in the Gothic Mode', *Modern Language Studies*, 33/1–2 (2003), 25.

9. Kathy Mezei and Chiara Briganti, 'Reading the House: a Literary Perspective', *Signs*, 27/3 (2002), 841.

10. Kate Ferguson Ellis lists three elements of the Gothic revision of the myth of the Fall: 'the subversion of primogeniture expressed in the theme of usurpation, the inadequacy of innocence as a defense against evil, and the validity of female rebellion against and autocratic father.' These revisions could also be seen as social critiques of the new family model that slowly emerged over the nineteenth century, which aggressively promoted the need for absolute privacy and a strict separation of spheres. Kate Ferguson Ellis, *The Contested Castle: Gothic Novels and the Subversion of Domestic Ideology* (Urbana IL: University of Illinois Press, 1989), p. 67.

11. Mezei and Briganti, 'Reading the House', 837.

12. Aileen S. Kraditor, 'Introduction', in A. S. Kraditor (ed.), *Up From the Pedestal: Selected Writings in the History of American Feminism* (Chicago IL: Quadrangle, 1968), pp. 3–24.

13. Barbara Welter 'The Cult of True Womanhood: 1820–1860', *American Quarterly*, 18/2–1 (1966), 151–74.

14. See Venetria K. Patton, *Women in Chains: the Legacy of Slavery in Black Women's Fiction* (Albany NY: SUNY Press, 2000).

15. Evelynn M. Hammonds, 'Toward a Genealogy of Black Female Sexuality: the Problematic of Silence', in J. Price and M. Shildrick (eds), *Feminist Theory and the Body: a Reader* (New York: Routledge, 1999), pp. 93–104.

16. Patricia Hills Collins, *Black Feminist Thought: Knowledge, Consciousness, and the Politics of Empowerment*, revised 10th anniversary edn (New York and London: Routledge, 2000 [1990]).

17. See also Toni Morrison, *Playing in the Dark: Whiteness and the Literary Imagination* (Cambridge MA: Harvard University Press, 1992).

18. Ellis reads the Gothic as an unyielding critique of the patriarchal ideology of the separation of spheres, which causes both men and women to struggle against and chafe under the constraints imposed by social expectations and gender role division. See also, Ellis, *The Contested Castle*. Yet, in the American interpretation of the Gothic, it is man's conflicting relationship with nature that comes to the fore. Richard Slotkin's well-known concept of regeneration through violence serves to shift the emphasis from the household onto the wilderness, where evil forces of human or inhuman origin await the solitary male hero. Hence, in Hawthorne's 'Young Goodman Brown' (1835) the house becomes polluted only after blasphemous knowledge has been (un)willingly acquired in the woods. In this reading, the contested familial space is supplanted by the dangerous liminality of wilderness, which threatens not only the house (which stands for civilisation) but, above all, the integrity of male identity. See also, Richard Slotkin, *Regeneration Through Violence: the Mythology of the American Frontier, 1600–1860* (Middletown CT: Wesleyan University Press, 1973).

19. Dave Bailey, *American Nightmares: the Haunted House Formula in American Popular Fiction* (Bowling Green OH: Bowling Green State University Popular Press, 1999), p. 21.

20. Bailey claims that modern haunted house tales, such as Robert Marasco's *Burnt Offerings* (1973) and Jay Anson's *The Amityville Horror* (1977), have eschewed the 'ontological uncertainty' of their late nineteenth-century predecessors in favour of a more straightforward embrace of the supernatural. In contrast to conventional ghost stories, ghosts and spectres are either treated perfunctorily or abandoned altogether in contemporary haunted house narratives; it is the semi-sentient house that comes to the forefront and channels whatever forces may be at work. Bailey, *American Nightmares*, p. 6.

21. See also Mikal J. Gaines, 'They Are Still Here: Possession and Dispossession in the 21st Century Haunted House Film', in F. Pascuzzi and S. Waters (eds),

The Spaces and Places of Horror (Wilmington DE: Vernon Press, 2020), pp. 179–202; Emanuelle Wessels, 'A Lesson Concerning Technology: the Affective Economies of Post-Economic Crisis Haunted House Horror in The Conjuring and Insidious', *Quarterly Review of Film and Video*, 32/6 (2015), 511–26; Kimberly Jackson, *Gender and the Nuclear Family in the Twenty-First Century Horror* (New York: Palgrave Macmillan, 2016).

22. Anneleen Masschelein, *The Unconcept: the Freudian Uncanny in Late-Twentieth-Century Theory* (Albany NY: SUNY Press, 2011), p. 131.

23. Here, Masschelein points to Julia Kristeva's foreignness in *Strangers to Ourselves*, Homi K. Bhabha's postcolonial unhomeliness, Anthony Vidler's *Archictural Uncanny* and Derrida's and Heidegger's writing on alienation, defamiliarisation and homelessness. For more, see Masschelein, *The Unconcept*, pp. 131–47.

24. See also Nicholas Royle, *The Uncanny* (Manchester: Manchester University Press, 2003), pp. 24–5.

25. Sigmund Freud, 'The Uncanny', in V. B. Leitch et al. (eds), *The Norton Anthology of Theory and Criticism* (New York: W. W. Norton & Company, 2001), p. 944.

26. Freud, 'The Uncanny', p. 930.

27. David Farrell Krell, 'Das Unheimliche; Architectural Sections of Heidegger and Freud', *Research in Phenomenology*, 22 (1992), 51.

28. Royle, *The Uncanny*, p. 1.

29. Terry Castle, *The Female Thermometer: Eighteenth-Century Culture and the Invention of the Uncanny* (Oxford: Oxford University Press, 1995), p. 8.

30. Castle, *The Female Thermometer*, p. 4.

31. Castle, *The Female Thermometer*, p. 17.

32. Fred Botting, *Limits of Horror: Technology, Bodies, Gothic* (Manchester: Manchester University Press, 2008), p. 7.

33. In her brilliant study of modern fantasy, Rosemary Jackson also refers to a secularisation of the uncanny and points to the vacuity associated with the uncanny as expressed in Heidegger's writing, with God's place remaining empty, an alternative region of the uncanny emerges close by. Jackson, *Fantasy*, p. 38.

34. Anthony Vidler, *The Architectural Uncanny: Essays in the Modern Unhomely* (Cambridge MA: MIT Press, 1992). p. 11.

35. Vidler, *The Architectural Uncanny*, p. 167.

36. Vidler, *The Architectural Uncanny*, p. 169.

37. Paulina Palmer, *The Queer Uncanny: New Perspectives on the Gothic* (Cardiff: University of Wales Press, 2012).

Notes • 189

38. Another significant aspect addressed by Palmer is the spectralisation of the homosexual, an issue discussed at length in the groundbreaking essay collection, Diana Fuss, *Inside/Out: Lesbian Theories, Gay Theories* (New York: Psychology Press, 1991), and in Terry Castle, *The Apparitional Lesbian: Female Homosexuality and Modern Culture* (New York: Columbia University Press, 1993). From a classic phallogocentric perspective, associations activated by the figures of a gay man and a lesbian woman point to disorder, the threat of contamination and menacing excess. It should be noted that Palmer's use of the queer uncanny is far wider than the definition employed in this chapter, as she discusses such themes as queer spectrality, transgender doubles and secrets and their disclosure. Palmer, *The Queer Uncanny*.

39. Palmer, *The Queer Uncanny*, p. 7.

40. Incidentally, all three novels were published in the Abyss line.

41. Charles Crow, *American Gothic* (Cardiff: University of Wales Press, 2009), p. 45.

42. See also '[Phil's] hand pressed the deck, and it was covered with something bumpy and scratchy, and the room stank of decomposition, salt, rotten things. The room went dark, completely black – and as he finished [vomiting] and squinted into the darkness, the bumpiness smoothed out, and the smell faded, but the light did not come back on' (p. 192).

43. Though this paradox is often reflected in real-life architecture, especially postmodern designs and the modernist 'l'espace indicible', it is in horror fiction that we encounter its finest manifestations. For more on Le Corbusier's 'l'espace indicible', see Anthony Vidler, *Warped Space: Art, Architecture, and Anxiety in Modern Culture* (Cambridge MA: MIT Press, 2000), p. 52–3.

44. Samuel Weber, 'The Sideshow, or: Remarks on a Canny Moment', *MLN*, 88/6 (1973), 1131.

45. Weber, 'The Sideshow', 1132–3.

46. Weber, 'The Sideshow', 1131.

47. Persephone Braham, 'Scylla and Charybdis', in J. A. Weinstock (ed.), *The Ashgate Encyclopedia of Literary and Cinematic Monsters* (Abingdon and New York: Routledge, 2014), p. 502–3.

48. Barbara Creed, *The Monstrous-Feminine: Film, Feminism, Psychoanalysis* (London and New York: Routledge, 1993), p. 106.

49. Creed, *The Monstrous-Feminine*, p. 27.

50. Jane M. Ussher, *Managing the Monstrous Feminine: Regulating the Reproductive Body* (London: Routledge, 2006), p. 2.

51. Reade killed the boy 'to do his witchery' (p. 135).

52. I will revisit monstrosity and the grotesque in more detail in Chapter 2.

190 • House of Horrors

53. This novel has little to offer in terms of diversity among the crew, apart from a few mentions of Ramón, a Black steward serving on *Pandora*, and when one of the main characters notices a ghost slave ship, incorporated by Reade and Scylla into their creation. However, the repeated refrain of 'blackness, thirst, loneliness' at various points in the novel, attributed to both Reade and Scylla, evokes a distant memory of the Middle Passage, the Transatlantic triangle trade and colonisation of the Pacific region. Despite the text disregarding any conspicuous Black presence, as the novel takes place among white Americans on a ship that enslaves other ships, that presence cannot be entirely denied.

54. Freud, 'The Uncanny', p. 940.

55. Koja's novel was jointly awarded the Bram Stoker Award for First Novel in 1991. The other winning novel is discussed in Chapter 3: Melanie Tem's *Prodigal*. *The Cipher* was also the first novel published in the acclaimed Abyss line.

56. VanderMeer views both the New Wave of science fiction and body-focused transgressive horror of the 1980s as two driving forces behind the New Weird. Incidentally, Kathe Koja was the co-editor of the second volume of an acclaimed, if short lived, anthology *Year's Best Weird Fiction*, together with the series editor Michael Kelly. VanderMeer, *www.jeffvandermeer.com/2009/06/28/the-new-weird-anthology-notes-and-introduction/* (last accessed 22 February 2023).

57. Steven Shaviro, 'Into the Funhole: Kathe Koja's The Cipher', *Genre*, 49/2 (2016), 214 (original emphasis).

58. Shaviro, 'Into the Funhole', 215.

59. The Funhole could also be approached via the 'abcanny', a concept theorised by China Miéville as a counterpart to the uncanny. More akin to 'abnormal' than to 'abject', which Miéville dislikes intensely, abcanny lies in the province of 'the unknown unknowns' rather than 'the unknown knowns' of the uncanny, and concerns unrecognisable monsters that have never been repressed due to their very unknowability. China Miéville, 'On Monsters: or, Nine or More (Monstrous) Not Cannies', *Journal of the Fantastic in the Arts*, 23/3(86) (2012), 385.

60. Vidler, *The Architectural Uncanny*, p. 147.

61. Steffen Hantke has suggested that a propensity to use unique objects in horror fiction, objects that resists the logic of capitalism (commodification), signals 'attempts to step outside industrial society altogether in search of radical otherness' (45). In his reading of *The Cipher*, Koja is not interested in magical objects that critique commodification or hark nostalgically to pre-industrial times, but rather in leaving the readers with 'a curious sense of emptiness or hollowness' (p. 49). The commodity has been expelled, and all that is left is a 'metaphysical absence' (p. 49). Steffen Hantke, 'Deconstructing Horror:

Commodities in the Fiction of Jonathan Carroll and Kathe Koja', *Journal of American Culture*, 18/3 (1995), 41–57.

62. Hantke, 'Deconstructing Horror', 52.

63. Dylan Trigg, *The Thing: a Phenomenology of Horror* (Winchester: Zero Books, 2014), p. 6.

64. Trigg, *The Thing*, p. 9.

65. Earlier in the novel Koja plants the suggestion of a monster in a video made when Nakota lowers a camera into the Funhole. Still, the continuously transforming record reveals only 'the ecstatic prance of self-evisceration, a figure carving itself, re-created in a harsh new form from what seemed to be its own hot guts, becoming no figure at all but the absence of one, a cookie-cutter shape and in but not contained by its outline a blackness, a vortex of nothing' (p. 56). The non-figure frightens Nicholas even more than the Funhole itself, yet he averts his eyes seconds before the black silhouette turns to face the camera. Interestingly, at a later point in the narrative, other characters begin to glimpse Nicholas on tape, as if he was already present in the Funhole un/reality. Nicholas, though, continues to see the same terrifying non-entity engulfed in nothingness.

66. Hantke, 'Deconstructing Horror', 52.

67. Mark Fisher, *Capitalist Realism: Is There No Alternative?* (Winchester: Zero Books, 2009), p. 34.

68. Paul M. Sammon's seminal splatterpunk anthology from 1990 featured only two women authors out of a possible seventeen. Five years later, almost half the featured authors were identified as women, including Kathe Koja, Poppy Z. Brite/Billy Martin, Nancy A. Collins, Lucy Taylor, Elizabeth Massie and Melanie Tem. Sammon acknowledged that 'this time, the emphasis is female . . . Kathe Koja. Nancy A. Collins. Roberta Lannes. Poppy Z. Brite. More than a dozen renegade femmes joining forces with rogue male counterparts like Martin Amis and Clive Barker', and warned his readers that '[t]he female contributors you are about to meet are not babes, broads, or chicks. Not bimbos, stereotypes, objects, or toys. They are *women*. Strong. Independent. Fiercely intelligent. Outraged, uninhibited, and dangerous as hell'. Paul M. Sammon, 'Introduction', in P. M. Sammon (ed.), *Splatterpunks II: Over the Edge* (New York: Tor Books, 1995), p. 17, 18 (original emphasis).

69. One cannot escape a feeling of jarring artificiality in how Brite/Martin constructs his literary worlds. They all appear insular and insulated, geared towards an extremely specific demographic – white Goth kids from comfortable middle-class backgrounds who will hungrily tick off all the obscure music references and appreciate androgyny (but still presented with a masculine bias), teen angst and transgressive gender expression, if not identity.

192 • House of Horrors

70. Zach appears 'faintly Asian' in an old schoolbook photo (p. 224), but Eddy's parents consider him American, not Asian-American. His jet-black hair and 'dark almond-shaped eyes' are the result of his mother's Cajun blood.

71. While explicit gay sex scenes in a horror novel were groundbreaking and scandalous twenty years ago, the fact remains that Zach and Trevor's relationship is fairly conventional, with Zach resisting the temptation to have sex outside his newly formed monogamous relationship.

72. Manuel Aguirre, 'Geometria strachu. Wykorzystanie przestrzeni w literaturze gotyckiej', trans. by Agnieszka Izdebska, in G. Gazda, A. Izdebska and J. Płuciennik (eds), *Wokół gotycyzmów: wyobraźnia, groza, okrucieństwo* (Kraków: Universitas, 2002), p. 20.

73. Aguirre, 'Geometria strachu', p. 23.

74. The artificiality of these spaces should come as no surprise as the Gothic has always taken place within an architectural charade. See also Spooner, *Contemporary Gothic*.

2. Grotesque Monsters and Hybrid Subjectivities

1. Mary Shelley, *Frankenstein; or, The Modern Prometheus*, 3rd edn, edited by D. L. Macdonald and K. Scherf (Ontario: Broadview Press, 2012 [1818]), p. 83.

2. Even in earlier, eighteenth and nineteenth-century texts, 'the monstrous, the hybrid and the disgusting are central' to Gothic aesthetics, and since the Gothic relies so heavily on transgression and its correlated affects, especially horror and terror, its affinity with the grotesque is understandable. Alison Milbank, 'Bleeding Nuns: a Genealogy of The Female Gothic Grotesque', in D. Wallace and A. Smith (eds), *The Female Gothic: New Directions* (Basingstoke: Palgrave Macmillan, 2009), p. 76.

3. Avril Horner and Sue Zlosnik analysed the comic turn in Gothic in their book-length 2004 study, rightly noting that due to its inherent hybridity, 'the roots of the Gothic lie in the comic as well as the tragic'. Avril Horner and Sue Zlosnik, *Gothic and the Comic Turn* (Basingstoke: Palgrave Macmillan, 2004), p. 7.

4. Catherine Spooner, *Contemporary Gothic* (London: Reaktion Books, 2006), p. 69.

5. Susana Araújo, 'The Gothic-Grotesque of *Haunted*: Joyce Carol Oates's Tales of Abjection', in K. Kutzbach and M. Mueller (eds), *The Abject of Desire: the Aestheticization of the Unaesthetic in Contemporary Literature and Culture* (Amsterdam: Rodopi, 2007), p. 89.

6. More precisely, the term was first applied to the ruins of Nero's palace

discovered in the late fifteenth century, and subsequently entered the vocabulary in relation to sixteenth-century painting and, later, the literature of Dante, Shakespeare, Rabelais and Cervantes. Justin Edwards and Rune Graulund, *The Grotesque* (London: Routledge, 2013), p. 5.

7. Mikhail Bakhtin, *Rabelais and his World*, trans. by Hélène Iswolsky (Cambridge MA: MIT Press, 1968), p. 317.

8. Bakhtin, *Rabelais and his World*, p. 281.

9. Wilson Yates, 'An Introduction to the Grotesque: Theoretical and Theological Considerations', in J. L. Adams and W. Yates (eds), *The Grotesque in Art and Literature: Theological Reflections* (Grand Rapids MI: Wm. B. Eerdmans Publishing, 1997), p. 26.

10. Bakhtin, *Rabelais and his World*, p. 317.

11. See Mary J. Russo, *The Female Grotesque: Risk, Excess and Modernity* (New York: Routledge, 1995), p. 5.

12. Milbank, 'Bleeding Nuns', p. 77.

13. Milbank, 'Bleeding Nuns', p. 77.

14. Milbank, 'Bleeding Nuns', p. 77.

15. Bakhtin, *Rabelais and his World*, p. 38.

16. Bakhtin, *Rabelais and his World*, p. 38–9.

17. Spooner, *Contemporary Gothic*, p. 69.

18. Spooner, *Contemporary Gothic*, p. 68–9.

19. Spooner, *Contemporary Gothic*, p. 68.

20. Rosi Braidotti, 'Signs of Wonder and Traces of Doubt: On Teratology and Embodied Differences', in J. Price and M. Shildrick (eds), *Feminist Theory and the Body: a Reader* (New York: Routledge, 1999), p. 292.

21. Erin Harrington, *Women, Monstrosity and Horror Film: Gynaehorror* (New York: Routledge, 2017), p. 184.

22. Harrington, *Women, Monstrosity and Horror Film*, p. 184.

23. Jane M. Ussher, *Managing the Monstrous Feminine: Regulating the Reproductive Body* (London: Routledge, 2006), p. 2.

24. Ussher, *Managing the Monstrous Feminine*, p. 3.

25. Ussher, *Managing the Monstrous Feminine*, p. 4.

26. Ussher, *Managing the Monstrous Feminine*, p. 4.

27. Ussher, *Managing the Monstrous Feminine*, p. 15. The monstrous reproductive body is also an abjected body (dirty and contaminating), uncontained and fecund, and 'with its creases and curves, secretions and seepages' is associated with the animal world, whereas the self-contained, unchangeable, 'proper' body is signified by the figure of a man or a prepubescent girl. Ussher, *Managing the Monstrous Feminine*, p. 7.

28. Sander L. Gilman, *Difference and Pathology: Stereotypes of Sexuality, Race, and Madness* (Ithaca NY: Cornell University Press, 1985).

29. Evelynn M. Hammonds, 'Black (W)holes and the Geometry of Black Female Sexuality,' *Differences* 6/2–3 (1994), 126–45; Evelynn M. Hammonds, 'Toward a Genealogy of Black Female Sexuality: the Problematic of Silence', in J. Price and M. Shildrick (eds), *Feminist Theory and the Body: a Reader* (New York: Routledge, 1999), pp. 93–104.

30. Lorraine O'Grady, '*Olympia's Maid*: Reclaiming Black Female Subjectivity,' in J. Frueh, C. L. Langer and A. Raven (eds), *New Feminist Criticism: Art, Identity, Action* (New York: Icon Editions, 1994), pp. 152–70.

31. Beverly Guy-Sheftall, 'The Body Politic: Black Female Sexuality and the Nineteenth-Century Euro-American Imagination', in K. Wallace-Sanders (ed.), *Skin Deep, Spirit Strong: the Black Female Body in American Culture* (Ann Arbor MI: University of Michigan Press, 2002), pp. 13–36.

32. Kaila Adia Story, 'Racing Sex – Sexing Race', in C. E. Henderson (ed.), *Imagining the Black Female Body* (New York: Palgrave Macmillan, 2010), pp. 23–43.

33. Sabine Strings, *Fearing the Black Body: the Racial Origins of Fat Phobia* (New York: NYU Press, 2019).

34. Russo, *Female Grotesque*, pp. 8–13.

35. Russo, *The Female Grotesque*, p. 7.

36. Russo, *The Female Grotesque*, p. 9.

37. Russo, *The Female Grotesque*, p. 12.

38. Russo, *The Female Grotesque*, p. 13.

39. Barbara Creed, 'Lesbian Bodies: Tribades, Tomboys and Tarts', in E. Grosz and E. Probyn (eds), *Sexy Bodies: the Strange Carnalities of Feminism* (London and New York: Routledge, 2013), p. 87.

40. Russo, *The Female Grotesque*, p. 1.

41. I understand 'female' as pertaining to all women, cis-women and trans-women alike.

42. While the painter is fictional, Michael Zulli 'became' Saltonstall and painted the two paintings which accompanied the publicity around *The Drowning Girl*. See also *https://greygirlbeast.dreamwidth.org/791852.html* (last accessed 20 February 2018).

43. Linda Williams, 'When the Woman Looks', in B. K. Grant (ed.), *The Dread of Difference: Gender and the Horror Film* (Austin TX: University of Texas Press, 1996), p. 21.

44. Rosi Braidotti, *Nomadic Subjects: Embodiment and Sexual Difference in Contemporary Feminist Theory* (New York: Columbia University Press, 2011), p. 224.

Notes • 195

45. Edwards and Graulund, *The Grotesque*, p. 114.

46. In a 2008 *Locus Magazine* interview, Kiernan made it clear that their propensity for narratives about body transformation correlates with their own experience of being trans: 'So, as a transsexual, how can I not write about the transmutation of flesh? How can I not write about having one mind, and a body that doesn't match?' See also, *www.locusmag.com/2008/Issue12_Kiernan. html* (last accessed 23 February 2023).

47. See the interview by Jeff VanderMeeer: *https://weirdfictionreview.com/2012/03/ interview-Caitlín-r-kiernan-on-weird-fiction/* (last accessed 12 February 2018)

48. See, for instance, Benjamin Noys and Timothy S. Murphy, 'Introduction: Old and New Weird', *Genre*, 49/2 (2016), 117–134; Roger Luckhurst 'The Weird: a Dis/orientation,' *Textual Practice*, 31/6 (2017), 1041–61; China Miéville, 'Weird Fiction,' in M. Bould (ed.) *The Routledge Companion to Science Fiction* (London and New York: Routledge, 2009), pp. 510–16.

49. See also Kristopher Woofter, 'Caitlín R. Kiernan's *The Drowning Girl* (2012) – Shirley Jackson', in S. Bacon (ed.), *Horror: a Reader* (Oxford: Peter Lang, 2019), p. 228.

50. Marilyn Farwell, *Heterosexual Plots and Lesbian Narratives* (New York and London: NYU Press, 1996), p. 98.

51. Farwell, *Heterosexual Plots*, p. 23.

52. 'Someday it's not going to seem so strange to people. At least, I like to hope it won't. I like to believe that someday it will be generally understood it's just how some people are. Gay. Straight. Transgender. Black. White. Blue eyes. Hazel eyes. Fish. Fowl. What the hell ever.' Kiernan, *The Drowning Girl*, p. 151.

53. Paulina Palmer, *Lesbian Gothic: Transgressive Fictions* (London: Cassell, 1999), p. 40.

54. Hélène Cixous, 'The Laugh of the Medusa', Signs, 1/4 (1976), 881.

55. Charles Crow, *American Gothic* (Cardiff: University of Wales Press, 2009), p. 158.

56. Sineating is a form of apotropaic magic which has not been extensively studied by anthropologists, but which has nonetheless survived in some Western folk traditions. For more see, Karin Kvideland, 'Sin-Eating', *International Society for Folk Narrative Research*, 35 (1984), 27–36.

57. All subsequent quotes from Elizabeth Massie's *Sineater* are from a non-paginated 2010 Kindle edition.

58. Sineater was released the same year as Bernard Rose's *Candyman*, and the texts bear a striking similarity in their representation of the supposed villain: an imposing male figure with a large overcoat, animalistic associations (bees,

196 • House of Horrors

foraging in the forest), who plays a significant role in the community and transgresses gendered and racialised norms.

59. In 1864, Missy Campbell's great-grandfather courageously stood his ground in the church against Union soldiers and thus cemented his position as the spiritual leader of Ellison. Although traditional Southern Baptism flourished in the following decades, the Campbells continued proselytising and persuading people to join them in sessions of snake-handling, witnessing and drinking poison. Elaborate wakes centred on sineating were part of this alternative spirituality that expanded alongside the official Baptist Chapter. In 1946, when one of Missy's ancestors, Orville Campbell, set fire to a bootlegger's cabin, three men 'drunk on the Spirit went into the inferno that was the cabin to prove their faith and were burned to ashes' (Part 1, Chapter 9). One of these men was Avery's father, and as a result, two-year-old Avery was taken in by an elderly woman. His orphan status meant his life belonged to the whole community. Ironically, it was Missy's own father who insisted on Avery becoming the new sineater since, as an orphan, he was perfect for the role. Despite hiding in the Baptist church, Avery was dragged out by the congregation and forced to take up the duties of the recently deceased sineater. Rather than living alone in the forest, Avery asked Lelia to become his wife to alleviate his loneliness.

60. Joel learns from his friend's letters that the friend's father, previously a Baptist preacher in Ellison, had left the town and stopped preaching altogether due to his feelings of responsibility for the death of Missy's daughter, Patsy. Misreading the mountain customs he believed to be 'fine because of their traditional value', his kindness towards Missy had devastating consequences (Part 2, Chapter 14). Accidentally seeing Avery in the forest, Patsy returned in a hysterical state and was locked in the shed by Missy. Reverend Mason told Missy to pray as God would surely guide her. Unfortunately for Patsy, Missy was guided to drive nails into her daughter's eyes.

61. In this timeline she meets two girls: a teenager Quinn who is showing the first signs of the 'sickness', and Eleanor, the adult daughter of Dawn, one of the Rust Maidens, desperately searching for answers about her mother.

62. Russo, *The Female Grotesque*, p. 56.

63. Catherine Driscoll, *Girls: Feminine Adolescence in Popular Culture and Cultural Theory* (New York: Columbia University Press, 2002), p. 2.

64. Carla Rice, *Becoming Women: the Embodied Self in Image Culture* (Toronto: University of Toronto Press, 2014), p. 159.

65. See also Michelle Hughes Miller, Tamar Hager and Rebecca Jaremko Bromwich (eds), *Bad Mothers: Regulations, Representations, and Resistance* (Bradford ON: Demeter Press, 2017).

Notes • 197

66. Rosemarie Garland Thomson, *Extraordinary Bodies: Figuring Physical Disability in American Culture and Literature* (New York: Columbia University Press, 2017 [1997]), p. 6.
67. Driscoll, *Girls*, p. 257.
68. With private and public borders becoming more porous through the rise of social media, attempts to reformulate girls' bedrooms as sites of resistance have been made over recent years. Audrey Wollen's 'Sad Girl Theory' is one such example, although it lacks a strong engagement with class, embodiment and race.
69. Interestingly, Kiste's novel contains several references to the triple moon symbol (two crescents embracing a full moon) that Phoebe and Jacqueline use as a secret message, and which Jacqueline later adopts as a way of reaching Phoebe through inanimate objects such as walls, glass shards and even soil. While Phoebe never elaborates on the appeal of this particular symbol, found randomly in a book by Jacqueline and Phoebe, it is associated with the Triple Goddess myths and is currently used in neopagan cosmologies and ecofeminist spirituality. Associations with an ancient female power and the tripartite female development (the maiden, the mother, and the crone) reverberate throughout the novel, but no connection to a female entity (such as Hecate) is ever made explicit.
70. Braidotti, *Nomadic Subjects*, p. 35.
71. Rosi Braidotti, *Transpositions: On Nomadic Ethics* (Cambridge: Polity Press, 2006), p. 11.
72. Braidotti, *Nomadic Subjects*, p. 171.
73. Braidotti, *Nomadic Subjects*, p. 23.
74. Rosi Braidotti, *Metamorphoses: Towards a Materialist Theory of Becoming* (New York: John Wiley & Sons, 2002), p. 181.
75. Kelly Hurley, 'Abject and *Grotesque*', in C. Spooner and E. McEvoy (eds), *The Routledge Companion to Gothic* (London: Routledge, 2007), p. 142.

3. Blood(y) Ties in Vampire Fictions

1. Ken Gelder, *Reading the Vampire* (London: Routledge, 2006 [1994]), p. ix.
2. Gina Wisker, 'Love Bites: Contemporary Women's Vampire Fictions', in D. Punter (ed.), *A New Companion to the Gothic* (Chichester: John Wiley & Sons, 2012), p. 236.
3. Wisker, 'Love Bites', p. 225.
4. Wisker, 'Love Bites', p. 229.

198 • House of Horrors

5. For instance, Lynda Hall argues that: '[a]ssuming complex voices and bodies from which to speak, the diverse boundaries and sites they defiantly queer, transgress, blur, and interrogate include: race, sex, gender, sexuality, nationality, geography, time, life/death, the inside/outside of the body, sanity/craziness, life/art, and dream/reality. They queer the "master narratives" of "normal" traditional white, heterosexual, male power and redefine the boundaries through taking the agency of writing their own and other's experiences into reality and visibility. As well as exploding the myth of the "family romance," they challenge many other assumed norms and oppressive privileges.' Lynda Hall, 'Passion(ate) Plays "Wherever We Found Space": Lorde and Gomez Queer(y)ing Boundaries and Acting In', *Callaloo*, 23/1 (2000), 394–5.

6. See Catherine Spooner, *Contemporary Gothic* (London: Reaktion Books, 2006).

7. See Fred Botting, 'Hypocrite Vampire . . .' *Gothic Studies*, 9/1, (2007), 16–34.

8. See also Veronica Hollinger, 'Fantasies of Absence: the Postmodern Vampire', in J. Gordon and V. Hollinger (eds), *Blood Read: the Vampire as Metaphor in Contemporary Culture* (Philadelphia PA: University of Pennsylvania Press, 1997), pp. 199–212.

9. See also Nina Auerbach, *Our Vampires, Ourselves* (Chicago IL: University of Chicago Press, 1995).

10. Jack Halberstam, *Skin Shows: Gothic Horror and the Technology of Monsters* (Durham NC and London: Duke University Press, 1995), p. 27.

11. Throughout, I refer to a ProQuest unpaginated version of the article, Sabine Meyer, 'Passing Perverts, After all? Vampirism, (in)Visibility, and the Horrors of the Normative in Jewelle Gomez' *The Gilda Stories*', *Femspec*, 9 (2002), 25–37.

12. Hollinger, 'Fantasies of Absence', p. 201.

13. Meyer, 'Passing Perverts, After all?'.

14. Meyer, 'Passing Perverts, After all?'.

15. Joan Gordon and Veronica Hollinger, 'Introduction: the Shape of Vampires', in Gordon and Hollinger (eds), *Blood Read*, p. 2.

16. Jules Zanger, 'Metaphor into Metonymy: the Vampire Next Door', in Gordon and Hollinger (eds), *Blood Read*, pp. 17–26.

17. Zanger, 'Metaphor into Metonymy', p. 19.

18. Jeffrey Andrew Weinstock, 'American Vampires', in J. Faflak and J. Haslam (eds), *American Gothic Culture: an Edinburgh Companion* (Edinburgh: Edinburgh University Press, 2016), p. 204.

19. Julia Kristeva, *Powers of Horror: an Essay on Abjection*, trans. by Leon S. Roudiez (New York: Columbia University Press, 1992).

20. Kristeva, *Powers of Horror*, p. 2.
21. Rosemary Jackson, *Fantasy: the Literature of Subversion* (London: Routledge, 2003 [1981]), p. 177.
22. Jackson, *Fantasy*, p. 177.
23. Kristeva, *Powers of Horror*, p. 93.
24. Robbie Duschinsky, 'Abjection and Self-identity: Towards a Revised Account of Purity and Impurity', *The Sociological Review*, 61/4 (2013), 712.
25. Duschinsky, 'Abjection and Self-identity', p. 721.
26. Duschinsky, 'Abjection and Self-identity', p. 722.
27. Xavier Aldana Reyes, *Horror Film and Affect: Towards a Corporeal Model of Viewership* (London: Routledge, 2016), p. 45.
28. For more on disgust, see Winfried Menninghaus, *Disgust: Theory and History of a Strong Sensation*, trans. by Howard Eiland and Joel Golb (Albany NY: SUNY Press, 2012 [2003]); William Ian Miller, *The Anatomy of Disgust* (Cambridge MA: Harvard University Press, 2009); Sara Ahmed, *The Cultural Politics of Emotion* (Edinburgh: Edinburgh University Press, 2014).
29. Kristeva, *Powers of Horror*, p. 2.
30. Menninghaus, *Disgust*, p. 1.
31. Hanjo Berressem, 'On the Matter of Abjection', in K. Kutzbach and M. Mueller (eds), *The Abject of Desire: the Aestheticization of the Unaesthetic in Contemporary Literature and Culture* (Amsterdam: Rodopi, 2007), p. 44.
32. Elizabeth Grosz, *Sexual Subversions* (Sydney: Allen & Unwin, 1989), pp. 77–8.
33. Kristeva, *Powers of Horror*, p. 12 (original emphasis).
34. Katherine J. Goodnow, *Kristeva in Focus: From Theory to Film Analysis* (New York and Oxford: Berghahn Books, 2010), p. 33.
35. Kristeva, *Powers of Horror*, p. 71.
36. Goodnow, *Kristeva in Focus*, p. 37.
37. Susana Araújo, 'The Gothic-Grotesque of *Haunted*: Joyce Carol Oates's Tales of Abjection', in Kutzbach and Mueller (eds), *The Abject of Desire*, p. 93.
38. Araújo, 'The Gothic-Grotesque of *Haunted*', p. 104.
39. See also Cedric Gael Bryant, '"The Soul Has Bandaged Moments": Reading the African American Gothic in Wright's *Big Boy Leaves Home*, Morrison's *Beloved*, and Gomez's *Gilda*', *African American Review*, 39/4 (2005), 541–53.
40. See also Judith E. Johnson, 'Women and Vampires: Nightmare or Utopia?', *The Kenyon Review*, 5/1 (1993), 72–80.
41. See also Jerry Rafiki Jenkins, 'Race, Freedom, and the Black Vampire in Jewelle Gomez's *The Gilda Stories*', *African American Review*, 46/2–3 (2013), 313–28.

200 • House of Horrors

42. Jewelle Gomez, 'Speculative Fiction and Black Lesbians', *Signs*, Theorizing Lesbian Experience, 18/4 (1993), 948. Kinitra D. Brooks in her book-length study of Black women's contemporary horror fiction rejects the term 'black women's speculative fiction' altogether as a harmful misnomer. In its stead, she proposes 'fluid fiction', a term that describes 'black women's purposeful blending of the genres of science fiction, fantasy, and horror' and signals a way out of 'the exhausted doctrines of genre fiction'. Kinitra D. Brooks, *Searching for Sycorax: Black Women's Hauntings of Contemporary Horror* (New Brunswick NJ: Rutgers University Press, 2018), p. 12.

43. See also Sauda Burch, 'Jewelle Gomez: the 20th Anniversary of *The Gilda Stories*. An Interview with Jewelle Gomez', *LambdaLiterary.com*, 12 July 2011, *https://lambdaliterary.org/2011/07/jewelle-gomez-the-20th-anniversary-of-the-gilda-stories/* (last accessed 12 February 2018).

44. Jerry Rafiki Jenkins, *The Paradox of Blackness in African American Vampire Fiction* (Columbus OH: Ohio State University Press, 2019), p. 25.

45. Paulina Palmer, 'Queer Transformations: Renegotiating the Abject in Contemporary Anglo-American Lesbian Fiction', in Kutzbach and Mueller (eds), *The Abject of Desire*, pp. 52–3.

46. Palmer, 'Queer Transformations', p. 53.

47. See Gina Wisker, 'Devouring Desires: Lesbian Gothic Horror', in W. Hughes and A. Smith (eds), *Queering the Gothic* (Manchester: Manchester University Press, 2011), pp. 123–41.

48. Jenkins, 'Race, Freedom, and the Black Vampire', 318.

49. Victoria Amador, 'Dark Ladies: Vampires, Lesbians, and Women of Colour', *Gothic Studies*, 15/1 (2013), 12.

50. Paulina Palmer, *Lesbian Gothic: Transgressive Fictions* (London: Cassell, 1999), p. 123.

51. Hall, 'Passion(ate) Plays', 401.

52. Hall, 'Passion(ate) Plays', 401.

53. Shannon Winnubst, 'Vampires, Anxieties, and Dreams: Race and Sex in the Contemporary United States', *Hypatia*, 18/3 (2003), 14.

54. Palmer, *Lesbian Gothic*, p. 122.

55. Palmer, *Lesbian Gothic*, p. 104.

56. Palmer, *Lesbian Gothic*, p. 124.

57. Hall, 'Passion(ate) Plays', 418.

58. Kathy Davis Patterson, '"Haunting Back": Vampire Subjectivity in *The Gilda Stories*', *Femspec*, 6/1 (2005), 40.

59. Barbara Creed, *The Monstrous-Feminine: Film, Feminism, Psychoanalysis* (London and New York: Routledge, 1993), p. 61.

Notes • 201

60. See also Bonnie Zimmerman, 'What Has Never Been: an Overview of Lesbian Feminist Literary Criticism', in V. B. Leitch et al. (eds), *The Norton Anthology of Theory and Criticism* (New York: W.W. Norton & Company, 2001), pp. 2340–59.

61. Jenkins, 'Race, Freedom, and the Black Vampire', 320.

62. Palmer, *Lesbian Gothic*, p. 103.

63. Hall, 'Passion(ate) Plays', 397.

64. Jack Halberstam, *In a Queer Time and Place: Transgender Bodies, Subcultural Lives* (New York and London: NYU Press, 2005), p. 10.

65. Jenkins, *The Paradox of Blackness*, p. 8.

66. Hollinger, 'Fantasies of Absence', p. 199.

67. Meyer, 'Passing Perverts, After all?'.

68. Christopher S. Lewis, 'Queering Personhood in the Neo-Slave Narrative: Jewelle Gomez's *The Gilda Stories*', *African American Review*, 47/4 (2014), 455.

69. Auerbach, *Our Vampires, Ourselves*, p. 184.

70. Auerbach, *Our Vampires, Ourselves*, pp. 185–6.

71. See also Jenkins's rebuttal of Auerbach in Chapter 1 of *The Paradox of Blackness*.

72. Auerbach, *Our Vampires, Ourselves*, p. 186.

73. Out of print for more than three decades, *Black Ambrosia* was re-issued by Valancourt Books in 2019 as part of their Paperbacks from Hell series showcasing popular, if underrated, horror fiction of the 1980s.

74. Lisa Kröger and Melanie R. Anderson, *Monster, She Wrote: the Women who Pioneered Horror and Speculative Fiction* (Philadelphia PA: Quirk Books, 2019), p. 183.

75. Deborah Caslav Covino, *Amending the Abject Body: Aesthetic Makeovers in Medicine and Culture* (Albany NY: SUNY Press, 2004), p. 4.

76. Covino, *Amending the Abject Body*, p. 13.

77. Covino, *Amending the Abject Body*, p. 28.

78. Halberstam, *Skin Shows*, pp. 16–17.

79. Milly Williamson, *The Lure of the Vampire: Gender, Fiction and Fandom from Bram Stoker to Buffy* (London and New York: Wallflower Press, 2005), p. 2.

80. Williamson, *The Lure of the Vampire*, p. 2.

81. Gina Wisker, *Horror Fiction: an Introduction* (London: A&C Black, 2006), p. 100.

82. Wisker, *Horror Fiction*, p. 127.

83. Throughout, I refer to a ProQuest unpaginated version of the article, Gina Wisker, 'Women's Horror as Erotic Transgression', *Femspec*, 3/1 (2001), 44–63.

84. Tem herself worked as a social worker.

202 • House of Horrors

85. After witnessing an earlier attack on her mother, she wrote in her diary that '[s]ometimes Mom and Ethan are like the same person. Sometimes they're like total strangers' (p. 50), a sentiment recalling both the semiotic lack of differentiation between a mother and an infant, and the sudden break that results in two separate subjectivities.

86. Carolyn Korsmeyer, *Savouring Disgust: the Foul and the Fair in Aesthetics* (Oxford: Oxford University Press, 2011), p. 128.

87. Kristeva, *Powers of Horror*, p. 96 (original emphasis).

88. Creed, *The Monstrous-Feminine*, p. 66.

89. Auerbach, *Our Vampires, Ourselves*, p. 6.

90. Imogen Tyler, 'Against Abjection', *Feminist Theory*, 10/1 (2009), 83.

91. Tina Chanter, 'The Exoticization and Universalization of the Fetish, and the Naturalization of the Phallus: Abject Objections', in T. Chanter and E. Płonowska Ziarek (eds), *Revolt, Affect, Collectivity: the Unstable Boundaries of Kristeva's Polis* (Albany NY: SUNY Press, 2012), p. 158.

92. Palmer, *Lesbian Gothic*, p. 53.

4. Spectral Kinship and Ghostly Selves

1. Renee L. Bergland, 'From *Indian Ghosts and American Subjects*', in M. del Pilar Blanco and E. Peeren (eds), *The Spectralities Reader: Ghosts and Haunting in Contemporary Cultural Theory* (New York: Bloomsbury Academic, 2013), pp. 377–8.

2. Terry Castle, *The Female Thermometer: Eighteenth-Century Culture and the Invention of the Uncanny* (Oxford: Oxford University Press, 1995), p. 125.

3. Castle, *The Female Thermometer*, p. 17.

4. Castle, *The Female Thermometer*, p. 184.

5. Maria del Pilar Blanco and Esther Peeren, 'Introduction: Conceptualizing Spectralities', in del Pilar Blanco and Peeren (eds), *The Spectralities Reader*, p. 2.

6. del Pilar Blanco and Peeren, 'Introduction: Conceptualizing Spectralities', p. 3.

7. del Pilar Blanco and Peeren, 'Introduction: Conceptualizing Spectralities', p. 5.

8. See also Roger Luckhurst, 'From "The Contemporary London Gothic and the Limits of the Spectral Turn"', in del Pilar Blanco and Peeren (eds), *The Spectralities Reader*, pp. 75–88.

9. See also Jacques Derrida, *Specters of Marx: the State of the Debt, the Work of Mourning and the New International*, trans. by Peggy Kamuf (New York and London: Routledge, 2012 [1993]).

Notes • 203

10. See also Avery Gordon, *Ghostly Matters: Haunting and the Sociological Imagination* (Minneapolis MN and London: University of Minnesota Press, 2008 [1997]).
11. See also Peter Buse and Andrew Scott (eds), *Ghosts: Deconstruction, Psychoanalysis, History* (New York: St Martin's Press, 1999).
12. See also del Maria Pilar Blanco and Esther Peeren (eds), *Popular Ghosts: the Haunted Spaces of Everyday Culture* (London: Bloomsbury Academic, 2010).
13. See also del Pilar Blanco and Peeren (eds), *The Spectralities Reader*.
14. The themes and specific topics covered by authors in these two anthologies, including, among others, pop-culture, commodification processes, replication, imitation and simulacra, photography and cinema, new media technologies and virtual reality, creepypasta and memology, cyberpunk aesthetics, memorial sites and museum space, speak to the malleability and analytical utility of ghosts.
15. del Pilar Blanco and Peeren, 'Introduction: Conceptualizing Spectralities', p. 1.
16. Nicholas Royle, *The Uncanny* (Manchester: Manchester University Press, 2003), p. 67.
17. Maria del Pilar Blanco and Esther Peeren, 'Introduction', in del Pilar Blanco and Peeren (eds) *Popular Ghosts*, p. xv.
18. del Pilar Blanco and Peeren, 'Introduction: Conceptualizing Spectralities', p. 9 (original emphasis).
19. Colin Davis, '*État présent*: Hauntology, Spectres and Phantoms', in del Pilar Blanco and Peeren (eds), *The Spectralities Reader*, p. 53.
20. See also Judith Butler, *Frames of War: When is Life Grievable?* (London: Verso Books, 2016); Judith Butler, *Precarious Life: the Powers of Mourning and Justice* (London: Verso Books, 2020).
21. Anneleen Masschelein, *The Unconcept: the Freudian Uncanny in Late-Twentieth-Century Theory* (Albany: SUNY Press, 2011), p. 139.
22. Masschelein, *The Unconcept*, p. 144.
23. Masschelein, *The Unconcept*, p. 146.
24. Maria del Pilar Blanco and Esther Peeren, 'Spectral Subjectivities: Gender, Sexuality, Race/Introduction', in del Pilar Blanco and Peeren (eds), *The Spectralities Reader*, p. 311. See also Gayatri Chakravorty Spivak, 'From 'Ghostwriting', in del Pilar Blanco and Peeren (eds), *The Spectralities Reader*, pp. 317–34.
25. Orlando Patterson, *Slavery and Social Death* (Cambridge MA: Harvard University Press, 1982).
26. Davis, '*État présent*', p. 54.
27. Davis, '*État présent*', p. 56.
28. Davis, '*État présent*', p. 56.

204 • House of Horrors

29. See also Julia Briggs, *Night Visitors: the Rise and Fall of the English Ghost Story* (London: Faber, 1977).

30. Srdjan Smajić, 'The Trouble with Ghost-Seeing: Vision, Ideology, and Genre in the Victorian Ghost Story', *ELH*, 70/4 (2003), 1107.

31. See also Brian Norman, *Dead Women Talking: Figures of Injustice in American Literature* (Baltimore MD: Johns Hopkins University Press, 2013).

32. See also Kathleen Brogan, *Cultural Haunting: Ghosts and Ethnicity in Recent American Literature* (Charlottesville VA: University Press of Virginia, 1998).

33. See also Jeffrey Andrew Weinstock (ed.), *Spectral America: Phantoms and the National Imagination* (Madison WI: Popular Press, 2004).

34. See also Julian Wolfreys, *Victorian Hauntings: Spectrality, Gothic, the Uncanny and Literature* (Basingstoke: Palgrave Macmillan, 2001).

35. Jeffrey Andrew Weinstock, 'Introduction: the Spectral Turn', in Weinstock (ed.), *Spectral America*, p. 4.

36. Weinstock, 'Introduction: the Spectral Turn', p. 5.

37. Abraham quoted in Paulina Palmer, *The Queer Uncanny: New Perspectives on the Gothic* (Cardiff: University of Wales Press, 2012), p. 38.

38. Lucie Armitt, *Twentieth-Century Gothic* (Cardiff: University of Wales Press, 2011), p. 148.

39. Armitt, *Twentieth-Century Gothic*, p. 148.

40. Sigmund Freud, 'The Uncanny', in V. B. Leitch et al. (eds), *The Norton Anthology of Theory and Criticism* (New York: W. W. Norton & Company, 2001), p. 940.

41. See also Elaine Showalter, 'Killing the Angel in the House: the Autonomy of Women Writers', *Antioch Review*, 32/3 (1973), 339–53.

42. See also Jane Kromm, 'The Feminization of Madness in Visual Representation', *Feminist Studies*, 20/3 (1994), 507–35.

43. Julia Kristeva, 'Talking about Polylogue', trans. by Sean Hand, in M. Eagleton (ed.), *Feminist Literary Theory: a Reader* (London: John Wiley & Sons, 2011), p. 286.

44. Brogan, *Cultural Haunting*, p. 9.

45. Jack Halberstam, *In a Queer Time and Place: Transgender Bodies, Subcultural Lives* (New York and London: NYU Press, 2005), p. 10.

46. Halberstam, *In a Queer Time and Place*, p. 10.

47. It is worth noting that when boys or men are subject to demonic/ghostly possession, their bodies are not turned into eroticised spectacles of corporeality. Rather, the influence of demonic presence surfaces through mind control, murderous urges and vague creepiness, as in *The Omen* (1976), *The Amityville Horror* (1979, 2005) and *Fallen* (1998).

48. A number of twenty-first-century possession horror films, such as *The Conjuring* (2013), *The Taking of Deborah Logan* (2014) and *Relic* (2020), have increasingly featured adult and even elderly women, reflecting various concerns relating to contested motherhood, ageing societies and the marginalisation of older women.

49. Amanda's consulting of these doctors is a veiled reference to the *Rosemary Baby*-type of possession narrative, as the advice provided assists the demon, whether intentionally or not. For instance, her physician tells Amanda to increase her salt intake, which actually strengthens this particular demon.

50. See also Jacques Derrida, *On Hospitality*, translated by Rachel Bowlby (Stanford CA: Stanford University Press, 2000).

51. Andrzej Marzec, *Widmontologia. Teoria filozoficzna i praktyczna artystyczna ponowoczesności* (Warsaw: Bęc Zmiana, 2015), p. 136.

52. Marzec, *Widmontologia*, p. 141.

53. Marzec, *Widmontologia*, p. 143.

54. Interestingly, the only other person who can see Naamah is the young daughter of Amanda's distant friend. As social norms and expectations have not yet been imposed on children, thus blocking their access to their own desires and those of others, perceptive children are a common trope in horror.

55. Carla Freccero, 'Queer Spectrality: Haunting the Past', in del Pilar Blanco and Peeren (eds), *The Spectralities Reader*, p. 342.

56. Christopher N. Okonkwo, *A Spirit of Dialogue: Incarnations of Ọgbáňje, the Born-to-die, in African American Literature* (Knoxville TN: University of Tennessee Press, 2008), p. 55.

57. See also Venetria K. Patton, *The Grasp that Reaches Beyond the Grave: the Ancestral Call in Black Women's Texts* (Albany NY: SUNY Press, 2013).

58. Jess Nevins, *Horror Fiction in the 20th Century: Exploring Literature's Most Chilling Genre* (Santa Barbara CA: Praeger, 2020), p. 189.

59. Christopher W. Okonkwo has noted that in the memoir co-authored with her mother, *Freedom in the Family: a Mother-Daughter Memoir of the Fight for Civil Rights*, Due recalls a constant fear of death during the turbulent decades of her childhood and youth. He has also emphasised Due's usage of West African conceptual imagery, which reverberates through her memories. See also Okonkwo, *A Spirit of Dialogue*.

60. Due, who majored in Nigerian literature, weaves themes and figures associated with West African spirituality and cultural heritage into *The Between*. The fact that Due had knowledge of African cosmology before writing *The Between* was confirmed in private correspondence with Okonkwo. See Okonkwo, *A Spirit of Dialogue*, p. 202, n. 11.

206 • House of Horrors

61. Brogan, *Cultural Haunting*, p. 2.
62. Brogan, *Cultural Haunting*, p. 4.
63. Brogan, *Cultural Haunting*, p. 12.
64. Kinitra D. Brooks, Alexis McGee and Stephanie Schoellman, 'Speculative Sankofarration: Haunting Black Women in Contemporary Horror Fiction', *Obsidian: Literature in the African Diaspora*, 42/1–2 (2016), 237–77.
65. Brooks, McGee and Schoellman, 'Speculative Sankofarration', 238.
66. Brooks, McGee and Schoellman, 'Speculative Sankofarration', 238.
67. Maisha L. Wester has emphasised that 'African American Gothic is particularly concerned with the horror of temporal collapse'. Maisha L. Wester, *American Gothic: Screams from Shadowed Places* (New York: Palgrave Macmillan, 2012), p. 27.
68. Achille Mbembe, 'From "Life, Sovereignty, and Terror in the Fiction of Amos Tutuola"', in del Pilar Blanco and Peeren (eds), *The Spectralities Reader*, p. 147.
69. Maria del Pilar Blanco and Esther Peeren, 'Spectropolitics: Ghosts of the Global Contemporary/Introduction', in del Pilar Blanco and Peeren (eds), *The Spectralities Reader*, p. 95.
70. Mbembe, 'From "Life, Sovereignty"', p. 133.
71. Patton, *The Grasp that Reaches Beyond the Grave*, p. 180.
72. Patton, *The Grasp that Reaches Beyond the Grave*, p. 180.
73. Patton has noted that the worlds of the living and dead are separated by water in Congo cosmology, and quotes Kruger-Kahloula's research on the 'Kalunga line': the water passage. It is Hilton's ancestor, Nana, who guides him over the Kalunga in the final scenes of the novel. Patton, *The Grasp that Reaches Beyond the Grave*, p. 189.
74. Interestingly, Patton draws attention to a multiplicity of meanings relating to this pin. Although it represents the medical profession in the novel and thus stands for Kaya's future, which is literally placed in Hilton's hands, it can also be taken to mean 'the image of the Mami Wata or Nne Mmiri, who controls the water entry to the physical world'. Patton, *The Grasp that Reaches Beyond the Grave*, p. 188. Soon after this exchange, Hilton dies and swims across the water to his grandmother.
75. tobias c. van Veen and Reynaldo Anderson, 'Fabulous Camps of the Black Fantastic: Sylvester James, Queer Afrofuturism, and Black Vernacular Becomings', in R. Anderson and C. R. Fluker (eds), *The Black Speculative Arts Movement: Black Futurity, Art+Design* (Lanham MD: Lexington Books, 2019), p. 219.
76. Patton, *The Grasp that Reaches Beyond the Grave*, p. 181.
77. Ogunyemi, quoted in Patton, *The Grasp that Reaches Beyond the Grave*, p. 131. For more on *ogbanje/abiku*, see also Chikwenye Okonjo Ogunyemi,

'An Abiku-Ogbanje Atlas: a Pre-Text for Rereading Soyinka's *Aké* and Morrison's *Beloved*', *African American Review*, 36/4 (2002), 663–78.

78. Okonkwo, *A Spirit of Dialogue*, p. 91–2.

79. For instance, the white woman from whom they bought their four-bedroom suburban house was happy that a Black family was interested in buying her place. She had been 'brought up by a black nanny in Virginia', 'always hired blacks to clean for her and became such good friends with them' and 'her husband had marched with Martin Luther King' (pp. 56–7). As they want the house, Dede and Hilton endure this 'benevolent' racism and bite their tongues as the woman repeatedly pinches Kaya's cheeks. Once they move in, however, they begin to be harassed by a number of their new, all-white neighbours.

80. In some of these dreams, Hilton's children are pleading for help as they die horrific deaths. In one such sequence, he sees the man inside the hearse again, beckoning him to follow. Death personified – the man with a powdered face and black sunglasses – encourages Hilton to take the final step and go quietly in his sleep. This uncanny figure in whiteface – perhaps a manifestation of Baron Samedi, a loa of the dead in Haitian Vodou – reverses the typical Western binary of whiteness and blackness, as it is whiteness that portends death and danger in Hilton's vision.

81. Nicolas Abraham, 'Notes on the Phantom: a Complement to Freud's Metapsychology', in N. Abraham and M. Torok, *The Shell and the Kernel: Renewals of Psychoanalysis, Volume 1*, ed. and trans. by Nicholas Rand (Chicago IL: University of Chicago Press, 1994), p. 171.

82. Okonkwo, *A Spirit of Dialogue*, p. 56.

83. Tom Gunning, 'To Scan a Ghost: the Ontology of Mediated Vision', in del Pilar Blanco and Peeren (eds), *The Spectralities Reader*, p. 216.

84. Gordon, *Ghostly Matters*, p. 115 (original emphasis).

85. All subsequent quotes from Ania Ahlborn's *Within These Walls* are from the non-paginated 2015 Kindle edition.

86. Italicised fragments signal the internal monologues of Jeanie and Lucas.

87. Jeanie is twelve when the narrative starts.

88. Sebastian Murken and Sussan Namini, 'Childhood Familial Experiences as Antecedents of Adult Membership in New Religious Movements: a Literature Review', *Nova Religio: Journal of Alternative and Emergent Religions*, 10/4 (2007), 18.

89. Murken and Namini, 'Childhood Familial Experiences', 28.

90. For instance, January, one of Halcomb's surviving followers, committed suicide with the poison used in 1983 a couple of months before the anniversary

208 • House of Horrors

of the massacre. In addition, Jeff's cell neighbour committed suicide after briefly speaking with him in 2010, while the guard who was on watch that day later killed his wife and then himself. Echo's mother, Maggie, killed herself during the 1980s, and Echo, after helping Halcomb's ghost capture Lucas and Jeanie, consumes arsenic and joins Halcomb's commune.

91. Interestingly, the findings by paranormal researchers included in the novel are inconclusive and the house does not appear to be haunted.

92. See also Kimberly Jackson, *Gender and the Nuclear Family in the Twenty-First-Century Horror* (New York: Palgrave Macmillan, 2016).

93. Gordon, *Ghostly Matters*, p. xvi.

94. Gordon, *Ghostly Matters*, p. 17.

95. del Pilar Blanco and Peeren, 'Introduction: Conceptualizing Spectralities', p. 9.

96. Palmer, *The Queer Uncanny*, p. 66.

97. See also Phyllis M. Betz, *The Lesbian Fantastic: a Critical Study of Science Fiction, Fantasy, Paranormal and Gothic Writings* (Jefferson NC: McFarland & Company, 2011).

98. Gordon, *Ghostly Matters*, p. 8.

99. Rosemary Jackson, *Fantasy: the Literature of Subversion* (London: Routledge, 2003 [1981]), p. 69.

Afterword

1. Fred Botting, *Limits of Horror: Technology, Bodies, Gothic* (Manchester: Manchester University Press, 2008), p. 175.

2. Elizabeth Grosz, *Volatile Bodies: Toward a Corporeal Feminism* (Bloomington IN and Indianapolis IN: Indiana University Press, 1994), p. 203.

Bibliography

Abraham, Nicolas, 'Notes on the Phantom: a Complement to Freud's Metapsychology', in N. Abraham and M. Torok, *The Shell and the Kernel: Renewals of Psychoanalysis*, Volume 1, ed. and trans. by Nicholas Rand (Chicago IL: University of Chicago Press, 1994), pp. 171–6.

Aguirre, Manuel, 'Geometria strachu. Wykorzystanie przestrzeni w literaturze gotyckiej', trans. by Agnieszka Izdebska, in G. Gazda, A. Izdebska and J. Płuciennik (eds), *Wokół gotycyzmów: wyobraźnia, groza, okrucieństwo* (Kraków: Universitas, 2002), pp. 4–32.

Ahlborn, Ania, *Within These Walls* (New York: Gallery Books, 2015), Kindle edn.

Ahmad, Aalya, 'Transgressive Horror and Politics: the Splatterpunks and Extreme Horror', in K. Corstorphine and L. R. Kremmel (eds), *The Palgrave Handbook to Horror Literature* (New York: Palgrave Macmillan, 2018), pp. 365–76.

Ahmed, Sara, *The Cultural Politics of Emotion* (Edinburgh: Edinburgh University Press, 2014).

Aldana Reyes, Xavier, *Body Gothic: Corporeal Transgression in Contemporary Literature and Horror Film* (Cardiff: University of Wales Press, 2014).

— (ed.), *Horror: a Literary History* (London: British Library, 2016).

— *Horror Film and Affect: Towards a Corporeal Model of Viewership* (London: Routledge, 2016).

— 'Post-Millennial Horror, 2000–16', in X. Aldana Reyes (ed.), *Horror: a Literary History* (London: British Library, 2016), pp. 189–214.

210 • House of Horrors

Amador, Victoria, 'Dark Ladies: Vampires, Lesbians, and Women of Colour', *Gothic Studies*, 15/1 (2013), 8–20.

Araújo, Susana, 'The Gothic-Grotesque of *Haunted*: Joyce Carol Oates's Tales of Abjection', in K. Kutzbach and M. Mueller (eds), *The Abject of Desire: the Aestheticization of the Unaesthetic in Contemporary Literature and Culture* (Amsterdam: Rodopi, 2007), pp. 89–105.

Armitt, Lucie, *Twentieth-Century Gothic* (Cardiff: University of Wales Press, 2011).

Arvin, Maile, Eve Tuck and Angie Morrill, 'Decolonizing feminism: challenging connections between settler colonialism and heteropatriarchy' *Feminist Formations*, 25/1 (2013), 8–34.

Ascari, Maurizio, *A Counter-History of Crime Fiction: Supernatural, Gothic, Sensational* (Basingstoke: Palgrave Macmillan, 2007).

Auerbach, Nina, *Our Vampires, Ourselves* (Chicago IL: University of Chicago Press, 1995).

Badley, Linda, *Writing Horror and the Body: the Fiction of Stephen King, Clive Barker, and Anne Rice* (Westport CT: Greenwood Publishing Group, 1996).

Bailey, Dale, *American Nightmares: the Haunted House Formula in American Popular Fiction* (Bowling Green OH: Bowling Green State University Popular Press, 1999).

Bakhtin, Mikhail, *Rabelais and his World*, trans. by Hélène Iswolsky (Cambridge MA: MIT Press, 1968).

Becker, Susanne, *Gothic Forms of Feminine Fictions* (Manchester and New York: Manchester University Press, 1999).

Bergland, Renee L., 'From Indian Ghosts and American Subjects', in M. del Pilar Blanco and E. Peeren (eds), *The Spectralities Reader: Ghosts and Haunting in Contemporary Cultural Theory* (New York: Bloomsbury Academic, 2013), pp. 371–92.

Berlant, Lauren, 'Intimacy: a Special Issue', *Critical Inquiry*, Intimacy, 24/2 (1998), 281–8.

— *The Female Complaint: the Unfinished Business of Sentimentality in American Culture* (Durham NC and London: Duke University Press, 2008).

Berlant, Lauren, and Michael Warner, '*Sex* in *Public*', *Critical Inquiry*, 24 (1998), 547–60.

Berressem, Hanjo, 'On the Matter of Abjection', in K. Kutzbach and M. Mueller (eds), *The Abject of Desire: the Aestheticization of the Unaesthetic in Contemporary Literature and Culture* (Amsterdam: Rodopi, 2007), pp. 19–48.

Bersani, Leo, and Adam Phillips, *Intimacies* (Chicago IL: University of Chicago Press, 2008).

Betz, Phyllis M., *The Lesbian Fantastic: a Critical Study of Science Fiction, Fantasy, Paranormal and Gothic Writings* (Jefferson NC: McFarland & Company, 2011).

Bienstock Anolik, Ruth, 'The Missing Mother: the Meanings of Maternal Absence in the Gothic Mode', *Modern Language Studies*, 33/1–2 (2003), 24–43.

Bloom, Clive, 'Horror Fiction: In Search of a Definition', in D. Punter (ed.), *A New Companion to the Gothic* (Chichester: John Wiley, 2012), pp. 211–23.

Botting, Fred, 'Hypocrite Vampire . . .' *Gothic Studies*, 9/1 (2007), 16–34.

— *Limits of Horror: Technology, Bodies, Gothic* (Manchester and New York: Manchester University Press, 2008).

Brabon, Benjamin A., and Stéphanie Genz, 'Introduction: Postfeminist Gothic', in B. A. Brabon and S. Genz (eds), *Postfeminist Gothic: Critical Interventions in Contemporary Culture* (Basingstoke: Palgrave Macmillan, 2007), pp. 1–15.

— (eds), *Postfeminist Gothic: Critical Interventions in Contemporary Culture* (Palgrave Macmillan, 2007).

Braham, Persephone, 'Scylla and Charybdis', in J. A. Weinstock (ed.), *The Ashgate Encyclopedia of Literary and Cinematic Monsters* (London: Routledge, 2014), p. 502–4.

Braidotti, Rosi, *Metamorphoses: Towards a Materialist Theory of Becoming* (New York: John Wiley & Sons, 2002).

— *Nomadic Subjects: Embodiment and Sexual Difference in Contemporary Feminist Theory* (New York: Columbia University Press, 2011).

— 'Signs of Wonder and Traces of Doubt: On Teratology and Embodied Differences', in J. Price and M. Shildrick (eds), *Feminist Theory and the Body: a Reader* (New York: Routledge, 1999), pp. 290–301.

— *The Posthuman* (Cambridge: Polity Press, 2013).

— *Transpositions: On Nomadic Ethics* (Cambridge: Polity Press, 2006).

Briggs, Julia, *Night Visitors: the Rise and Fall of the English Ghost Story* (London: Faber, 1977).

Brite, Poppy Z. (Billy Martin), *Drawing Blood* (New York: Dell Abyss, 1993).

— (ed.), *Love in Vein: Twenty Original Tales of Vampiric Erotica* (New York: HarperPrism, 1994).

— (ed.), *Love in Vein: 18 More Tales of Vampiric Erotica* (New York: HarperPrism, 1994).

Brooks, Kinitra D., *Searching for Sycorax: Black Women's Hauntings of Contemporary Horror* (New Brunswick NJ: Rutgers University Press, 2018).

Brooks, Kinitra, Alexis McGee and Stephanie Schoellman, 'Speculative Sankofarration: Haunting Black Women in Contemporary Horror Fiction', *Obsidian: Literature in the African Diaspora*, 42/1–2 (2016), 237–77.

212 • House of Horrors

Brogan, Kathleen, *Cultural Haunting: Ghosts and Ethnicity in Recent American Literature* (Charlottesville VA: University Press of Virginia, 1998).

Bryant, Cedric Gael, '"The Soul Has Bandaged Moments": Reading the African American Gothic in Wright's *Big Boy Leaves Home*, Morrison's *Beloved*, and Gomez's *Gilda*', *African American Review*, 39/4 (2005), 541–53.

Burch, Sabine, 'Jewelle Gomez: the 20th Anniversary of *The Gilda Stories*. An Interview with Jewelle Gomez', *LambdaLiterary.com*, 12 July 2011, *https://lambdaliterary.org/2011/07/jewelle-gomez-the-20th-anniversary-of-the-gilda-stories/* (last accessed 12 February 2018).

Buse, Peter, and Andrew Scott (eds), *Ghosts: Deconstruction, Psychoanalysis, History* (New York: St Martin's Press, 1999).

Bussing, Sabine, *Aliens in the Home: the Child in Horror Fiction* (Westport CT: Greenwood Press, 1987).

Butler, Judith, *Frames of War: When is Life Grievable?* (London: Verso Books, 2016).

— *Precarious Life: the Powers of Mourning and Justice* (London: Verso Books, 2020).

— *Undoing Gender* (New York: Psychology Press, 2004).

Carroll, Noël, *The Philosophy of Horror; or, Paradoxes of the Heart* (New York and London: Routledge, 1990).

Castle, Terry, *The Apparitional Lesbian: Female Homosexuality and Modern Culture* (New York: Columbia University Press, 1993).

— *The Female Thermometer: Eighteenth-Century Culture and the Invention of the Uncanny* (Oxford: Oxford University Press, 1995).

Chanter, Tina, 'The Exoticization and Universalization of the Fetish, and the Naturalization of the Phallus: Abject Objections', in T. Chanter and E. Płonowska Ziarek (eds), *Revolt, Affect, Collectivity: the Unstable Boundaries of Kristeva's Polis* (Albany NY: SUNY Press, 2012), pp. 149–80.

Cixous, Hélène, 'The Laugh of the Medusa', *Signs*, 1/4 (1976), 875–93.

Clasen, Mathias F., *Why Horror Seduces* (New York: Oxford University Press, 2017).

Clover, Carol J., *Men, Women, and Chain Saws: Gender in the Modern Horror Film – Updated Edition* (Princeton NJ and Oxford: Princeton University Press, 2015 [1992]).

Clute, John, *The Darkening Garden: a Short Lexicon of Horror* (Cauheegan: Payseur & Schmidt, 2006).

Cohen, Jeffrey Jerome, 'Monster Culture (Seven Theses)', in J. J. Cohen (ed.), *Monster Theory: Reading Culture* (London and Minneapolis MN: University of Minnesota Press, 1996), pp. 3–25.

Collins, Michael J., 'Culture in the Hall of Mirrors: Film and Fiction and Fiction and Film', in T. Magistrale and M. A. Morrison (eds), *A Dark Night's Dreaming: Contemporary American Horror Fiction* (Columbia SC: University of South Carolina Press, 1996), pp. 110–22.

Collins, Patricia Hills, *Black Feminist Thought: Knowledge, Consciousness, and the Politics of Empowerment*, revised 10th anniversary edn (New York and London: Routledge, 2000 [1990]).

Cooke, Jennifer, 'Making a Scene: Towards an Anatomy of Contemporary Literary Intimacies', in J. Cooke (ed.), *Scenes of Intimacy: Reading, Writing and Theorizing Contemporary Literature* (London and New York: Bloomsbury Academic, 2013), pp. 3–21.

Covino, Deborah Caslav, *Amending the Abject Body: Aesthetic Makeovers in Medicine and Culture* (Albany NY: SUNY Press, 2004).

Creed, Barbara, 'Lesbian Bodies: Tribades, Tomboys and Tarts', in E. Grosz and E. Probyn (eds), *Sexy Bodies: the Strange Carnalities of Feminism* (London and New York: Routledge, 2013), pp. 86–103.

—— *The Monstrous-Feminine: Film, Feminism, Psychoanalysis* (London and New York: Routledge, 1993).

Crow, Charles L., *American Gothic* (Cardiff: University of Wales Press, 2009).

Datlow, Ellen (guest editor), 'Women Destroy Horror: Special Issue', *Nightmare Magazine*, 25 (2014).

Davies, Cristyn, and Kerry H. Robinson, 'Reconceptualising Family: Negotiating Sexuality in a Governmental Climate of Neoliberalism', *Contemporary Issues in Early Childhood*, 14/1 (2013), 39–50.

Davis, Colin, '*État présent*: Hauntology, Spectres and Phantoms', in M. del Pilar Blanco and E. Peeren (eds), *The Spectralities Reader: Ghosts and Haunting in Contemporary Cultural Theory* (New York: Bloomsbury Academic, 2013), pp. 53–60.

Deleuze, Gilles, and Félix Guattari, *Kafka: Towards a Minor Literature*, trans. by Dana Polan, foreword by Réda Bensmaïa (Minneapolis MN: University of Minnesota Press, 1986 [1975]).

Derrida, Jacques, *On Hospitality*, trans. by Rachel Bowlby (Stanford CA: Stanford University Press, 2000).

—— *Specters of Marx: the State of the Debt, the Work of Mourning and the New International*, trans. by Peggy Kamuf (New York and London: Routledge, 2012 [1993]).

Driscoll, Catherine, *Girls: Feminine Adolescence in Popular Culture and Cultural Theory* (New York: Columbia University Press, 2002).

Due, Tananarive, *The Between* (New York: Harper Collins, 1995).

Duschinsky, Robbie, 'Abjection and Self-identity: Towards a Revised Account of Purity and Impurity', *The Sociological Review*, 61/4 (2013), 709–27.

Edelman, Leo, *No Future: Queer Theory and the Death Drive* (Durham NC: Duke University Press, 2004).

Edwards, Justin, and Rune Graulund, *The Grotesque* (London: Routledge, 2013).

Ellis, Kate Ferguson, *The Contested Castle: Gothic Novels and the Subversion of Domestic Ideology* (Urbana IL: University of Illinois Press, 1989).

Engstrom, Elizabeth, *Black Ambrosia* (New York: Tor Horror, 1988).

Farwell, Marilyn, *Heterosexual Plots and Lesbian Narratives* (New York and London: NYU Press, 1996).

Fisher, Mark, *Capitalist Realism: Is There No Alternative?* (Winchester: Zero Books, 2009).

Foucault, Michel, *The History of Sexuality, Vol. 1: an Introduction*, trans. by Robert Hurley (New York: Vintage Books, 1990 [1978]).

Fraser, Nancy, and Axel Honneth, *Redistribution or Recognition? A Political-Philosophical Exchange* (London and New York: Verso Books, 2003).

Freccero, Carla, 'Queer Spectrality: Haunting the Past', in M. del Pilar Blanco and E. Peeren (eds), *The Spectralities Reader: Ghosts and Haunting in Contemporary Cultural Theory* (New York: Bloomsbury Academic, 2013), pp. 335–59.

Freud, Sigmund, 'The Uncanny', in V. B. Leitch et al. (eds), *The Norton Anthology of Theory and Criticism* (New York: W.W. Norton & Company, 2001 [1919]), pp. 929–52.

Frow, John, *Genre* (Abingdon: Routledge, 2005).

Fuss, Diana (ed.), *Inside/Out: Lesbian Theories, Gay Theories* (New York: Psychology Press, 1991).

Gabb, Jacqui, *Researching Intimacy in Families* (Basingstoke: Palgrave Macmillan, 2008).

Gaines, Mikal J., 'They Are Still Here: Possession and Dispossession in the 21st Century Haunted House Film', in F. Pascuzzi and S. Waters (eds), *The Spaces and Places of Horror* (Wilmington DE: Vernon Press, 2020), pp. 179–202.

Gelder, Ken, *Reading the Vampire* (London: Routledge, 2006 [1994]).

Giddens, Anthony, *The Transformations of Intimacy: Sexuality, Love and Eroticism in Modern Societies* (Stanford: Stanford University Press, 1992).

Gilman, Sander L., *Difference and Pathology: Stereotypes of Sexuality, Race, and Madness* (Ithaca NY: Cornell University Press, 1985).

Gomez, Jewelle, 'Speculative Fiction and Black Lesbians' *Signs*, Theorizing Lesbian Experience, 18/4 (1993), 948–55.

— *The Gilda Stories* (London: Sheba Feminist Press, 1991).

Goodnow, Katherine J., *Kristeva in Focus: From Theory to Film Analysis* (New York and Oxford: Berghahn Books, 2010).

Gordon, Avery, *Ghostly Matters: Haunting and the Sociological Imagination* (Minneapolis MN and London: University of Minnesota Press, 2008 [1997]).

Gordon, Joan, and Veronica Hollinger, 'Introduction: the Shape of Vampires', in J. Gordon and V. Hollinger (eds), *Blood Read: the Vampire as Metaphor in Contemporary Culture* (Philadelphia PA: University of Pennsylvania Press, 1997), pp. 1–7.

Gran, Sara, *Come Closer* (New York: Soho Press, 2003).

Grixti, Joseph, *Terrors of Uncertainty: the Cultural Contexts of Horror Fiction* (London: Routledge, 1989).

Grosz, Elizabeth, *Sexual Subversions* (Sydney: Allen & Unwin, 1989).

— *Volatile Bodies: Toward a Corporeal Feminism* (Bloomington IN and Indianapolis IN: Indiana University Press, 1994).

Gunning, Tom, 'To Scan a Ghost: the Ontology of Mediated Vision', in M. del Pilar Blanco and E. Peeren (eds), *The Spectralities Reader: Ghosts and Haunting in Contemporary Cultural Theory* (New York: Bloomsbury Academic, 2013), pp. 207–44.

Guran, Paula, 'Interview. Jeanne Cavalos: Abyss, Odyssey & Beyond', *DarkEcho* (1996), *https://web.archive.org/web/20170720153344/http://www.darkecho.com/darkecho/archives/cavelos.html* (last accessed 21 November 2020).

— 'Interview. Jeanne Cavalos: Scientist, Editor, Writer, Teacher . . .', *DarkEcho* (1998), *www.darkecho.com/darkecho/archives/cavelos2.html* (last accessed 5 October 2013).

Guy-Sheftall, Beverly, 'The Body Politic: Black Female Sexuality and the Nineteenth-Century Euro-American Imagination', in K. Wallace-Sanders (ed.), *Skin Deep, Spirit Strong: the Black Female Body in American Culture* (Ann Arbor MI: University of Michigan Press, 2002), pp. 13–36.

Halberstam, Jack, *In a Queer Time and Place: Transgender Bodies, Subcultural Lives* (New York and London: NYU Press, 2005).

— *Skin Shows: Gothic Horror and the Technology of Monsters* (Durham NC and London: Duke University Press, 1995).

— *The Queer Art of Failure* (Durham NC and London: Duke University Press, 2011).

Hall, Lynda, 'Passion(ate) Plays "Wherever We Found Space": Lorde and Gomez Queer(y)ing Boundaries and Acting In', *Callaloo*, 23/1 (2000), 394–421.

Hammonds, Evelynn M., 'Black (W)holes and the Geometry of Black Female Sexuality,' *Differences*, 6/2–3 (1994), 126–45.

— 'Toward a Genealogy of Black Female Sexuality: the Problematic of Silence', in J. Price and M. Shildrick (eds), *Feminist Theory and the Body: a Reader* (New York: Routledge, 1999), pp. 93–104.

216 • House of Horrors

Hanich, Julian, *Cinematic Emotion in Horror Films and Thrillers: the Aesthetic Paradox of Pleasurable Fear* (London and New York: Routledge, 2011).

Hantke, Steffen, 'Deconstructing Horror: Commodities in the Fiction of Jonathan Carroll and Kathe Koja', *Journal of American Culture* 18, No. 3 (1995), 41–57.

—— 'The Decline of the Literary Horror Market in the 1990s and Dell's Abyss Series', *The Journal of Popular Culture*, 41/1 (2008), 56–71.

—— 'The Rise of Popular Horror Fiction', in X. Aldana Reyes (ed.), *Horror: a Literary History* (London: British Library, 2016), pp. 159–87.

Harrington, Erin, *Women, Monstrosity and Horror Film: Gynaehorror* (New York: Routledge, 2017).

Hendrix, Grady, *Paperbacks from Hell: the Twisted History of '70s and '80s Horror Fiction*, with Will Errickson (Philadelphia PA: Quirk Books, 2017).

Holder, Nancy, *Dead in the Water* (New York: Dell Abyss, 1994).

Holland-Tell, Linda J., *As American as Mom, Baseball, and Apple Pie: Constructing Community in Contemporary American Horror Fiction* (Bowling Green OH: Bowling Green State University Popular Press, 2001).

Hollinger, Veronica, 'Fantasies of Absence: the Postmodern Vampire', in J. Gordon and V. Hollinger (eds), *Blood Read: the Vampire as Metaphor in Contemporary Culture* (Philadelphia PA: University of Pennsylvania Press, 1997), pp. 199–212.

Horner, Avril, and Sue Zlosnik, *Gothic and the Comic Turn* (Basingstoke: Palgrave Macmillan, 2004).

—— (eds), *Women and the Gothic: an Edinburgh Companion* (Edinburgh: Edinburgh University Press, 2016).

Hurley, Kelly, 'Abject and Grotesque', in C. Spooner and E. McEvoy (eds), *The Routledge Companion to Gothic* (London: Routledge, 2007), pp. 137–46.

Jackson, Kimberly, *Gender and the Nuclear Family in the Twenty-First-Century Horror* (New York: Palgrave Macmillan, 2016).

Jackson, Rosemary, *Fantasy: the Literature of Subversion* (London: Routledge, 2003 [1981]).

Jancovich, Mark, *Horror* (London: Batsford, 1992).

Janicker, Rebecca, *The Literary Haunted House: Lovecraft, Matheson, King and the Horror in Between* (Jefferson NC: McFarland & Company, 2015).

Jenkins, Jerry Rafiki, 'Race, Freedom, and the Black Vampire in Jewelle Gomez's *The Gilda Stories*', *African American Review*, 46/2–3 (2013), 313–28.

—— *The Paradox of Blackness in African American Vampire Fiction* (Columbus OH: Ohio State University Press, 2019).

Johnson, Colleen L., 'Perspectives on American Kinship in the Later 1990s', *Journal of Marriage and Family*, 62/3 (2000), 623–39.

Johnson, Judith E., 'Women and Vampires: Nightmare or Utopia?', *The Kenyon Review*, 5/1 (1993), 72–80.

Jones, Darryl, *Sleeping with the Lights On: the Unsettling Story of Horror* (Oxford: Oxford University Press, 2018).

Joshi, S. T., *The Evolution of the Weird Tale* (New York: Hippocampus Press, 2004).

— *The Modern Weird Tale* (Jefferson, NC: McFarland & Company, 2001).

Keesey, Pam (ed.), *Daughters of Darkness: Lesbian Vampire Stories* (Pittsburgh: Cleis Press, 1998).

Kiernan, Caitlín R., 'Caitlín R. Kiernan: Transmutations', *Locusmag.com*, 31 December 2008, *www.locusmag.com/2008/Issue12_Kiernan.html* (last accessed 12 February 2018).

— 'Open this Mouth Wide, and Eat Your Heart', *greygirlbeast.dreamwidth.org*, 9 September 2011, *https://greygirlbeast.dreamwidth.org/791852.html* (last accessed 20 February 2018).

— *The Drowning Girl: a Memoir* (New York: ROC, 2012).

King, Stephen, *Danse Macabre* (New York: Simon and Schuster, 2011 [c. 1981]).

Kiste, Gwendolyn, *The Rust Maidens* (Carbondale IL: Trepidatio, 2018), Kindle edn.

Koja, Koja, *The Cipher* (New York: Dell Abyss, 1991).

Korsmeyer, Carolyn, *Savouring Disgust: the Foul and the Fair in Aesthetics* (Oxford: Oxford University Press, 2011).

Kraditor, Aileen S., 'Introduction', in A. S. Kreditor (ed.), *Up From the Pedestal: Selected Writings in the History of American Feminism* (Chicago IL: Quadrangle, 1968), pp. 3–24.

Krell, David Farrell, 'Das Unheimliche; Architectural Sections of Heidegger and Freud', *Research in Phenomenology*, 22 (1992), 43–61.

Kristeva, Julia, *Powers of Horror: an Essay on Abjection*, trans. by Leon S. Roudiez (New York: Columbia University Press, 1992).

— 'Talking about Polylogue', trans. by Sean Hand, in M. Eagleton (ed.), *Feminist Literary Theory: a Reader* (London: John Wiley & Sons, 2011), pp. 284–6.

Kromm, Jane, 'The Feminization of Madness in Visual Representation', *Feminist Studies*, 20/3 (1994), 507–35.

Kröger, Lisa, and Melanie R. Anderson, *Monster, She Wrote: the Women Who Pioneered Horror and Speculative Fiction* (Philadelphia PA: Quirk Books, 2019).

Kutzbach, Konstanze, and Monika Mueller (eds), *The Abject of Desire: the Aestheticization of the Unaesthetic in Contemporary Literature and Culture* (Amsterdam: Rodopi, 2007).

Kvideland, Karin, 'Sin-Eating', *International Society for Folk Narrative Research*, 35 (1984), 27–36.

Levine, Nancy E., 'Alternative Kinship, Marriage, and Reproduction', *Annual Review of Anthropology*, 37 (2008), 357–89.

Lewis, Christopher S., 'Queering Personhood in the Neo-Slave Narrative: Jewelle Gomez's *The Gilda Stories*', *African American Review*, 47/4 (2014), 447–59.

Lewis, Tyson, and Daniel Cho, 'Home Is Where the Neurosis Is: a Topography of the Spatial Unconscious', *Cultural Critique*, 64 (2006), 69–91.

Luckhurst, Roger, 'From "The Contemporary London Gothic and the Limits of the Spectral Turn"', in M. del Pilar Blanco and E. Peeren (eds), *The Spectralities Reader: Ghosts and Haunting in Contemporary Cultural Theory* (New York: Bloomsbury Academic, 2013), pp. 75–88.

— 'The Weird: a Dis/orientation,' *Textual Practice*, 31/6 (2017), 1041–61.

Marks, Laura U., *The Skin of the Film: Intercultural Cinema, Embodiment, and the Senses* (Durham NC and London: Duke University Press, 2000).

Martin, Billy, 'I'm Basically Retired (For Now)', *LiveJournal*, 9 June 2010, *http://docbrite.livejournal.com/2010/06/09/* (last accessed 20 November 2020).

Marzec, Andrzej, *Widmontologia. Teoria filozoficzna i praktyczna artystyczna ponowoczesności* (Warszawa: Bęc Zmiana, 2015).

Masschelein, Anneleen, *The Unconcept: the Freudian Uncanny in Late-Twentieth-Century Theory* (Albany NY: SUNY Press, 2011).

Massie, Elizabeth, *Sineater* (Crossroad Press, 2010 [1992]). Kindle edn.

Mbembe, Achille, 'From "Life, Sovereignty, and Terror in the Fiction of Amos Tutuola"', in M. del Pilar Blanco and E. Peeren (eds), *The Spectralities Reader: Ghosts and Haunting in Contemporary Cultural Theory* (New York: Bloomsbury Academic, 2013), pp. 131–49.

Menninghaus, Winfried, *Disgust: Theory and History of a Strong Sensation*, trans. by Howard Eiland and Joel Golb (Albany NY: SUNY Press, 2012 [2003]).

Meyer, Sabine, 'Passing Perverts, After all? Vampirism, (in)Visibility, and the Horrors of the Normative in Jewelle Gomez' the Gilda Stories', *Femspec*, 9 (2002), 25–37 (a non-paginated ProQuest version), *www.proquest.com/scholarly-journals/passing-perverts-after-all-vampirismvisibility/docview/200082364/se-2?accountid=14887* (last accessed 6 December 2021).

Meyers, Helene, *Femicidal Fears: Narratives of Female Gothic Experience* (Albany NY: SUNY Press, 2001).

Mezei, Kathy, and Chiara Briganti, 'Reading the House: a Literary Perspective', *Signs*, 27/3 (2002), 837–46.

Miéville, China, 'On Monsters: or, Nine or More (Monstrous) Not Cannies', *Journal of the Fantastic in the Arts*, 23/3 (86) (2012), 377–92.

— 'Weird Fiction', in M. Bould, A. M. Butler, A. Roberts and S. Vint (eds), *The Routledge Companion to Science Fiction* (London and New York: Routledge, 2009), pp. 510–6.

Milbank, Alison, 'Bleeding Nuns: a Genealogy of The Female Gothic Grotesque', in D. Wallace and A. Smith (eds), *The Female Gothic: New Directions* (Basingstoke: Palgrave Macmillan, 2009), pp. 76–97.

Miller, Michelle Hughes, Tamar Hager and Rebecca Jaremko Bromwich (eds), *Bad Mothers: Regulations, Representations, and Resistance* (Bradford ON: Demeter Press, 2017).

Miller, William Ian, *The Anatomy of Disgust* (Cambridge MA: Harvard University Press, 2009).

Moers, Ellen, *Literary Women* (Garden City NY: Doubleday, 1976).

Moretti, Franco, 'The Dialectic of Fear', *New Left Review*, 136 (1982), 67–85.

Morgensen, Scott Lauria, *Spaces Between Us: Queer Settler Colonialism and Indigenous Decolonization* (Minneapolis MN: University of Minnesota Press, 2011).

Morrison, Toni, *Playing in the Dark: Whiteness and the Literary Imagination* (Cambridge MA: Harvard University Press, 1992).

Morton, Lisa, 'Women Destroy Horror! Roundtable Interview: Linda Addison, Kate Jonez, Helen Marshall, and Rena Mason', *Nightmare Magazine*, Women Destroy Horror: Special Issue, 25 (2014), 179–93.

Muñoz, José Esteban, *Cruising Utopia: the Then and There of Queer Futurity* (New York: NYU Press, 2009).

Muraco, Anna, 'Intentional Families: Fictive Kin Ties Between Cross-Gender, Different Sexual Orientation Friends', *Journal of Marriage and Family*, 68 (2006), 1313–25.

Murken, Sebastian, and Sussan Namini, 'Childhood Familial Experiences as Antecedents of Adult Membership in New Religious Movements: a Literature Review', *Nova Religio: Journal of Alternative and Emergent Religions*, 10/4 (2007), 17–37.

Myers, E. C., 'Interview: Ellen Datlow', *Nightmare Magazine*, 4 (2013), *www.nightmare-magazine.com/nonfiction/interview-ellen-datlow/* (last accessed 19 October 2021).

Ndalianis, Angela, *The Horror Sensorium: Media and the Senses* (Jefferson NC: McFarland & Company, 2012).

Nevins, Jess, *Horror Fiction in the 20th Century: Exploring Literature's Most Chilling Genre* (Santa Barbara CA: Praeger, 2020).

— 'Conceptualizing Varieties of Space in Horror Fiction', in K. Corstorphine and L. R. Kremmel (eds), *The Palgrave Handbook to Horror Literature* (New York: Palgrave Macmillan, 2018), pp. 441–56.

Ng, Andrew Hock Soon, *Women and Domestic Space in Contemporary Gothic Narratives: the House as Subject* (New York: Palgrave Macmillan, 2015).

Norman, Brian, *Dead Women Talking: Figures of Injustice in American Literature* (Baltimore MD: Johns Hopkins University Press, 2013).

Noys, Benjamin, and Timothy S. Murphy, 'Introduction: Old and New Weird', *Genre*, 49/2 (2016), 117–34.

O'Grady, Lorraine, 'Olympia's Maid: Reclaiming Black Female Subjectivity', in J. Frueh, C. L. *Langer and A. Raven (eds)*, New Feminist Criticism: Art, Identity, Action (New York: Icon Editions, 1994), pp. 152–70.

Ogunyemi, Chikwenye Okonjo, 'An Abiku-Ogbanje Atlas: a Pre-Text for Rereading Soyinka's *Aké* and Morrison's *Beloved*', *African American Review*, 36/ 4 (2002), 663–78.

Okonkwo, Christopher N., *A Spirit of Dialogue: Incarnations of Ọgbañje, the Born-to-die, in African American Literature* (Knoxville TN: University of Tennessee Press, 2008).

Palmer, Paulina, *Lesbian Gothic: Transgressive Fictions* (London: Cassell, 1999).

— 'Queer Transformations: Renegotiating the Abject in Contemporary Anglo-American Lesbian Fiction', in K. Kutzbach and M. Mueller (eds), *The Abject of Desire: the Aestheticization of the Unaesthetic in Contemporary Literature and Culture* (Amsterdam: Rodopi, 2007), pp. 49–68.

— *The Queer Uncanny: New Perspectives on the Gothic* (Cardiff: University of Wales Press, 2012).

Patterson, Kathy Davis, '"Haunting Back": Vampire Subjectivity in *The Gilda Stories*', *Femspec*, 6/1 (2005), 35–57.

Patterson, Orlando, *Slavery and Social Death* (Cambridge MA: Harvard University Press, 1982).

Patton, Venetria K., *The Grasp that Reaches Beyond the Grave: the Ancestral Call in Black Women's Texts* (Albany NY: SUNY Press, 2013).

— *Women in Chains: the Legacy of Slavery in Black Women's Fiction* (Albany NY: SUNY Press, 2000).

del Pilar Blanco, María, and Esther Peeren, 'Introduction', in M. del Pilar Blanco and E. Peeren (eds), *Popular Ghosts: the Haunted Spaces of Everyday Culture* (London: Bloomsbury Academic, 2010), pp. ix–xxiv.

— 'Introduction: Conceptualizing Spectralities', in M. del Pilar Blanco and E. Peeren (eds), *The Spectralities Reader: Ghosts and Haunting in Contemporary Cultural Theory* (New York: Bloomsbury Academic, 2013), pp. 1–27.

— (eds), *Popular Ghosts: the Haunted Spaces of Everyday Culture* (London: Bloomsbury Academic, 2010).

— 'Spectral Subjectivities: Gender, Sexuality, Race/Introduction', in M. del Pilar Blanco and E. Peeren (eds), *The Spectralities Reader: Ghosts and Haunting in Contemporary Cultural Theory* (New York: Bloomsbury Academic, 2013), pp. 309–16.

— 'Spectropolitics: Ghosts of the Global Contemporary/Introduction', in M. del Pilar Blanco and E. Peeren (eds), *The Spectralities Reader: Ghosts and Haunting in Contemporary Cultural Theory* (New York: Bloomsbury Academic, 2013), pp. 91–7.

— (eds), *The Spectralities Reader: Ghosts and Haunting in Contemporary Cultural Theory* (New York: Bloomsbury Academic, 2013).

Pinedo, Isabel Cristina, *Recreational Terror: Women and the Pleasures of Horror Film Viewing* (Albany NY: SUNY Press, 1997).

Ptacek, Kathryn (ed.), *Women of Darkness* (New York: Tom Doherty Associates, 1989).

— *Women of Darkness II: More Original Horror and Dark Fantasy by Contemporary Women Writers* (New York: Tom Doherty Associates, 1990).

Punter, David, *The Literature of Terror: a History of Gothic Fictions from 1765 to the Present Day*, vol. 2 (New York: Routledge, 2013 [1996]).

Renner, Karen J., *Evil Children in the Popular Imagination* (New York: Palgrave Macmillan, 2016).

— (ed.), *The Evil Child in Literature, Film and Popular Culture* (London and New York: Routledge, 2013).

Rice, Carla, *Becoming Women: the Embodied Self in Image Culture* (Toronto: University of Toronto Press, 2014).

Rifkin, Mark, *When Did Indians Become Straight? Kinship, the History of Sexuality, and Native Sovereignty* (Oxford: Oxford University Press, 2011).

Royle, Nicholas, *The Uncanny* (Manchester: Manchester University Press, 2003).

Rubenstein, Roberta, 'House Mothers and Haunted Daughters: Shirley Jackson and Female Gothic', *Tulsa Studies in Women's Literature*, 15/2 (1996), 309–31.

Russo, Mary J., *The Female Grotesque: Risk, Excess and Modernity* (New York and London: Routledge, 1995).

Sammon, Paul M., 'Introduction', in P. M. Sammon (ed.), *Splatterpunks II: Over the Edge* (New York: Tor Books, 1995), pp. 17–8.

— (ed.), *Splatterpunks: Extreme Horror* (New York: St Martin's Press, 1990).

Scahill, Andrew, *The Revolting Child in Horror Cinema: Youth Rebellion and Queer Spectatorship* (New York: Palgrave Macmillan, 2015).

Sedgwick, Eve Kosofsky, *The Coherence of Gothic Conventions* (New York: Arno Press, 1980).

Shaviro, Seven, 'Into the Funhole: Kathe Koja's *The Cipher*', *Genre*, 49/2 (2016), 213–29.

Shelley, Mary, *Frankenstein; or, The Modern Prometheus*, 3rd edn, ed. by D. L. Macdonald and K. Scherf (Ontario: Broadview Press, 2012 [1818]).

Showalter, Elaine, 'Killing the Angel in the House: the Autonomy of Women Writers', *Antioch Review*, 32/3 (1973), 339–53.

Slotkin, Richard, *Regeneration Through Violence: the Mythology of the American Frontier, 1600–1860* (Middletown CT: Wesleyan University Press, 1973).

Smajić, Srdjan, 'The Trouble with Ghost-Seeing: Vision, Ideology, and Genre in the Victorian Ghost Story', *ELH*, 70/4 (2003), 1107–35.

Snyder, Lucy A., 'An Historical Overview of Classic Horror Novels', *Nightmare Magazine*, Women Destroy Horror: Special Issue, 25 (2014), 169–73.

Sobchack, Vivian, *Carnal Thoughts: Embodiment and Moving Image Culture* (Berkeley CA and Los Angeles CA: University of California Press, 2004).

Spivak, Gayatri Chakravorty, 'From 'Ghostwriting', in M. del Pilar Blanco and E. Peeren (eds), *The Spectralities Reader: Ghosts and Haunting in Contemporary Cultural Theory* (New York: Bloomsbury Academic, 2013), pp. 317–34.

Spooner, Catherine, *Contemporary Gothic* (London: Reaktion Books, 2006).

— 'Crime and the Gothic', in Ch. J. Rzepka and L. Horsley (eds), *A Companion to Crime Fiction* (Chichester: Wiley-Blackwell, 2010), pp. 245–57.

Story, Kaila Adia, 'Racing Sex – Sexing Race', in C. E. Henderson (ed.), *Imagining the Black Female Body* (New York: Palgrave Macmillan, 2010), pp. 23–43.

Strings, Sabine, *Fearing the Black Body: the Racial Origins of Fat Phobia* (New York: NYU Press, 2019).

Tallbear, Kim, 'Making Love and Relations Beyond Settler Sex and Family', in A. Clarke and D. Haraway (eds), *Making Kin Not Population* (Chicago IL: Prickly Paradigm Press, 2018), pp. 145–63.

Tem, Melanie, *Prodigal* (E-Reads, 1999 [1991]).

Thomson, Rosemarie Garland, *Extraordinary Bodies: Figuring Physical Disability in American Culture and Literature* (New York: Columbia University Press, 2017 [1997]).

Todorov, Tzvetan, *The Fantastic: a Structural Approach to a Literary Genre*, trans. from the French by Richard Howard, with a foreword by Robert Scholes (Ithaca NY: Cornell University Press, 1975).

Tompkins, Jane, *Sensational Designs: the Cultural Work of American Fiction, 1790–1860* (New York: Oxford University Press, 1985).

Triggs, Dylan, *The Thing: a Phenomenology of Horror* (Winchester: Zero Books, 2014).

Tuttle, Lisa (ed.), *Skin of the Soul: New Horror Stories by Women* (London: Women's Press, 1990).

Tyler, Imogen, 'Against Abjection', *Feminist Theory*, 10/1 (2009), 77–98.

Ussher, Jane M., *Managing the Monstrous-Feminine: Regulating the Reproductive Body* (London: Routledge, 2006).

Wallace, Diana, and Andrew Smith (eds), *The Female Gothic: New Directions* (Basingstoke: Palgrave Macmillan, 2009).

Weber, Samuel, 'The Sideshow, or: Remarks on a Canny Moment', *MLN*, 88/6 (1973), 1102–33.

Weinstock, Jeffrey Andrew, 'American Vampires', in J. Faflak and J. Haslam (ed.), *American Gothic Culture: an Edinburgh Companion* (Edinburgh: Edinburgh University Press, 2016), pp. 203–21.

— 'Introduction: the Spectral Turn', in J. A. Weinstock (ed.), *Spectral America: Phantoms and the National Imagination* (Madison WI: Popular Press, 2004), pp. 3–17.

— (ed.), *Spectral America: Phantoms and the National Imagination* (Madison WI: Popular Press, 2004).

Welter, Barbara, 'The Cult of True Womanhood: 1820–1860' *American Quarterly*, 18/2 (1) (1966), 151–74.

Wessels, Emanuelle, 'A Lesson Concerning Technology: the Affective Economies of Post-Economic Crisis Haunted House Horror in *The Conjuring* and *Insidious*', *Quarterly Review of Film and Video*, 32/6 (2015), 511–26.

Wester, Maisha L., *American Gothic: Screams from Shadowed Places* (New York: Palgrave Macmillan, 2012).

Weston, Kath, *Families We Choose: Lesbians, Gays, Kinship* (New York: Columbia University Press, 2013 [1991]).

Whitney, Sarah E., *Splattered Ink: Postfeminist Gothic Fiction and Gendered Violence* (Urbana IL: University of Illinois Press, 2016).

Williams, Anne, *Art of Darkness: a Poetics of Gothic* (Chicago IL: University of Chicago Press, 1995).

Williams, Linda, 'Film Bodies: Gender, Genre, and Excess', *Film Quarterly*, 44/4 (1991), 2–13.

Williams, Linda, 'When the Woman Looks', in B. K. Grant (ed.), *The Dread of Difference: Gender and the Horror Film* (Austin TX: University of Texas Press, 1996), pp. 15–34.

Williams, Tony, *Hearths of Darkness: the Family in the American Horror Film, Updated Edition* (Jackson MS: University of Press of Mississippi, 2014 [1996]).

Williamson, Milly, *The Lure of the Vampire: Gender, Fiction and Fandom from Bram Stoker to Buffy* (London and New York: Wallflower Press, 2005).

Winnubst, Shannon, 'Vampires, Anxieties, and Dreams: Race and Sex in the Contemporary United States', *Hypatia*, 18/3 (2003), 1–20.

Wisker, Gina, *Contemporary Women's Gothic Fiction: Carnival, Hauntings and Vampire Kisses* (London: Palgrave Macmillan, 2018).

— 'Devouring Desires: Lesbian Gothic Horror', in W. Hughes and A. Smith (eds), *Queering the Gothic* (Manchester: Manchester University Press, 2011), pp. 123–41.

— *Horror Fiction: an Introduction* (London: A&C Black, 2006).

— 'Love Bites: Contemporary Women's Vampire Fictions', in D. Punter (ed.), *A New Companion to The Gothic* (Chichester: John Wiley & Sons, 2012), pp. 224–38.

— 'Women's Horror as Erotic Transgression', *Femspec*, 3/1 (2001), 44–63.

Wood, Robin, 'The American Nightmare: Horror in the 70s', in M. Jancovich (ed.), *Horror, the Film Reader* (London: Routledge, 2002), pp. 25–32.

Wolfreys, Julian, *Victorian Hauntings: Spectrality, Gothic, the Uncanny and Literature* (Basingstoke: Palgrave Macmillan, 2001).

Woofter, Kristopher, 'Caitlín R. Kiernan's *The Drowning Girl* (2012) – Shirley Jackson', in S. Bacon (ed.), *Horror: a Reader* (Oxford: Peter Lang, 2019), pp. 227–33.

VanderMeer, Jeff, 'Interview: Caitlín R. Kiernan on Weird Fiction', *Weird Fiction Review*, 12 March 2012, *https://weirdfictionreview.com/2012/03/interview-Caitlín-r-kiernan-on-weird-fiction/* (last accessed 12 February 2018).

VanderMeer, Jeff, 'The New Weird Anthology – Notes and Introduction', *JeffVanDerMeer.com*, 28 June 2009, *www.jeffvandermeer.com/2009/06/28/the-new-weird-anthology-notes-and-introduction/* (last accessed 19 October 2014).

van Veen, tobias c., and Reynaldo Anderson, 'Fabulous Camps of the Black Fantastic: Sylvester James, Queer Afrofuturism, and Black Vernacular Becomings', in R. Anderson and C. R. Fluker (eds), *The Black Speculative Arts Movement: Black Futurity, Art+Design* (Lanham MD: Lexington Books, 2019), pp. 217–30.

Vidler, Anthony, *The Architectural Uncanny: Essays in the Modern Unhomely* (Cambridge MA: MIT Press, 1992).

— *Warped Space: Art, Architecture, and Anxiety in Modern Culture* (Cambridge MA: MIT Press, 2000).

Yates, Wilson, 'An Introduction to the Grotesque: Theoretical and Theological Considerations', in J. L. Adams and W. Yates (eds), *The Grotesque in Art and Literature: Theological Reflections* (Grand Rapids MI: Wm. B. Eerdmans Publishing, 1997), pp. 1–68.

Yael, Ben-zvi, *Native Land Talk: Indigenous and Arrivant Rights Theories* (Hanover NH: Dartmouth University Press, 2018).

Zanger, Jules, 'Metaphor into Metonymy: the Vampire Next Door', in J. Gordon and V. Hollinger (eds), *Blood Read: the Vampire as Metaphor in Contemporary Culture* (Philadelphia PA: University of Pennsylvania Press, 1997), pp. 17–26.

Zimmerman, Bonnie, 'What Has Never Been: an Overview of Lesbian Feminist Literary Criticism', in V. B. Leitch et al. (eds), *The Norton Anthology of Theory and Criticism* (New York: W.W. Norton & Company, 2001), pp. 2340–59.

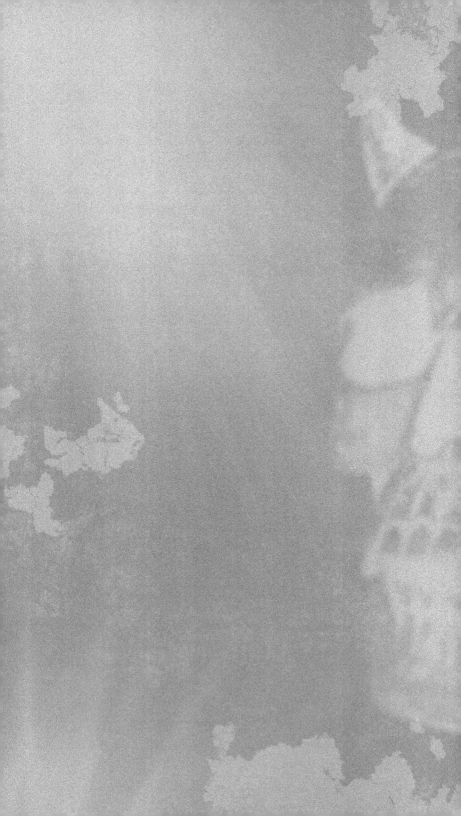

Index

abiku 153

abjection 6, 19, 27, 62, 75, 91, 94–5, 97–103, 106–7, 110, 112–13, 115, 118, 121, 123–4, 126, 128–9, 130–1

Abyss (Dell Publishing imprint) 9–10, 12

adolescence 83–5, 112, 121, 161–2

Age of Reason 34, 133
    see also Enlightenment

Ahlborn, Ania 139, 158–9, 161, 165, 170
    Within These Walls (2015) 20, 137, 139, 158–68, 170

anisotropy 51

anti-materialism 113–14

archaic mother 34, 36, 117–18, 131

architectural uncanny 29–30

Bakhtin, Mikhail 35, 56, 58–9

Barker, Clive 4, 7

becoming 39–40, 58, 69, 89–90, 104

Black femininity 61, 104, 130, 155–6

Black masculinity 139, 155–6

blackness 77, 106

body genre 7

bourgeoisie 17, 24–5, 29–31, 43, 167
    see also middle class

Butler, Judith 15–16, 60–1, 135
    see also performativity of gender

cannibalism 31, 35, 50, 79, 100, 144

Cavelos, Jeanne 9, 12

community 15, 56–7, 74–5, 78–88, 96–7, 103–4, 112–13, 150, 163–4
    see also social body

corporeality 13, 26, 39, 55–7, 60, 129, 131, 140–1, 145–6, 169, 174
    lesbian corporeality 64
    vampiric corporeality 112

cults 41, 44, 66–7, 127, 139, 159, 163–4, 167–8

cultural haunting 138, 150

228 • House of Horrors

dark eroticism 50, 91, 110, 116
deconstruction 25, 28, 59, 96, 103, 137
Deleuze, Gilles 14, 88–9, 104
demon 140
Derrida, Jacques 28, 134–8, 147–8, 150–1
doubling 36, 49, 67, 72–3, 140, 166, 169
disability 84
dis/ease 6–7, 60, 65, 124
dispossession 140–1
domesticity 14, 26, 84–5
domestic abuse 14, 85
Dracula (1897) 93, 96, 101, 111, 115
Due, Tananarive 10–12, 97, 139, 150–3, 155, 157
    The Between (1995) 19–20, 139, 150–8
    The Good House (2003) 26–7

écriture feminine 73
Engstrom, Elizabeth 10–12, 97–8, 109–11, 119, 130
    Black Ambrosia (1988) 12, 19, 97, 108–20, 130
Enlightenment 6, 28–9, 133–4, 154
    see also the Age of Reason
epistemological instability 94, 158, 168, 170
excess 6, 8, 30, 45–6, 48–9, 58–61, 64, 67, 76–8, 91, 98, 100, 130

familial secrets 8, 17–18, 25, 37, 71, 126, 136, 139, 148, 165
family of choice 14, 45, 105, 169
    see also queer families
fantastic 3, 6, 12, 28, 64–5, 73, 76, 98–9

Foucault, Michel 60–1
Frankenstein (1818) 55
Freud, Sigmund 27–8, 32, 134–5
friendship 14–16, 85–6, 91, 126, 149

gender binary 16, 74, 174
gender roles 42, 82–3
ghost stories 134, 137–8, 158, 169
girlhood 82–4, 87–8, 145, 162–3, 169
Gomez, Jewelle 10–11, 97, 102–7, 121, 130
    The Gilda Stories (1991) 19, 97, 101–9, 130
Gothic 6, 8–12, 20, 25, 28–9, 46, 49, 51, 56, 59, 91, 93, 96, 101, 134–5, 139, 150, 166
    African-American Gothic 102, 150, 155
    American Gothic 26, 137
    Female Gothic 9, 101–2
    lesbian Gothic 103, 105–6, 130
    postmodern Gothic 95
Gothic heroine 25, 59, 166
Gothic romances 8, 25
Gothic transgression 45
Gothic vestigiality 8, 25, 43
Gothic-Carnivalesque 59
Gran, Sara 11, 139, 145–6
    Come Closer (2003) 20, 139–49, 169
grotesque 18, 35, 55–9, 61–2, 64, 67–9, 73, 75, 79–81, 83, 88–91
    female grotesque 35, 56, 61–3, 74, 78–9, 91, 74, 78–9, 83, 88, 90–1

male grotesque 74–6, 78–81, 91

Romantic grotesque 59, 62

Guattari, Félix 14, 88–9, 104

haunted house 17, 23–7, 30–1, 34, 43–5, 50, 133, 166

haunting 67, 70–1, 122, 133–41, 148, 15, 158–9, 166–9

transgenerational haunting 18, 50, 71, 139–40, 150

see also cultural haunting; spectrality

hauntology 28, 135–7, 148

heteronormativity 14–6, 20, 30, 48, 68–9, 84, 90, 96, 103–5, 108, 130–1

heterotopia 18, 27

Holder, Nancy 9–10, 31, 50–1

Dead in the Water (1994) 18, 24, 31–6, 50–1

homophobia 44, 47–8, 104

horror vacui 33

horror anthologies 10–12, 97, 138

hospitality 135, 147–8

hostipitality 148

hybridity 33–6, 64, 68–70, 76, 90, 94, 107

identity 7, 34, 62, 83, 89, 100–1, 105, 144, 150, 156–8

see also naming

impurity 26, 98–9

intimacy 7, 13–16, 24–5, 68–9, 126, 174

invisibility 30, 45–6, 106–7, 168

Jackson, Shirley 5, 11, 169

jouissance 19, 105, 129

the Kabala (Kabbalah) 146

Kiernan, Caitlín R. 3, 10–12, 63–5, 68–70, 72–3, 91

The Drowning Girl: a Memoir (2012) 13, 18, 63–73, 174–5

King, Stephen 3, 5–6, 10, 102, 137

kinship 4, 12, 13–16, 51, 65, 72–3, 103–5, 130, 150, 163, 169

Kiste, Gwendolyn 82–3, 85, 91

The Rust Maidens (2019) 18, 57, 82–91

Koja, Kathe 9–10, 12, 18, 37–9, 43, 51–2, 120

The Cipher (1991) 9, 18, 24, 37–43, 50–2, 120

Kristeva, Julia 60, 98–100, 112, 124, 126, 128–9, 141

madness 61, 64, 71–2, 110, 141, 147

Martin, Billy (Poppy Z. Brite) 3, 9–12, 30, 43–5, 50–1, 97, 108

Drawing Blood (1993) 13, 18, 24, 43–52, 174–5

Exquisite Corpse (1994) 50

Massie, Elizabeth 10–11, 74, 91

Sineater (1993) 18, 57, 74–81, 91

materiality 4, 12–13, 24, 38–9, 51, 133–4, 169

see also corporeality

maternal figure 32–3, 42, 116–17, 130–1, 163

matrilineality 63, 65, 72–3, 104

menarche 121, 126

menstruation 60, 121, 126, 131

mermaid 66–7, 70, 73

meta-fiction 66, 73

230 • House of Horrors

middle class 15, 19–20, 24–6, 29–30,
43, 113–14, 116, 120, 127, 129,
130–1, 139, 144, 155, 167
see also bourgeoisie
mise en abyme 51
minor literature 2–3, 14
misandry 120, 141
monstrous 34, 55–6, 60, 63, 78,
95–6, 101, 122, 145
monstrous bodies 18, 56, 59–60,
101
monstrous feminine 34, 60,
105–6
monstrous-maternal 60
Morrison, Toni 11–12, 26, 102
The Beloved (1987) 26, 102, 155
*Playing in the Dark: Whiteness
and the Literary Imagination*
(1992) 26
motherhood 60, 71, 84–5, 95, 101,
104, 107, 120

naming 31, 42, 47, 103–5, 159,
162–4
see also identity
narcissism 37, 106
neuroatypicality 72, 91
New Weird 37, 64–5, 175
nomadic subjectivity 88–9
non-human 59–60, 62, 76–8, 89–90,
110–11, 120
nuclear family 4, 14–16, 18–20, 23,
25, 45, 65, 83–4, 101, 128, 131,
139, 167
numinosum 29, 51

Oates, Joyce Carol 5, 10–11
Oedipal complex 93, 101, 123, 128
ogbanje 153–4, 158

ostranenie 28
otherness 18, 38, 51, 59–61, 77, 97,
100, 102, 109, 121, 134–6, 139,
148

patchwork family 35
patriarchy 8–9, 59, 68, 83–4, 101,
103–4, 106, 109, 141, 159, 164,
167
subversion of patriarchy 56, 59,
68, 104, 106, 109
performativity of gender 15, 60–1
phallogocentrism 70, 91, 102, 141,
174
phantom 29, 136–7, 157–8
possession horror 83, 145
post-human 88–90
predatory lesbian trope 63–4, 106,
116
primal scene 101, 105–7, 121, 123–6

queer desire 45–6, 48, 50, 68, 144
queer families 15–16, 45, 65, 105,
108
see also family of choice
queer uncanny 30, 46, 50

racialisation 7, 138
repression 6, 10, 28–9, 37, 39, 45–6,
91, 134, 138–40, 150
reproduction 15–16, 34, 48, 57, 60,
74–5, 78, 93, 95, 97–8, 100,
105, 107, 119, 129–30
reproductive rights 83–4
Rice, Anne 5, 11, 96, 102, 109, 120
Romanticism 56, 59, 133

sankofarration 151, 154, 157
Scylla 33–6

sea Gothic 31

sexual violence 14, 106, 117, 126, 131, 142, 145
  grooming 122, 126, 161
  incest 25, 35, 50, 98, 123–5
  rape 101, 105–16, 114, 116, 125, 164–5

Shelley, Mary 55

social body 62, 112–13
  see also community

Southern Gothic 8, 74, 80, 137

spectral turn 134–5, 138–9

spectrality 17, 19–20, 29, 133–40, 147, 150–1, 159, 166, 168, 169–70
  see also haunting

spectrality studies 134–7

speculative fiction 11, 38, 102–3, 109, 150–1

Stoker, Bram 93

subjectification 101–3, 117–18, 124, 138, 148, 157–8
  see also nomadic subjectivity

succubus 115–16, 141

suicide 41–2, 47, 66–7, 70–1, 160, 162, 167

Tem, Melanie 9–10, 97–8, 120–2, 131
  Desmodus (1995) 108
  Prodigal (1991) 19, 97, 120–9, 131, 167

transgression 7–8, 30, 45, 58, 60–1, 68, 75, 82, 89–90, 94, 119, 147

trauma 45, 50, 106, 117, 138, 151, 174

transgenerational trauma 20, 24, 136, 139

teratology 59, 86–7, 90
  see also monstrous

uncanny 17–18, 24, 26–34, 36–7, 39, 43, 45–6, 49, 51, 62–3, 72, 134–5, 140
  Das Unheimliche 27–8

unhuman 39–40

wandering subject 153–4

white underclass 43

whiteness 14, 19, 26, 90, 127, 174

white femininity 82, 139, 155–6

also in series

Lindsey Decker, *Transnationalism and Genre Hybridity in New British Horror Cinema* (2021)

Stacey Abbott and Lorna Jowett (eds), *Global TV Horror* (2021)

Michael J. Blouin, *Stephen King and American Politics* (2021)

Eddie Falvey, Joe Hickinbottom and Jonathan Wroot (eds), *New Blood: Critical Approaches to Contemporary Horror* (2020)

Darren Elliott-Smith and John Edgar Browning (eds), *New Queer Horror Film and Television* (2020)

Jonathan Newell, *A Century of Weird Fiction, 1832–1937* (2020)

Alexandra Heller-Nicholas, *Masks in Horror Cinema: Eyes Without Faces* (2019)

Eleanor Beal and Jonathan Greenaway (eds), *Horror and Religion: New literary approaches to Theology, Race and Sexuality* (2019)

Dawn Stobbart, *Videogames and Horror: From Amnesia to Zombies, Run!* (2019)

David Annwn Jones, *Re-envisaging the First Age of Cinematic Horror, 1896–1934: Quanta of Fear* (2018)